# Teaching Art to Young Children 4–9

## 2nd Edition

D0496153

# Teaching Art to Young Children 4–9

## 2nd Edition

## Rob Barnes

London and New York

First published 2002 by RoutledgeFalmer
11 New Fetter Lane, London EC4P 4EE

Simultaneously published in the USA and Canada
by RoutledgeFalmer
29 West 35th Street, New York, NY 10001

*RoutledgeFalmer is an imprint of the Taylor & Francis Group*

© 2002 Rob Barnes

Typeset in Garamond by Keystroke, Jacaranda Lodge, Wolverhampton
Printed and bound in Great Britain by
Biddles Ltd, Guildford and King's Lynn

Cover image: 'Fox by Moonlight' by Naiomi Holzer, age 9.

All rights reserved. No part of this book may be reprinted
or reproduced or utilised in any form or by any electronic,
mechanical, or other means, now known or hereafter invented,
including photocopying and recording, or in any information
storage or retrieval system, without permission in writing from
the publishers.

*British Library Cataloguing in Publication Data*
A catalogue record for this book is available from the British Library

*Library of Congress Cataloguing in Publication Data*
A catalog record has been requested

ISBN 0–415–25474–4

# Contents

# List of Illustrations

**Colour Plates**

The following colour plates appear between pp. 80 and 81.

## Monochrome Illustrations

## Charts

# Foreword

All aspects of education should be questioned for their relevance in the curriculum. Long-established activities can become a tradition or habit but not necessarily fulfil the needs of children and the community. In writing this book Rob Barnes explains and justifies the wide range of concerns which are at the heart of education, with clarity and depth. Many aspects of the subject are covered theoretically and with sound practical ideas and advice.

Art provides us with a prime means of learning, understanding and communicating. In this way it is significant across the curriculum. Without the skills involved, our children can be denied access to extensive areas of knowledge and the opportunity for individual responses.

Teaching is a creative process and in art and design activities the approach of the teacher is critical. We can teach by supplying set pieces for our pupils to imitate or we can create situations in which pupils develop self-confidence, working on the basis of their own experience, extending their understanding, discovering, satisfying their curiosity and gaining pleasure. The good teacher will accept children, whatever their ability, and will harness and enhance their imaginative and natural talents.

Rob Barnes's understanding of the needs of children and his sensitivity to their individuality enable him to suggest an extensive range of approaches to the teaching situation. These provide a rich source of guidance and stimulation for anyone involved with children. For the thoughtful reader this book can be the source of reassurance and satisfaction as a teacher and ensure relevance and pleasure for the pupils.

*Norman Manners*

Norman Manners
Art Consultant

# Preface to the Second Edition

I have revised this book mainly to take account of changes in art education. There are additional chapters and more about developing skills and using themes leading to art activities. Existing chapters have been expanded or revised. There is also a chapter about using digital images generated by computers, cameras and scanners. A chapter about the curriculum and activities is derived from art education's more enduring features. Using the work of famous artists receives more attention and I have added photographs of children's work within the new chapters. There are also additional colour plates. An obvious aim in this new expanded edition has been to preserve the original content where this was appropriate, but update some of the earlier material since the introduction of the UK National Curriculum. I was tempted to refer extensively to research, government documents, schemes and expected outcomes. Some broad reference to the UK National Curriculum is inevitable, but I decided to keep this to a minimum because readers over the years have said that the content already closely fits 'best practice'. Teachers may find that expected outcomes in art are actually less interesting than unexpected outcomes. I hope so.

Research into art education has been published by the *Journal of Art and Design Education*. The undoubted contribution this has made to art education is acknowledged by the author.

*Rob Barnes, 2001*

# Acknowledgements

Particular thanks are expressed to all those teachers and students who over the years have helped form the ideas contained in this book. It is not possible to mention them all by name but special thanks must be extended to Jane Barker, Dinah Birnie, Mavis Eccles, Sheila Gillies, Claire Goodman, Norman Manners, Ann Meades, Liz Molander, Mary Mundey, Amanda Parker, Jill Shea, Rachel Smith, Molly Turner, Sylvia Turner, Cathy Whalen and Julie Whyte. Grateful thanks are also due to the staff and children of Catton Grove First School, Clover Hill First School, Heartsease First School, Ipsley First School, Knowland Grove First School, Lakenham First School, Lyng C.P. School, Nelson First School, Northfields First School, West Earlham First School and Wray Primary School.

Seven children, whose work has been collected over a period of time, deserve special mention. They are Adam Ballard, Richard and Peter Barnes, Rebecca Bryant, Naomi Holzer, Toby Whalen and Mary Wright.

Reproductions of work by Van Gogh and Monet courtesy of The Bridgeman Art Library.

# 1 Making links

Creative activities confront how we feel about things. Expressing a mood, emotion, or temperament through art becomes as valid as responding to another person, a moving sight, or a meaningful experience. Both responding and expressing through art puts us in touch with qualities which are part of what makes us human. As such they give special significance and meaning to what we see with our eyes and the inner eye of the mind. They touch on part of us that nothing else can.

For children, art can be a means whereby they reconstruct and assimilate the experiences they have had. What might have been an incomplete inner vision can become clear enough for them to give meaning to what they encounter and can help to build up concepts of themselves in relation to the world. Nowhere is this more obvious than when young children cannot read or write. Their early art provides them with a personal language which describes the world they live in through the shapes and symbols they make when they draw. By adult standards those symbols are often poorly executed, even inadequate, but they are unique to the children who did them and crucial to their development. Clumsy and primitive the drawings may be, but they record an experience of perception and a stage reached in a child's personal growth and awareness.

Most of us who are teaching would want to help this process and try to find ways of developing children's artistic learning. By intuition we might find our way. More likely we might look at prevailing schemes and the National Curriculum. Some of this would inspire, but some would be vague and meaningless. Learning objectives are hard to determine if we are only presented with finished pieces of children's work to puzzle over. Making links between principles and practice has traditionally proved difficult. In art teaching, an ethos of apparently vague and random objectives still characterizes many classrooms. It could be argued that the teachers should make these links for themselves but that would be to ignore the problems most of us have in putting theory into practice. An understanding of principles, the essential part of any theory, does not automatically lead to good practice. Nor does good practice mean that principles of art teaching are understood.

It is not difficult to find children enjoying their artwork, coping with what we asked them to do and controlling materials. But how do we know if they are really learning anything? Are they engaged in anything worthwhile? Painting a cardboard box bright red all over may be enjoyable. It may be interesting, but has it any educational value to the child so industriously occupied in doing it?

The themes in this book are intended to bring together principles and practice so that effective art teaching can evolve. Since the first edition of this book, the UK National Curriculum and schemes in art have been published. Art has moved onwards as it always does, embracing the digital image, 'installations', 'land art' and 'performance art'. Despite this, teachers still want to know basic things like how children draw, producing original artwork, and what value art offers. Like most views on art and design, the arguments and suggestions set down here can undoubtedly be challenged. Art thrives on its multiplicity of viewpoints and its unwillingness to be governed by any hard and fast rules. For that reason, conceptual models have been avoided in favour of arguments which try to touch more on the experience of teaching art than on its various theories. The intention is to examine principles and practice together rather than try to separate them entirely. A frequently made assumption is that the two can successfully be divided and analysed. Yet though one may be associated with thinking, the other with doing, they are not necessarily separable nor do they always prove to be helpful by being treated in this way.

Another, and perhaps less obvious, aim is to discuss art teaching in a context of 'creative teaching'. Teachers are far more creative in their thinking than they often suspect, and art can be a way of using this creativity across the whole curriculum. To that end, many ideas in this book will be found to cover a far wider range of curricular interests than art alone. In the year 2001, art schemes published by the Qualifications and Curriculum Authority (QCA) endorsed that position by making numerous links with other subjects. A creative teacher makes these links in any case, realizing that children do not learn piecemeal subject by subject, even if we conveniently structure curriculum documents as if they do.

Not many decades ago we would have believed that art was for a few gifted children. Nowadays, the majority of children are regarded as being creative and their artwork is readily cited as evidence of their creativity. The shift in viewpoint has partly resulted from the influence of a variety of educationists as well as changes in the way we see our roles as parent and teacher. In Victorian times, children were viewed as imperfect adults. Now they have qualities which we recognize make them perfectly childlike and capable of producing imaginative 'Child Art'. They are no longer seen as inadequate small adults but as being able to produce artwork with special qualities which no adult could hope to emulate. We expect children to be taught as individuals as well as being part of a group, and we have organized our education system so that individual learning is valued.

We also expect that children will do more in their artwork than just copy. Deliberately to teach children to copy would not fit any principle of individual learning or creativity and we would rightly think a narrow way of working had been prescribed. The UK National Curriculum firmly put the study of art and

*Figure 1* A Thinking Face. Age 6. 370 × 500 mm.

artists in context, but some of this has resulted in mindless copying of masterworks. Some principles are already formed in our minds and affect how we approach teaching art. Others, like working from reproductions of famous paintings, need to be understood. From sound principles we can then plan children's work more purposefully so that it promotes their learning, besides just being enjoyable.

Imposing one view of art teaching would be a fruitless exercise. We still have every right as teachers to choose where we stand. Children learn successfully despite experiencing different methods of art teaching and different schemes. The very differences we see in good practice only reflect the variety of excellence which is possible. For that reason the examples which appear in this book should be treated with some caution and carefully considered rather than blindly accepted as good or bad. The same is true of published government schemes, most of which date quickly. A lot depends on the perceptions we bring with us and these inevitably influence our preference for working one way rather than another. We can be a slave to the detail of a published scheme, but there is no reason to be constrained unless we choose to be.

What works for one teacher may not work for us. But examples, such as the one which follows, have a knack of illuminating our own views by their realistic and concrete nature, even if they do not coincide with our own preferences. A slight shift of principle or practice often arises when one particular way of working has been found wanting. And in this example, the effect on children's work was considerable, the change of tack a result of personal choice.

> I used to think of providing different things for children to do each day. Then I discovered you really have to listen to them talking about their experiences so you can get them to record and extend their thinking. They must use ideas from things they themselves experience at first hand. They need to handle things because at this age, tactile experience is very important. If they can feel and experience for themselves they produce work of far greater vitality than if I'd planned what they should do and forced it on them.
>
> (First school headteacher)

In choosing to work from one principle rather than another we are bound to be guided by what succeeds. But how are we to know what good practice is? We could be told that this or that piece of work demonstrated good practice and try to emulate the examples. But we would be no better than the pupils we criticize for copying. The successful art teachers are often those who have discovered ways of developing their own ideas without resorting to copying those of the teachers they see around them. Ideally, each of us should gain enough understanding about art teaching to know what we are looking at and assess if anything is being learned by the child who painted that bright red box.

Even intuitively good teachers will talk about artwork in a way which eventually reveals they are working from firmly held principles. They may be unable to analyse their own teaching, yet determined to produce original work, or to give guidance without being over-directive. Or they may want pupils to be problem-solvers in their artwork.

> We were discussing mazes and this led on to a lot of work in drama . . . we acted out what it was like to go through a maze . . . what you might meet along the way. Then the children went on to draw their own mazes. They could choose from a variety of drawing materials and I told them the mazes had to function . . . they could choose whether or not to draw them out in rough first. We discussed hedges and whether they might meet good or bad things in their maze. One boy drew his mum as a good thing to meet . . . there were a lot of pots of gold and some children saw mazes as patterns to be embellished. They're used to decorating things because I teach a great deal through pattern, so it's not very surprising that they bring it into their mazes.
>
> (Teacher of 6-year-olds)

From what is said, and from the illustrations (Figure 2, Plate 2), we know that a principle operating is that children are expected to come up with their own solutions. There is some link with previous experience of patternwork and we know the topic of mazes crosses subject barriers. The teacher is also concerned that the children choose from a wide variety of drawing materials. We also sense that the work in progress is inventive and contains a design problem, one which makes children think artistically when they embellish it with pattern.

What we do not know is how the maze project came to be planned and developed. Even if the teacher appeared to work spontaneously, the frame of reference and understanding of art teaching was clearly crucial. In the example the teacher began by involving her children in drama, then art. She linked the two and indicated a principle of her own art teaching by allowing children to choose materials. But we are given only a glimpse of her teaching process, rather as if we have been invited too late into the classroom. We may be intrigued or even impressed by the end-products we see, but are left ignorant of most of the attitudes which permeate her work.

End-products do not readily reveal principles in the same clear way that a financial statement produces a balance of figures. We could analyse some forms of artwork to our heart's content without discovering anything more momentous than the fact that paint was mixed thickly or thinly. Understanding principles and how they link with practice is a task associated more closely with processes than with puzzling over finished artwork as if it held the ultimate key.

Fortunately we are not wandering through a maze trying to find pots of gold along the route. We already bring to art teaching our own experience and

*Figure 2* Maze Picture. Age 6. 300 × 210 mm.

perception. There must be very few teachers who do not regularly see children occupied in drawing or painting, or who have never tried it out for themselves. Even if the experience was limited, art teaching need not remain the province of a specialist or artistically gifted teacher. There is plenty of good art teaching being done by teachers whose own artistic abilities are slight. Many of them give their children confidence through joining them in learning what art is all about rather than setting themselves apart as experts. Their understanding grows as they develop expertise from uncertain but potentially promising beginnings.

The new century has seen educational practice embrace terms like 'delivery' and emphasize skills. Accountability has transformed much creative teaching into 'expected outcomes', certainties rather than uncertainties. Yet to be uncertain is a feature of much creative thinking. How else would we break new ground or have a single original thought? From uncertainty can grow a genuine confidence in working creatively with children and a surprising discovery of their ability to amaze us with their innocent originality. They will inevitably teach us a great deal about art through what they produce. But we are also in a position to create the best possible climate for their creative work to evolve. Almost all we need as a starting point is a mind open to the persuasion that art has value. From there we can encourage, motivate and guide children in what for many of them will be a lasting and influential early experience of art.

*Figure 3* Children Painting.

# 2 The value of art

Any value that art might have in the eyes of our culture is something that has to be the concern of schools, as well as the rest of society. Otherwise we ignore what makes us human. Art is part of the human condition and contrasts sharply with our more specific needs to invent things and make discoveries through technology. Art does not function in the same sense that technology has produced for us the microchip computer. Artistic values are less concerned with function and more associated with what they do for us in a learning, civilizing and enriching capacity. As such they are easily called into dispute, largely because they deal with immeasurable qualities, often because they defy conclusive proof. If we are to be convinced by arguments for the value of art then our yardstick is more one of human experience than scientific testing.

The shifting sands of curriculum design have seen the status of art change. The late 1990s saw the arts in schools somewhat displaced by concerns for numeracy, literacy, assessment scores and inspections. Fortunately teachers are creative enough to smuggle their own ideas into what they teach and there is enthusiasm and interest which is hard to extinguish. Art survives in schools because of the enlivening effect it has on pupils and teachers alike. Pockets of creative teaching will always refuse to be overshadowed by obsessions with target-setting and performance indicators. Something in the human spirit transcends the day-to-day round of necessary skill acquisition and assessment.

From the beginning of our existence we have needed to make forms which express the values which make us human beings whose imaginative gifts distinguish us from other animals. The silicon chip is no substitute for our imagination and senses, and throughout the centuries art has been practised to articulate, refine and give expression to our visual sense. The evidence of art in galleries and buildings across the world points to a fundamental need in us to make visual expression of who and what we are. In more recent times our education has been as much to do with the way we live, our relationships and judgements, as it has with our intellectual understanding. The notion of an educated person rests not solely with scientific and intellectual achievement. In the final analysis we might hold our wisdom and ability to make good judgements more valuable as assets in a civilized society. At the end of the fifteenth century we could hardly have claimed that Leonardo da Vinci's scientific achievements were the sum total of his fame or education. He expressed his worth through art as well as science in that rare combination which makes for genius.

How would he have fared in today's English primary school with its literacy, numeracy and regime of inspections? He would discover that where teachers really believe in the value of art they often have to fight hard to justify its importance for children's learning. There are many teachers who are ready to champion a one-sided set of intellectual values and see art as providing for the emotions and nothing more. If they think that schools are entirely for developing the intellect, then it doubtless becomes very hard to make a good case for art's inclusion as a subject in the curriculum. Fortunately the fight for its inclusion as a National Curriculum subject in our schools was won long ago. But if its place alongside basic subjects is to be fully realized we must look carefully at what value it has.

## Learning to see

Children may be literate in the usual sense of the term, but development of visually sensitive or visually literate children is a fundamental reason for doing art. If we understand that literacy means we can read and write, it can also be applied in art to looking and drawing. Of course artists do far more than look and draw. To develop an awareness of and receptivity to visual things includes all the things we associate with artistic pursuits. Artists, for example, invent, imagine and analyse, as well as apply colour, sculpt and assemble things. But all these activities contribute to what educates children artistically by making them literate in a particularly visual way.

Through a sharpened visual sense they learn to see much more and to see with greater insight than they otherwise would. For them, trees which were rather generalized perceptions become objects of close observation and significance. They become personal and special to the child as viewer of them. The flight of a bird, the form of a sea shell, or the twisted roots of a tree, all have aesthetic qualities which visual literacy makes it possible to experience. And part of becoming visually aware is for children to discover the enjoyment of being able to see with the eye of the artist who is awake to the appearance of the surrounding world. By developing the ability to see in far more specific ways, children can begin to disregard what is merely superficial and allow themselves to become attentive to the more subtle qualities and changes of form which are present in everything their eyes and minds rest on.

The close attention that children can bring to looking allows them to concentrate on much more than each form in isolation. When their visual sensitivity is undeveloped they tend to focus on one thing at a time and draw quite separate objects surrounded by space. Art can help them to perceive the world in a greatly extended way so that they then begin to assimilate a variety of perceptions in relation one to another. What was previously placed as an object in a drawing on its own can gradually become part of a complete network of related shapes.

With a heightened perception, usually when children are older, the paper is often treated more as a whole and the content is organized to include combinations of objects together.

At the heart of perception is expression. As long ago as 1966, Arnheim said that before we perceive in an analytical way, we perceive the expressive or feeling-character of things. He described this as a skill necessary for survival when we respond to facial expression to determine how friendly or hostile other people are. We can imagine instances when children are more aware of the expressive character which objects display than of what they actually are. Some objects become frightening and others lovable through children's perception of them. And in this, the expressive characteristics of what they experience play an undeniable role in their relationship to them, and in the way they incorporate them into their artwork.

Without our developing visual literacy the rather commonplace remains so. Most people at some time or another have picked up stones from a beach and flung them into the sea for the pleasure of doing something quite useless. Sooner or later they will pick up a stone and examine it for its rounded form or its qualities of colour or decoration. Such awareness develops when we have the time to stop and look at things for ourselves. But in the classroom we have the chance to develop this perception much further by deliberately making time for looking at things through the processes of art.

The qualities that an object like a beach pebble can convey are an important part of its whole character. Though children will examine their world in a variety of other ways, such as by measuring and describing in words, their visual discrimination of things is vital to their ultimate understanding of them. No amount of words can really describe an irregular shape quite so accurately as a drawing does. And the way children interpret everyday objects through drawing is often far superior to their looking at photographs. Even if we discount for the moment any expressive, artistic qualities drawings have, as a way of making children look closely they are unique. Biologists will quickly point out that photographs do not very adequately convey the structure of things but drawings can provide an interpretation which is scientifically sound as well as instructive.

It is true that before the age of 6, children tend to draw what they know rather than what they see. But in a class of 6-year-olds there can regularly be a great deal of searching drawing going on, which is as much hard work as anything else they do. Learning to see is rarely something children find easy, and as one teacher says,

> This idea that art isn't hard work is a fallacy. When they're really working hard at drawing, some of them find it very difficult just as they find language and number difficult. I've made them look long and hard many times at the shape of things around them and now none of them say 'I can't draw', any more than they say 'I can't read or write' . . . They were drawing these sticky buds and it was fascinating to listen to them talking to each other about their drawings and saying things like 'Look, it's got a horseshoe

shape on it. Is that why it's called a Horse Chestnut?' . . . all this talking
. . . a lot of language work comes out of it . . . someone describes the outside
of the buds as being like toffee . . . they're engrossed in looking and
analysing what they see.

The same teacher spoke about the frustration some of her children experience
when they draw.

> I have one little boy who's very good at drawing but some days he will get
> so frustrated that he leaves his drawing unfinished. He doesn't want to see
> it again. Other days he is so carried away with what he is doing his face is
> a picture of joy. Some days it goes well, some days it doesn't.

In that sense, art is no different from the rest of the curriculum. Yet it presents
children with the task of dealing with special visual qualities that no other
subject offers. The ability to perceive those qualities is bound to emerge over a
long period of time and is a result of a necessary repeated involvement in art.
As we grow up we learn to discriminate between more complex qualities than
ever a child can, and may even become like a connoisseur or specialist in certain
specific judgements. The wine connoisseur, for instance, is a good example
of the development of a sharpened sense of taste for wine. Connoisseurs spend
the time needed to refine their experience of tasting wines and base their
judgements partly on previous known good wines they have sampled. Through
art, we begin to see qualities which have visual subtlety, such as the many shades
of colour to be found in a field of grass, patterns made by clouds in the sky, the
different colours to be found in brickwork, or the variety of shapes in fallen
leaves. The value of art persists a long time in education. Dewey (1934) in *Art
as Experience* said,

> To think effectively in terms of relations of qualities is as severe a demand
> on thought as to think in terms of symbols, verbal and mathematical.
> Indeed since words are easily manipulated in mechanical ways, the produc-
> tion of a work of genuine art probably demands more intelligence than
> does the so-called thinking that goes on among those who pride themselves
> on being 'intellectuals'.

Attending to special qualities which things have includes not only what
children take in with their eyes but what they eventually give out in their art.
Through using art materials children learn to deal with colour, shape, line,
texture and tone (by which is meant the lightness and darkness of things). These
formal elements of art are a constant source of wonder to children who are
motivated to explore art media to see what they are like. Even though they
must look first in order to create anything, it naturally is not long before the
artwork itself demands their close attention, just as their surroundings have
done. In turn, attention to the subject-matter or content of artwork, the lines,

the colours and the shapes, is helped and hindered by the materials which are used. The resulting work is a compromise between what the artist wants to do and what the medium will actually allow. Those qualities which Dewey speaks of constantly present themselves as the children try to interpret the world through their artistic thinking and the media they use.

There is value just in being confronted by new and different materials. Left to their own devices, children might by chance use a variety of media, but the sensitive art teacher can ensure that they find out about, and make comparisons between, the nature of different materials. This can be approached through problem-solving (see Chapter 12) and, for young children, by means of structured play. Practice in handling various materials is part of any young child's education. Observing the world is not enough. Handling materials and finding out what they do demands a different kind of thinking and the development of a variety of physical skills.

This is very apparent when children use clay or Plasticine. Three-dimensional materials pose a different set of problems to solve from the two-dimensional ones of flat paper and drawing. A child working on paper organizes the world into two-dimensional symbols. But using clay gives children the opportunity to mould and express a three-dimensional world in a three-dimensional way.

Children become more fluent in their creative ideas the more often they tackle creative projects. Like success breeding success, fluency can be a feature of continual involvement in creative thought. Children can learn to rely on quite illogical thought processes to arrive at new solutions. Trusting in what may amount to intuition or good guesses can be bad practice in an intellectual process of thought. But in the arts it is more or less a way of life, and for children, a valuable way of coping with the qualities of life which refuse to submit to rational or intellectual thought.

A long-term aim of developing visual literacy is to make children so aware of their surroundings that they go on looking when they grow up. The richness of nature, for instance, can be experienced through art precisely because of art's appropriateness as a way of knowing the world. Developing visual sensitivity, we can argue, is important for producing artistically educated and aware adults who actually care what the things around them look like. There is of course nothing wrong with being trained to earn a living but this is hardly the same as being educated. Without art being taught in schools, we can imagine children being less open to artistic enrichment in later life than they are now. Or if they were open to appreciating art, the judgements they might make would be founded more on ignorance than on knowledge and awareness.

Talking about art as a way of knowing suggests that what we are dealing with is a form of intelligence. The idea is not new (see Witkin, 1974; Ross, 1983). Or if not intelligence itself, then it is a code we have developed so that we can understand reality as it exists for us. We see things not as they are, but as we are. The private code of artistic sensitivity becomes our window for viewing reality and for each one of us it can be as different as Chinese and

A creature with forty-nine heads.

*Figure 4* Creature from *James and the Giant Peach*. Age 6. 750 × 480 mm.

English are as languages. In Chinese some words do duty both for nouns and verbs so that objects are also events that are happening (Watts, 1957). This is confusing to Western minds but what is apparent is that the perception of reality differs for all of us according to the particular way of knowing we develop. For children, art is not meant merely to be an alternative way of knowing, but is part of the way they learn to trust what their senses tell them.

Where subject areas in schools are blurred, as they often are for young children, to treat art as a separate and unconnected way of knowing is to deny its effect on other forms of learning. Children need to be involved in art to complete their understanding of what they see and to educate their visual sense, not only for producing art, but for learning in a rounded and meaningful way. The general progress of children and their competence in basic skills appears to benefit where they are involved in a programme of learning which includes art in its list of activities.

Quite simply, the development of a visual sense seems to make children more alive and identified with the world. Whenever we learn something new our way of knowing the environment is transformed. We have gained awareness we previously did not have. Children who are alive to their world often display a curious exploratory and adventuresome spirit. They are 'participators' in life whose knowledge, gained through a variety of subjects, spurs them on to know more. They may not grow up to be creators of art later in life, but if they cannot become artists, they can at least learn to appreciate the art that other adults do.

Wisdom is acquired rather than received. Each of us has to construct our own fundamental concept of what it means to learn to see. Immersed in the making of images and objects, it is easy to lose sight of what art offers as a way of comprehending the world. Art encourages us to understand and give meaning to what we see. Perhaps as old men and women we will remember only what had meaning for us, what we learned about life and what deeply affected us. We will certainly include what we saw and if we are lucky may even be aware that changes took place in our visual perception of things. The trees we drew, the plants, the houses, the people, all affected our perceptions of them.

If children look carefully enough, the object they draw can change their private ignorance of its appearance. Pablo Picasso once said, 'I do not seek, I find.' This describes learning to see very well. Through a heightened perception, a well-developed habit of seeing, children can move from 'looking' to 'finding' without always needing to be directed to do so. The fact that they have developed the habit of seeing has wider implications and may well influence the whole of the rest of their curriculum. We do not yet understand why children who are involved in creative work seem to develop academically as a spin-off. But if it is true that they do, then art's place on the school timetable would seem to be influential, if not indispensable.

## Art and the individual

Education has seen as one of its main functions the development of individuality through teaching each child according to his or her particular strengths, talents, or needs. An essential characteristic of creativity is that ideas are put together to produce something new to the individual. We could hazard a guess that the really great breakthroughs in discovery and invention in our time have not happened without creative thinking coming fairly high up on the list of ingredients necessary for success. It is odd then that if we value what individuals can do through creative thinking, we do not give it more specific attention in schools. The very ability which is given such low status in some classrooms is actually what is needed in order to create something new for our society. Being inventive, being what we call creative, should be a prime concern of education and the individual. No more so than in our current society, where change comes upon us so quickly that the flexibility of thought which we associate with creativity is almost a prerequisite for keeping pace.

Through art children can learn to adapt and change ideas in an imaginative way. Imagination, in the form of mental pictures and fragments of memory, is a tool whereby as individuals we enhance our experience and mentally try things out. Art encourages children to visualize in the eye of the mind whatever might be, as well as what was and is. They learn to make comparisons between what they visualize in the mind and what ends up on paper as a piece of artwork. In encouraging children to use their imagination through art, we also help them to visualize fresh ideas, which can often give them confidence to try out new things for themselves. Much of the fantasy we attach to imagination may seem to be of little practical use but it can act as a stepping-stone to the solution of everyday problems. It may be that the truly creative thinkers as children become those adults later on in life who can see positive alternatives where others fail to envisage them.

Art sessions give children the chance to allow their individuality to be expressed through tangible form. Those very qualities which make art individual are the ones which demonstrate to others that there is more than one way to interpret things. In a field where there are no 'right' answers, individuals learn that art can be a celebration of diversity, a celebration of individuality for its own sake. Teachers can do a great deal to foster this individuality by appreciating each piece of work a child does for its very uniqueness of expression. Contrast this with classrooms where the teacher always does the problem-solving by producing stereotypes to be copied (see Chapter 3). The reason for art being undervalued by these teachers may well lie in the fact that their children have never had the experience of making their own individual contributions. We can hardly value what children have never had the chance to produce. In stereotyped art, uniqueness and individuality never become serious considerations.

If we want children's art to be individual, we need hardly be surprised if sometimes we fail to understand the work they produce. Being creative, as a teacher or child, can mean being uncertain, failing, as well as evolving new and interesting viewpoints. To fail is human, but to accept failure and live with uncertainty is a hard lesson which art often helps children come to terms with through their work. In this, the teacher's attitude is crucial and demands an accepting and encouraging response to individual work rather than a critical one. Learning to value the kind of thinking which has taken effort and courage, in order to make an individual statement, is surely what in the end makes teaching art worthwhile.

## Art as an expression of feeling

Art is often described as the subject on the timetable through which children release their feelings. There is an idea, still prevalent in some schools, that the only good reason for doing art is for children to release emotions which have become pent up through doing academic work. Art is looked on as a purgative process through which the emotions have their outlet. In fact, children can be just as pent up doing art as they can be doing basic subjects like maths or language. Many of them give an impression of having pent-up emotions when really all that has happened is that they have run out of energy to concentrate. Traditionally, numeracy and literacy tend to be done in the morning. It is not surprising that art is assumed to be an emotional release if it always appears to be done just when children are less able to cope with giving their best attention. That, coupled with an atmosphere of enjoyment and expression of feeling, marks it out as a strong candidate for being therapeutic. So it can be, but if it is only for the release of the emotions, then its value is associated more with psychiatry than expressive art.

Although there is little doubt that feelings can be released through art, if this were all that art could do for children then it would rightly deserve low status as a subject. Without a great deal of alternative mental activity, such as problem-solving, discriminating, or decision-making, all that children would do was unload their feelings. What they actually created would not really matter. And if emotional unloading were the sole purpose of art, then art sessions would need to be organized rather like psychotherapy, with the teacher acting as psychiatrist. Herbert Read (1943) probably knew exactly how emotional release could become some teacher's platform for defending art. He described the art teacher as being like a 'psychic midwife', a medical missionary of the mind who was ready to deliver the artistic babies produced by the class.

Art may be a therapeutic release, but it also has the function of communicating to others through its organization of form and content. As a cathartic unloading of feeling it becomes no more valuable than the worst examples of what used to be called 'Free Expression' (see Chapter 3). Art as therapy is legitimately part of the programmes in special schools and hospitals, but its place in the general school curriculum is earned in more worthwhile ways.

Critics and educationists alike have readily accepted that art is an expression of feelings rather than a release for them. The translation of inner feelings into a concrete and public form characterizes the expression of visual form. When we look at what art does for us, feeling or emotional response is essentially what makes it live and communicate its message. If works of art do not affect us in some way it is doubtful that what we are encountering is really what can be called art. The very practice of doing art in schools inevitably draws on children's feelings about themselves and allows them to use that part of themselves which can never fully be articulated through words. Indeed feelings are readily destroyed by being put into words, unless they can find expression in a poetic sense, rather than cold-blooded description.

Through art children can identify their feelings with the subject-matter they choose to interpret. Each time they paint, or draw, or make something in clay, the subject becomes part of their lives through the production of what is called (Witkin, 1974) 'feeling form'. In that sense they do indeed paint out their feelings of excitement, fear, anger, or joy in what they express (Plate 3). Yet for children, and maybe for adults, being able to identify with the subject is part of their overall progress towards finding meaning in what they do. For some children, the feelings they associate with their subject are clearly profound. Like the experience many of us have when we see the greatest works of art, or listen to the finest musical performance, children can derive assurance from their best experiences in art, that life is made worthwhile and given significance. As Robert Hughes (1980) said of art,

> The purpose of art is to close the gap between you and everything that is not you and thus proceed from feeling to meaning.

## Deciding on what to value

Within minutes of waiting inside school premises it is often possible to absorb and sense the way in which art is valued. Whilst the outside catchment area of a school may be drab and boring, a real contrast can be found inside. There is of course a danger that art for display in the school becomes 'window dressing' for parents and important visitors. But the character of a school is to a great extent expressed by what it puts on the walls of its building. No amount of 'window dressing' compensates for bad art teaching so to value art mainly for the contribution it makes to display alone is not a very good reason for doing it. In fact, display as a reason for doing art can easily lead to a cul-de-sac of thought which (Chapter 3) sees end-products as the only foundation of art teaching.

A lively environment for children is quite another matter. Children thrive on seeing examples of work displayed which provoke their thinking and stimulate their curiosity. If artistic learning is to happen, then making the classrooms visually stimulating is an essential thing to do. By making the classroom look interesting and alive a teacher also demonstrates involvement and commitment. We express our educational values in everything we display, from the children's work itself, right down to the presentation of everyday materials and equipment.

Whatever finds its way to the walls of the classroom is usually only a selection of what is available. So it matters much more what value teachers put on what the children do in their art sessions rather than what a few have produced for display. Emphasizing the unique and special values that are peculiar to art gives it an importance which goes a long way towards teaching children that it has worth in its own right. This is nothing to do with how frequently art appears on the timetable but with the quality of it as an experience when it does take place.

When art becomes no more than a glorified visual aid for other subjects it loses out on the very values which make it worth doing. Here we are on dangerous ground. It is in topics such as history and other social studies, that the place of art is most frequently misunderstood (see Chapter 6). To all intents and purposes, history-related artwork ought to offer a number of opportunities for doing creative work. Making models, drawing pictures of Viking ships, for instance, or making maps all call for artistic skills. But they hardly constitute the real value of art in children's education. In work based on history topics (which is not the same thing as working from themes), art is often used to fulfil a rather secondary and illustrative role. It is a servant to the topic or a resource for another subject. Whilst the value of this is self-evident when children appear to be using all forms of learning within one topic, if what is done merely adds weight to the information they write about, art is robbed of its unique and creative dimension. Without counter-balancing by allowing topics to aid art, instead of the other way round, a restricted and impoverished version of artistic learning easily becomes the day-to-day practice.

Now this might seem to be over-critical of much excellent learning that is possible through the humanities. Yet it does bear closer scrutiny because the trap it is laying is an easy one to fall into. It is very difficult to be convinced that art is not getting a fair deal when we see children industriously working away producing illustrations and models. To any outsider there seems to be plenty of art going on and enough impressive-looking examples to satisfy the need for display around a general theme. Where then is the problem? Surely art must take second place in some topics?

Of course, it sometimes does. This is not a serious problem so long as we recognize what is happening and do not misconstrue it to be the whole art education programme. As a regular servant to the topic, art makes itself a slightly worrying companion to what is factual, rather than what is imaginative or expressive. The desire to link art with facts is a very strong one and the rationale quite clear in some teachers' minds. As one teacher puts it,

> I believe that art is valuable in that it gives a visual representation of the written work children do. It gives more meaning to the factual work and provides added interest to the topic.

It does. But making it play such a subservient role means that its creativity is swamped by factual considerations. There is nothing wrong with making any one particular subject the centre of our own teaching style, but we need to understand what each subject has to offer, so the best can be made of it. This is especially true in first schools where subject barriers are usually not clearly defined. How guilty might we feel if each subject in turn was used as a support for topic work? Would we say that we believed language was important in that it made the facts in the topics clearer? Would we say that the reason for doing maths was to measure things in history? Or would we more honestly say that language and mathematics could grow out of work on the topic just as the topic might provide some imaginative starting points for art?

The problem to be resolved in doing history, geography or science topics is that as children become engrossed in fact-gathering and analysis, they tend to overemphasize this aspect to the exclusion of being creative. Who, after all, wants a new and creative shape for a Viking ship, or some creative spellings? There is almost always a huge bank-balance of facts around to be taken account of. We can, though, have creative paintings of Viking ships and a creative use of words without ignoring the fact that their shape or spelling are somewhat fixed.

The teacher who seemed so concerned with art as a way of illustrating facts also thought it could be valuable to encourage the development of physical skill. With very young children this might be true but hardly something special to art. Children learn fine motor skills even through using a knife and fork, so to applaud art as a way of learning these skills does not count for very much. Any more than the fact that children on the whole tend to enjoy art gives it greater or less value than other enjoyable activities.

Perhaps a nightmare vision of art teaching is one where art is never valued as anything but a recreation or leisure activity. Leisure is a by-product of art which can sometimes devalue it rather than act as its driving force. Schools are not leisure centres and the fact that so much art is done in people's leisure time does not necessarily divorce it from hard work. To describe art as a leisure activity is to be in ignorance of how artistic learning occurs. If we disregard learning through the senses, and allow art to become a recreation, then what passes for art in schools need hardly be taken seriously. The fact that schools have television sets and video equipment could just as easily be connected in our minds with leisure. Yet we would not point to these as having no educational value because the content of television programmes for schools is assumed to be linked with education. If teachers find they treat art merely as a leisure activity, rather than as learning which happens to be enjoyable as well, then they should look very carefully at its content to find out what is missing.

There are many instances in which the arts have rejected the concept of being a diversion rather than making a serious contribution to life. As David Best (1985) points out,

> The seriousness of the arts consists partly but significantly in the fact that what is expressed in them feeds back into life, in the insights given into the human condition and other aspects of life. When the arts lose this seriousness they atrophy.

Art educators in this century have held different views on what are the most crucial values of art. Each one of us has the right to decide for ourselves what artistic values we emphasize above all others. Learning to see, art and the individual and art as expression of feeling are the three strands of value described here. There are many others, but at the core of most theories of artistic value lies uniqueness. Herbert Read (1943) and Elliot Eisner (1972), particularly, had a high regard for the unique qualities which only art offers. They saw uniqueness as a yardstick for testing the value of art.

Many teachers will sum up the value of art in terms of its promoting a child's sense of personal worth. They view art as a way in which a child can gain confidence and a sense of being wanted, or his view of the world becoming accepted. Art teaching has the characteristic of giving us a free hand in a free syllabus, the content of which is rarely mapped out in advance. By intuition and common sense we might make good judgements about those values which we see as vital. But if we are ever to teach art with any conviction and insight, then some of what is valuable in art will need our consideration, not least because our own value system conditions how we teach.

# 3 Producing original artwork

When art is well organized and well taught, children produce work which has a flair and originality about it. No two pieces of work look alike and children delight in experimenting with ideas, solving problems and making decisions about their artwork. Watch any group of children who are totally absorbed in their painting. When they are really engrossed they show a willingness to create something which is often new and individual. To the onlooker they seem to be living in a world dictated by themselves in terms of colour, shape and line depicting their experiences. Their work has life to it and tells us things about them which we could never understand merely through words.

There are times when children are self-motivated to work but, more usually, sensitive teaching is needed to get the very best artwork even with the youngest of children. For teachers who do not think of themselves as specialists the every-day planning of creative activities for young children can be problematic. They may lack confidence in their own abilities and feel anxious about doing art alongside other areas of the curriculum. Most likely, children will use a separate part of the school for music or physical education but art will have to be fitted in wherever it can be organized within the classroom. Not only that but a teacher will need to be inventive to devise interesting art projects. There are very few useful textbooks and magazine articles in comparison with language learning or mathematics.

A common difficulty is one of persuading children they can draw. Taken together with the recurring task of devising creative projects of value, it may well seem as if other areas of the curriculum are by comparison a good deal easier to manage.

## Three suspect solutions

Producing original artwork is both rewarding and stimulating to do, largely because we can make use of children's uninhibited flair for the original. Before examining useful approaches to art teaching, though, we need to look at three apparent solutions, which really do not help matters at all. They are unfortunate, though sometimes popular, strategies, which need to be understood in order to avoid confusion. It would be easy enough to criticize these three by declaring them the province of the lazy or uncaring teacher. But that will not do. We need to see why they persist and what their attraction is. Why do they appear solutions, yet in reality are rather limited ways of working?

The first of these solutions is to send children away into an available part of the classroom to paint or draw unaided. They do whatever they like. Sometimes this is misnamed 'Free Expression' even though in the end it is neither very free nor is it particularly expressive. When this is done, art is sometimes regarded by the teacher as being too spontaneous to need teaching. All that seems necessary is to provide the materials, invite the children to start, and stand well clear.

Many headteachers, with good experience of the disasters which can happen to children who are left to their own devices, are eager to criticize 'Free Expression'. This probably has its roots in a time when unfettered experience of art and its materials was the fashion in schools. It was as if the children were too artistically angelic to be influenced at all by their teacher. The experience they were having was considered enough in itself, and the work produced was sacrosanct.

Few teachers would disagree that at the nursery and infant stages children need to explore new materials for themselves. Their spontaneous language of pictorial symbols expresses their experience long before they are able to write things down. In fact teachers are much more likely at this stage to play an enabling role, rather than formally teach art. They will know that the youngest of children usually need to explore over and over again what for them are new materials. But teachers will still need to support, stimulate and encourage their pupils in what they do. It is some time before any skill with the materials they try out is developed by children, and to repeat their experience with a particular medium is an important part of their early development.

What then of older infants? Can they simply carry on with the teacher leaving them to it? Quite a number of teachers are adamant about their non-intervention in art. They believe that the child's art is an end in itself. After all, if the adult artist views art as a rather personal matter, then why should this not be the same for a child? They see their role as to provide materials, set the scene and disappear. The child is expected to produce artwork automatically and any involvement by the teacher is thought of as contamination of the art process. True, the dangers of being rigid and over-directive are avoided, yet almost anything the child produces becomes acceptable as art, regardless of what it is. How attractive this is for the teacher who believes in it. When quite mindless artwork is produced the teacher cannot be held responsible. Evaluating what has been done is not necessary and the children's development can just be left to chance, or assumed to be taking place. The quality of the work does not matter either, because there were never any established aims for what was attempted by the children.

Only the most creative pupils manage to survive this for long. Other children regularly become bored when they are left to do what they like and some are greatly relieved when they are allowed to stop working. Having lost faith in their work they are bewildered by the teacher's encouragement of their efforts and begin to associate this freedom with dissatisfaction rather than enjoyment. Privately they often feel angry with themselves and frustrated by not being able to think of more to do to their paintings. Subsequently, many of them lose confidence and repeat the same images over and over again, instead of trying anything new.

In other areas of the curriculum we would not give out books and expect that children would learn to read, or present practical maths equipment and expect learning to begin automatically. Yet in art sessions it is often assumed that the materials themselves will usually be enough to start children off. It does seem that the teacher who allows this to happen displays a serious lack of responsibility. Children who are bored by their art sessions almost cry out to be given at least some small extension of their experience. And their teacher should be the one to do this if only to relate art to the rest of the curriculum. However good the help offered by a visiting parent or classroom helper, the teacher has the ultimate responsibility for art. If this responsibility is not taken up, then it is difficult to be convinced the subject is either understood or valued as part of children's learning. More likely it has turned into a purely recreational activity through which children learn very little. They are no better or worse for the experience they have of doing art.

Left to themselves children will make marks on paper but how spontaneously and creatively they do it is questionable. Inside the classroom all too often a considerable amount of messing about with materials has been mistaken for art activity. Much of it is characterised by runny unmanageable paint (see Chapters 9 and 16). Perhaps not so much in playgroups because it is there we can see children painting with great gusto; but when children reach school age their needs change and their artwork demands much more than encouragement from a well-intentioned adult.

We each have our own priorities for what we think is important. And opting out of any part of the school curriculum obviously leaves time for doing other things we might see as more worthwhile. For some teachers there is apparently a very clear division between what they see as being work, and art. Their priorities dictate that it is only when children have finished work that they can do art. Which is to suggest that little actual learning takes place when children are engaged in using materials like paint and crayons rather than workcards and exercise books. If art is looked on by the teacher as being other than another kind of work, in turn this is transmitted to the children. They most likely grow to see it as a not very serious activity, one similar to being let out to play.

The other two solutions taken up concern teacher-directed approaches which are at the opposite extreme from the rather *laissez faire* nature of 'Free Expression'. Teacher-directed art is any art that is controlled by the adult in such a way that the end-product is predetermined. This is often in evidence when teachers provide children with a ready-made kit of parts for them to assemble into a final product. Educational suppliers' catalogues show commercially produced versions which may be anything from sticky paper shapes to quite complex craft kits. Colour photographs display the finished product and associated kit of parts to make the difficult look easy. Clean children are photographed in a clean room doing clean work. The various art and craft kits produced commercially are not a serious threat to artistic development largely because of their cost. Few children ever use them for long enough because they cannot be afforded in quantity. Some specialist kits even come into the category of a headteacher's executive toy rather than an educational kit. Most of them have a certain novelty interest and a take-home product at the end.

More difficult to justify are the art kits which teachers collect together themselves for the children to assemble. Actually making these kits for children takes a lot of time and effort on the part of the teacher and any helpers. It really is hard work. But the resulting artwork is so stereotyped and identical that there is very little which could be called original about it. An example would be a kit designed by an adult from which the children made a clown puppet in order to 'develop their skills in handling materials'. All the parts would be the same. A paper cone or card tube for the body, card shapes duplicated with outlines, paper spots for eyes, a piece of cork for a nose and wool for the hair. The teacher might begin by showing a finished example she has made to motivate the children. They follow a step-by-step sequence of instructions and at the end of the day all the clowns look very similar to one another.

What the children produce by this method is generally less skilful than the teacher's example. Such rigid conditions have been set up that there are very few decisions the children can take about their puppets. The design is an adult one, not a child's, and such changes as there are to the facial expression or colour of the clown hardly make it original 'Child Art'.

What a lost opportunity this is. Most of the possible problem-solving is being done for the children as if they were incapable themselves. Some of them will be quite disappointed with their puppets as they compare them with the best examples they can see. Others will have been given so much help that they hardly need to have been there in the first place. They are the ones who go home with what amounts to a free gift from their teacher.

There is a lot of pressure on teachers to do this instead of letting children produce art for themselves. It is particularly strong in schools where 'Child Art' is not really very well understood or highly valued.

> I very often feel under pressure from the head, inspectors and parents to help children by doing work for them. When I put up a display I can see parents don't understand Child Art. But they do understand adult art. I had a parent come into school today and outside the classroom were clowns drawn by another teacher and coloured by her children. I'm sure she thought her child had done the drawing as well. Even other teachers are condescending about Child Art and spend hours working themselves into the ground doing friezes for the walls. When they see what my children do, they seem to think it is because I can't draw. I feel I have to defend what the children

do by themselves because it doesn't fit in with the rest of the artwork in the school.

(Teacher)

To produce work which looks just like its neighbour confirms children in the belief that there is a right way to do art. This often rests on the experience they have of seeing teachers do things for them and of copying examples they are given. When we consider that there are already many instances when children are shown 'right' ways, for example, to form letter shapes, add, subtract or use practical apparatus, this is not a surprising reaction. The expectation that they will be shown how to do art the right way is hardly a shock to the system. It fits in well with a variety of things teachers already do. By controlling a step-by-step procedure to produce art, a teacher does nothing children would find revolutionary. But in the end almost all the invention and creativity is taken out of their work.

Although kits the teacher designs for children rarely leave much room for change they can nearly always be made much more creative than they are. It is difficult to believe that at Christmas time the many models of Father Christmas made from card tubes and cotton wool need all look so similar. In one art session a far greater range of materials can be used with very little more preparation on the teacher's part. Cotton wool is not the only material for white beards. Why, for instance, should all the models be the same size? Could a choice be given? There are a variety of ways of decorating even the most similar of Christmas shapes with different paper or fabric belts, buckles, buttons and boots. Assembling a kit in only one way is not a very worthwhile use of children's time. There are better things to do and more creative ways to do them.

The third solution is one arrived at to overcome the challenge of teaching children to draw. Substitutes for drawing, like templates or teacher-drawn outlines, are imposed in order to 'make the work look better'. If templates are used, so goes the argument, children can achieve success in producing their work. They are unable to draw things too small to be filled in with colour, and they take much longer to finish so there are fewer problems about not having plenty to do. If they are left to draw for themselves they become frustrated and do not bother to take care with what they are doing.

My children get very disruptive sometimes if they can't draw and then art becomes a real chore. If I'm trying to cope with thirty children I can't spend time helping them to draw. When I draw big outlines for them first, the children work very well for me and do some impressive work.

(Teacher)

The temptation to give out a template around which a child draws or to draw for children seems irresistible. Many children enjoy filling in outlines with colour and some will do this all day if they are allowed. When children are drawing round outlines and filling in they are certainly less demanding to teach, and we could even be convinced the artwork was the children's if it was they who actually made the marks. But at the heart of the practice is a desire to produce an image which has an adult sophistication. It is hard to understand quite what a child derives from drawing round, say, a three-quarter view of an elephant, but it is done in some classrooms. Privately we might frown at ourselves for doing the drawing for children, but publicly will we pin the work to the wall?

Taken to its logical conclusion we could imagine the aspiring art student years later attending her first life-drawing class at art school. 'Where's the template?' she asks as she has never drawn with anything else. Of course she would not be let anywhere near her art school had she not shown ability. But did the drawing skill emerge as if by chance? At the very least she must have demonstrated her talent to be given a chance to study. We all know how unskilled adults can feel about their own drawing ability. With embarrassed pride they will often claim not to be able to draw a straight line (or add up fractions, or knock a nail in the wall, or to be much more than tone deaf). But such drawing ability as there is was never developed by using a template or having the outlines drawn by anyone else. We learn things like drawing by doing it ourselves and templates ultimately have nothing to do with it. Teachers who use such devices are probably not so much concerned with drawing as with coping with the difficulties of surviving the school day. Templates are a way of keeping children busy without actually having to grasp the nettle of teaching them art.

Any teacher who is stuck with these particular substitutes for drawing has not really considered how children learn. If it is true that whenever they draw they are assimilating their experience by reconstructing it, then that reconstruction is remarkably different from the way an adult interprets things. Look at the drawing which is illustrated in Figure 5. It is something of a puzzle. To many adults it looks like a fish with fins and a tail. The 5-year-old has decorated it with lines and spots like the patterns seen on fishes. Yet what the child drew was his experience of seeing his teacher play the guitar. The guitar moved about as she played so we see a variety of positions for the neck of the instrument and more than one set of strings. There are obvious confusions about the strings and metal frets. In conversation with him, however, it turned out that the part that really interested him was doing all the spots. They were not decoration at all, but represented the places his teacher put her fingertips to make the notes. Part of the drawing at the bottom shows the hole in the main body of the guitar.

As adults we have to adjust to a different kind of interpretation which does not follow the silhouette outline we expect to see. Had a template been used or the teacher drawn the guitar, then that boy's individual experience would never have been reconstructed as he knew it. To impose an adult concept of drawing would have been to hold back his development because an adult's drawing would have as little relation to his experience as his drawing does to ours. More than this, to set up adult standards as the ones to follow is grossly to undervalue

*Figure 5* Age 5. 450 × 340 mm.

what children can do. It is inevitable that in comparison with adults' drawings those done by children will look primitive. They need to be judged alongside development in mathematics or language and if genuinely a child's will be equally childlike.

## Finding a balance

So far, ways of coping have been mentioned which are thought to be unhelpful. In writing about the use of templates it is worth pointing out that there are still creative uses to which they can be put. Not all descriptions of these apparent solutions need be so negative. Geometric shapes can be drawn round as a basis for patternwork, and some of the older children may be able to cut out their own templates for repeating shapes (Plate 35 and Figure 40). Provided that the outcome of the art is not adult and predetermined, templates have their uses. Outlines and templates for work in maths are commonly used as well and here they are appropriate to the learning which is going on. In art, colouring books, which are the most prevalent form of predetermined art, can of course be made creative if children change what is drawn already. But to pursue this when there are better ways for children to learn through art would be neither profitable nor particularly appropriate in schools. There are some colouring books which offer choice of shape, but these are the exception. Even creative use of these colouring books is best left to a wet afternoon at home.

Predetermined, teacher-directed ways of working can have the effect of undermining children's self-confidence and independence of thought. Instead of becoming used to making their own artistic decisions, the security they derive is gained from 'getting things right in the teacher's eyes'. They become dependent, rewarding to teach maybe, but miss out on the very individuality which creative work is meant to encourage. They are being mechanical, doing without thinking, and learning that art can be wrong and right. There is a case cited in a book called *Borderliners*, by the writer Peter Hoeg, of a child who discovered that the only way to gain a gold star for his work was to fill in the background carefully. His teacher praised time spent doing this, whether or not it was appropriate.

It is not easy to find a good balance between over-directing children's art and simply leaving them to do as they please. There are many teachers who have tried to avoid structuring art and found out later that their children needed much clearer guidelines. Having endured the experience of seeing children mess about with art materials they quickly imposed a rigid style of working as an antidote. Teacher-directed work may be bad for children but many teachers have preferred it to having their art sessions get out of hand. If the extremes are to be avoided then we must look for structures which are not inflexible but at the same time practical enough to work well in the classroom.

A first step towards this is to consider and reassess how art activities are planned in the first place. Very often what happens is that we decide what the end-product will be and set about devising the means to produce it. A not unreasonable way of doing things we might think. We decide, for instance, the children will paint a picture of 'Our Street' and we see in our mind's eye what it will look like. Then we sort out the materials necessary to start. The children are given a good idea of what things they might see in the street and how they might paint them, then off they go. Or we see a piece of artwork made with tissue paper and foil perhaps, collaged and well displayed. We like the effect of it so want to try it out with our own class. Each time the procedure we adopt is the same. Think of the end-product and work backwards to the beginning to find out how to make it possible for children to do.

Without seeing examples of artwork done by other people we would never tune in to what children are capable of. But in reality the creative process (and the learning experience) lies in the gap which exists between the glimmer of an idea and its final tangible product. Creativity, it could be said, lies in the gap between intention and outcome, means and not just ends.

One of the best ways of reinforcing this is to say that *the more clearly defined the end-product* is in our minds before we start, *the less creative it is likely to be* in the end.

Now this does not suit teaching very well. After all, teachers need to be clear about their ideas and transmit enthusiasm to children so that they feel able to cope. There is nearly always an end-product produced as the result of any creative work which is going on. In fact the end-product, to a certain extent, is what identifies the creative process which has taken place. Defined end-products are attractive because we know exactly what to prepare and what we are all supposed to be doing. Being vague and indecisive is no virtue. It smacks of impractical theory which has no place in the classroom. There are constraints like the rationing of materials, organization of time and distribution of work-space to consider. A clearly envisaged end-product can actually appear to be the most promising line of approach for us to think about.

Since we are surrounded by so many end-products it is not surprising they have such a hold over our thinking. Well before they reach school age, children encounter all sorts of products such as toys, furniture, houses and their own playthings. Even in their early scribbles they begin to learn that there is a connection between action and the end-product. Wooden building bricks, Lego and cardboard boxes link 'making' with 'made' and support the child's view of how he thinks the world exists (Feldman, 1982). As adults we also experience seeing end-products as the aim of a variety of occupations. The technical wizardry is much less apparent than the product which has evolved as a result of it. And even in the world of art it is the end-product which dominates the galleries of the world.

Children become conditioned from a very early age to expect to take home from playschool some artistic end-product. And with help from parents the emphasis on valuing end-products has begun. To abandon the artistic take-away in playgroups would require exceptional courage. Letting children have artwork to take home is often proof that they in fact did something with their play. In providing for end-products at the playschool stage, a habit is formed which need not necessarily spill over into infant schools, but often it does. Many children already come to their first art sessions at school to find that their experience of playschool art is largely reinforced.

No wonder there is so much resistance to art being seen as a language of expression. When there is a clear end-product in mind it is easier to see our way. There is always something to make. We can even consider the skills that are necessary to make things an end in themselves and point to folding, sticking and colouring-in as achievements in their own right. When we plan art activities solely with the end-product in mind, children can make things endlessly with-out our needing to consider why. Art as a language of expression on the other hand may well be a fine description of how we might see art. But has it anything to offer for the day-to-day business of planning purposeful learning?

In fact art as a 'language of expression' generally finds its way into the descriptions used by art educators to encompass a variety of desirable qualities. Feeling, expression, communication and, more obviously, colour, form, line, texture, tone and pattern are associated with it, much in the same way that sound qualities are part of music. Essentially, art as a language describes the way we express our relation to the world through visual means rather than words. How this is linked to practical planning of art activity lies in the way it can be brought into operation long before any organizational details determine what will happen. We examine first the qualities we think are important ingredients for the art session.

This can more easily be understood by taking an example found in industrial design. Supposing we were working as the designer of a new racing car. We might have *speed* in mind as an essential quality we needed. *Speed* could not be found anywhere in the component parts of the car or in its final appearance as an end-product. *Speed* is associated with what we expect the car will do.

If the truly creative part of artistic growth does not lie only in making end-products, then we must look at what children *do*, as well as what they have *made*. If we cannot be entirely certain about what they are to produce as an end-product (and of course we must have a rough idea), then we will need to give very clear guidance about what they are asked to do. Though there will be a 'mental sketch' held in our heads as to what the likely end-product will be, by concentrating on the process, individuality can become a vital ingredient, conformity the exception.

This might in some instances be as simple as getting children to decide what shape to draw, finding out how to solve a problem, or trying out three different ways of doing the same thing. Instead of being dogmatic about the final picture we wanted for 'Our Street', we would be asking them to make choices about the way they went about it. There would be the chance for more interpretation and they could arrive at a variety of end-products, not one. The children would, for example, examine the difference between one kind of window and another, one chimney and another, and build up their own detailed mental images of how they see things in terms of shapes and colours. They would be encouraged to make changes as the design progressed and extend their awareness of shape and colour through the individual decisions they made. Windows and doors would be their own windows and doors, special and personal to them rather than determined for them by an adult.

For the teacher it is not so much end-products which must be emphasized as the *process* which will lead children to produce original work. Besides asking 'What can they put in a picture of their own street?', we need to ask ourselves,

- 'How can they develop their expression through art?' (By being introduced to the variety of shapes of windows, doors, and the brickwork around them?)
- 'How can they become more aware of their surroundings?' (Encourage them to look, compare and collect examples, pictures, photographs.)
- 'How can I develop their confidence to experiment?' (By rewarding and encouraging different and original solutions to problems?)
- 'How can they use their feelings in what they do?' (Through drama, stories, music and discussion?)

And more specifically,

- 'How can I get them thinking carefully about shape and pattern?'
- 'How can I develop their skills in colour-mixing?'
- 'How can they develop their drawings?'

Such questions (which are developed in Chapter 6) are ones which directly influence what we ask children to do. Within one piece of artwork they may be asked to think of several things even if they are very young and inexperienced artists. To help them, rough preliminary drawings might be suitable as a way of beginning, or comparison of photographs of buildings could be another stimulus to their thinking. The planning to make this possible does not happen by chance but is carefully structured to allow for as much flexibility as possible in the final results.

When children are dealing with artistic ideas, standards of achievement cannot be pointed to in the same way as with folding, sticking, filling in neatly, or using a brush. These are basic skills which may or may not lead to invention, feeling, expression and imagination, all qualities children can display through their artwork. When we consider what children will do and how their minds are occupied, we deal with important bricks from which to build up artistic learning.

One reason why being clear about the process is important is that it is much more likely to make the climate of the classroom one of thought as well as activity. Compare this with planning which is based on end-products only. If children are not really thinking about their own original artwork they are more inclined to follow the teacher's planned formula. Yet as simple a strategy as asking them to make three or four decisions themselves about their artwork avoids the predetermined, end-product thought-trap. There are promising opportunities for bringing variety into the process and accepting many interpretations of what is asked of children in the production of art. They will then have taken responsibility for themselves. For them the aims can be several, the choices many and the results quite individual.

# 4 How children draw

It is very tempting to show children how to draw. Often what happens is that a method or stereotype is taught and the children copy it. There are plenty of well-known stereotypes to be found. The zigzag shape of a Christmas tree so frequently found is surely more to do with adult concepts of a tree than what a child would draw. Yet many of these stereotypes are shown with the best of intentions. Children see how to draw birds by joining up two circles, or fishes by adding to an oval shape. Or they learn to draw a shape for themselves and repeat it over and over again. When they develop their own repeated symbols this is quite natural to them and part of their evolving perception. But when shapes are forced on them by an adult, then progress may be somewhat held back.

Around the age of 7, or even earlier, children can become dissatisfied with the symbolic drawings which they have done and are likely to say that they cannot draw properly. Perhaps they pick this up from adults or they simply develop a fear of drawing something they find complicated. Very rarely do they say this when they are pattern-making, printing, or drawing abstract shapes. Flat shapes are not so difficult as dealing with space. More usually the response 'I can't draw' arises from trying to draw animals or the human figure. There are well-known difficulties like trying to draw someone's nose or a person sitting cross-legged. But apart from these especially difficult problems most children are capable of making a very good attempt to draw what they can see or imagine.

The difficulty a teacher has in persuading children to draw can partly be solved by understanding what they are capable of doing. The heart of the problem, though, lies in finding ways in which children can even begin to draw what they obviously find difficult. What do children think about when they try out the first marks on paper? What exactly does a teacher need to bring to their attention? Fundamental to teaching young children to draw are

- looking at pattern
- looking at shape
- practice in drawing patterns and shapes
- acceptance and encouragement by the teacher
- refusing to draw for children.

For those children who find drawing is a problem, pattern proves to be a good starting place. The search for pattern can begin with flat surfaces where the problems of drawing a three-dimensional world on two-dimensional paper are lessened. This is not a method of teaching drawing, but a good way to begin looking because what is being drawn can be thought about in simple stages. A child who cannot draw a cat, for example, can often draw a pattern of the markings on a cat's fur. Decisions about stripes, lines, or other patterns can be tackled without the complication of an outline. Inevitably, working on the pattern associated with cat fur involves looking more closely than usual at a cat or pictures of cats. From there it is a much smaller step to look more closely at the shape the cat might be. Drawing a pattern may also provide just the necessary incentive to make an extra effort to look for a shape to put it in. From observation of cat-fur patterns grows the intense looking and trial and error needed to determine the cat's shape.

Similarly, a class might start out by looking at the patterns to be found on tree bark or stones. Classroom collections of pattern, rubbings from bark and drawings of pattern might be made. All these create such an interest in looking and finding out which patterns came from which trees, that it is almost impossible not to discover something about the shape of trees and stones at the same time. The one activity has a natural relationship to the other. Wax-crayon rubbings or drawings which show changes of pattern can be cut into shapes to define an outline. The simplest of collections can provide material for discussion and comparison of shape.

The way we can learn to draw shapes by making comparisons is intriguing. Our brains already have the capacity for comparing shapes and this is a sufficiently sophisticated skill to enable us to recognize people we know. We compare what we see with previously known facial measurements and their relationships, which our brain has memorized. Such comparisons with known shapes are also used when we try to draw. We compare with the known and more consciously analyse what we see in order to translate our vision to paper. With young children the process can be turned into a shape game, which includes

- looking for circles
- looking for squares
- looking for anything which is almost straight
- comparing curves and straights with each other
- looking for shapes which change when they are moved, or when we see them from a different angle
- looking for sharply defined edges, or pointed, spiked shapes.

Deciding what shape things are is usually a process of comparing with the extremes, such as straight against circle, curve against straight, or curve in comparison with a circle. A curved shape can sometimes be analysed by asking to what extent it is similar to, or different from, a circle or a straight line. We can ask what the straightest part of the curve is. What is the most curved? Which is the longest? Which the shortest? These are questions which help us to define what we are looking at by inviting judgements about similarities and differences. When children are working from memory, the process is a similar one but requires questions which trigger previous memories of particular shapes. An example of these kinds of questions comes from a game of the five-minute sort where children are not given any answers but are made to visualize for themselves. The aim is to build up a strong mental image, sometimes supported by a further search for reference material, such as pictures, photographs and videotapes.

## Cat and mouse

CAT  Is its head bigger or smaller than its body?
Can you imagine it with its back arched?
Can you show me the shape in the air with your finger?
Has it got its claws out?
Is it sitting down? Stretching? Standing? What do you think it's doing?
Where does it put its tail?
What kind of tail is it?
Is it angry or friendly?
How do you know?
What markings has it on its fur?

MOUSE  Do you think it has a round nose? A pointed nose? A flat nose? Turned up?
How long is its tail?
Is its body bigger at the back or in the middle?
Where do its whiskers go?
Has it got toes?
Are they like yours? What are they like?

Professional book illustrators use reference material such as photographs for their drawings, and to expect children to draw without looking at some reference is to ask a lot of them. They find animals difficult to draw in any case, especially if they are unfamiliar with them. At the stage where 5-year-olds draw a cat much as they would a human being the problem does not arise. They use a symbol for a cat and typically give it a human face. Older children draw in a more visually realistic way and need to develop their skills in observation and translate these on to paper. Each time they make comparisons of shape they develop their drawing skill a fraction more. We can think of this process as one where the act of drawing creates the need to have another look and make comparisons. In turn, looking leads to another drawing, which again promotes further observation.

Anyone who can draw a cat from memory has usually studied its shape very carefully. The drawing is done from a 'mental vocabulary' of the experience of seeing cat shapes. Each time children practise looking and drawing they add to the mental vocabulary they have acquired through the process. Their development, like that of a musician who practises music, can only take place through continual exposure to looking and drawing, comparing, contrasting, making marks and responding to them. In the end the only 'right' shapes to draw are the ones the children have found for themselves.

If we want children to progress, then attempts to tidy up drawings or draw for them are not helpful. They are counter-productive. Acceptance of children's most primitive attempts to draw is very important because without acceptance they will probably give up. It takes considerable mental effort for them to produce a drawing, and by not valuing what they do, we inevitably erode their motivation.

If we as teachers find children's efforts embarrassingly bad we are defining our own problem not theirs. They will not progress by having us force on them an adult concept of shape or pattern because at the primitive early stages of drawing they need to work through one drawing problem to arrive at another. If they are allowed to use one drawing rather like a stepping-stone to another, they will usually learn far more quickly than when an adult interferes.

When children have done their best and faced up to the difficulties of asking themselves what shape they think things are, we have little right to be dissatisfied with the results. Such drawings are not necessarily good by our adult standards but can be excellent expressions of the way children think.

## Examples from teachers

Examining what teachers say about drawing can reveal a variety of commonly experienced problems and a few useful solutions.

> Some children come to me having been to playschool, some straight from home, and they are all enthusiastic about exploring with art materials. At the age of 5 they don't have inhibitions about using paint but some do about drawing. If a child says 'Can you draw this for me?' I always get them to look and talk about it. This week we're looking at the shape of fruit and vegetables so I've set up a display in my classroom. They can touch, smell, and look at them. Today each child had to make comparisons between various shapes. An apple was like a football shape and we compared the curve of a banana with the edge of a reading book. We sorted the fruit and vegetables into sizes and we discussed how apples grew attached by the stalk. Later I had them making fruit shapes out of Plasticine so they could keep changing the shape.
>
> (Teacher of 5-year-olds)

The 'I can't draw' response usually happens when children are trying to achieve a realistic likeness (of an animal, for instance). My own reaction is one of sympathy – I was virtually thrown out of the art class at the age of 13 because I could never do it and I had the feeling of failure. But I don't give help to any child in the form of doing the drawing. Instead, I ask the child to explain the problem – is it part of a figure he cannot do? Or has he no idea where to start? I get him to close his eyes and try to see the shape and size and pattern. I might also ask him how it feels – soft, furry, spiky? . . . I also ask other children and between us we build up a picture of what it looks like. I let them look at books but not just to copy.

(Teacher of 7- to 8-year-olds)

All that happens if you show them how to draw is that they repeat your stereotype. If they copy from books or trace them they get stuck and don't seem to progress. It's like a formula which they go on repeating. So we spend a lot of time looking and comparing one shape with another.

(Teacher of 6-year-olds)

I play a classroom game where we all look at the same object to see how many different things we can see and compare.

(Teacher of 8-year-olds)

When they're looking I get them to simplify things by cutting paper shapes in black paper. It's not easy but it makes them think about shape.

(Teacher of 9-year-olds)

I get them to look at a bicycle which I prop up against a window. It's such a flat shape against the window in the classroom that it is almost two-dimensional. The children can draw it and build up their own confidence by finding they know a lot about it already, and a lot more than they thought they did.

(Teacher of 9-year-olds)

We can assess children's drawings by seeing them as an interpretation of what they themselves have experienced. In the end, we may criticize pupils for not looking hard enough but clearly we cannot criticize them for being at their particular stage of development.

Children enjoy drawing things which they are attached to or like very much. A group of children who bring in something from home, a toy or a teddy bear, will generally make a good job of drawing it because they know it so well. A familiar toy has its shape well and truly embedded in a child's consciousness and proves to be a very productive way to encourage careful observation. They can find out which is the fattest part of the toy, which the thinnest, and the act of bringing in a toy to draw also gives endless opportunities for discussion and work in other areas of the curriculum.

With most drawing problems, solutions lie in reconsidering the appearance of the object being drawn, rather than giving attention to the shortcomings of the drawing. When children are drawing something, especially something unfamiliar, the teacher's role is to talk more about the object they are drawing than the drawing itself. The importance of this teaching point cannot be emphasized too strongly. Another careful look at the source of reference for the drawing will bring about new decisions for whatever the child feels is not going well. Changes we might suggest to be made to their drawing, rather than to their observation, are often counter-productive. They are simply our own imagery. After all, which one of us has the right to impose our own literal vision on children's imaginative eyes?

## Children's imagery

Much as we might like to think that children move clearly from one stage of drawing to another, their progress is not so smooth. We cannot say that drawings are always typical of a particular age range. Yet some understanding of what is going on is essential if we are to know what can be expected. Years ago, Kellogg (1969) and Gardner (1980) wrote about the stages children go through from scribble through symbolism and schema to visual realism. Although children usually follow these stages, they also defy the rules and produce combinations of stages. The 5-year-old who drew the picture shown in Figure 6 used a combination of symbolic and realistic drawing. The drawing of himself is typical for a 5-year-old but the drawing of the school is not. He

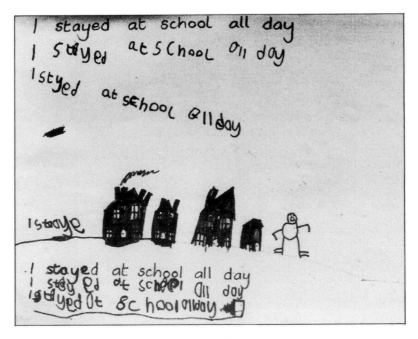

*Figure 6*  I Stayed at School All Day. Age 5. 365 × 250 mm.

*Figure* 7 House Stereotype. Age 6. 340 × 290 mm.

*Figure* 8 Houseface. Age 5. 295 × 210 mm.

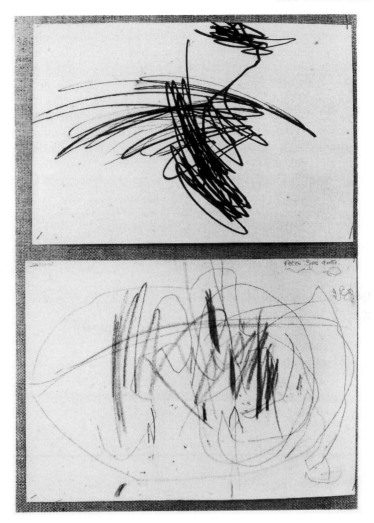

*Figures 9, 10* Scribble. Age 3. 290 × 420 mm.

has looked carefully at the number of chimneys and windows. The windows are not simply placed at each corner (see Figure 7) but are set in from the edge of the brickwork as they would be in reality. Why then is there a mixture of styles?

A useful way to interpret the two styles is to think of how children reconstruct their experiences. At the moment of drawing, this particular child (who lived close to the school) looked at the school buildings and drew what he could see. He counted the chimneys and windows and kept looking at the school from outside. When he put himself in the picture he was certainly not working from a full-length mirror, and reconstructed his knowledge of himself by producing a symbol as large as the school. He still drew himself the largest because at this stage he considers he is the most important feature of the drawing. Yet he does not worry at all about combining inner thoughts and outer vision in the one piece of work. The distinctions an adult might make are not there. Even houses and people can become fused together in a child's mind as a drawing begins as one thing and ends up looking like another (Figure 8).

Typically, what can be expected from 2–4-year-olds is scribble. Scribble is to drawing what babbling is to talk. From rather random marks they make when they first are given paper and crayons, children develop enough control to make the scribble more ordered and intentional. They like scribbling and will repeat the activity just for the fun of it. Occasionally within their scribbles they will find images by accident such as boats, people, houses and themselves. If asked, they will invent subject-matter for the pictures even when none existed. Parents

*Figure 11* Daddy, Peter, Mum. Age 3. 350 × 150 mm.

*Figure 12* Daddy with a Big Face. Age 4. 580 × 350 mm.

*Figure 13* Hills and Scribble. Age 5. 450 × 320 mm.

often ask what things have been drawn and their children become very practised at giving answers, even if they have to invent these.

Their first really recognizable and intentionally drawn shapes are circles or oval shapes. Before long these become 'Me', 'My Mum' or 'My Dad'. As we can see from the example in Figure 12, a pre-school child will sometimes add expression to the face. The most important symbols are nearly always the largest, often representing the child himself, and there is no sense of perspective or space as we know it. When such drawings are produced it is not uncommon to find children returning to scribble within a few seconds of concentrated drawing. They still enjoy scribbling, even though they can draw symbols, and are reluctant to give it up. Art materials are as yet fairly new to children of this age and playing with them is just as important as doing any drawing. At school the scribbling is still there (Figure 13). Houses are drawn but scribble is still included.

In the symbolic drawings of people, a private code is used and we more or less have to read the image as if it were a word. Symbols for people are drawn almost looking like tadpoles. They have no neck, sometimes no body, arms, fingers, or toes. Quite what meaning can be attached to this kind of drawing is uncertain. It is a very dangerous practice to read too much into children's drawings and we are very often misled. We can say that these drawings describe more how they think of themselves than what they actually see when they look. They are not very aware of their own neck and their head feels big in comparison with the rest of their bodies. They cannot see their shoulders, so the way they draw turns out to be a satisfactory description of how they feel they are, rather than a very recognizable likeness.

*Figure 14* Mum Frightened by a Spider. Age 5. 255 × 175 mm.

*Figure 15* Blackbird. Age 6. 280 × 330 mm.

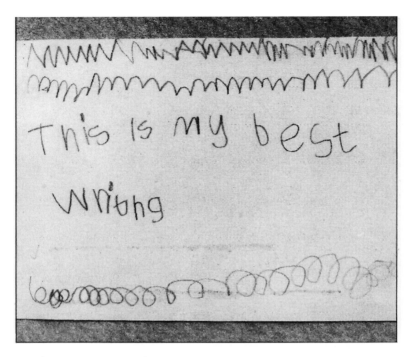

*Figure 16* My Best Writing. Age 5. 250 × 150 mm.

*Figure 17* Writing/Landscape. Age 6. 305 × 180 mm.

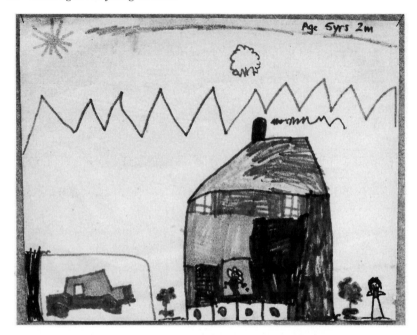

*Figure 18*  X-Ray House. Age 5. 310 × 240 mm.

When children draw from experience of looking, they often draw expressive essentials which adults miss. The character of a spider (Figure 14) is shown as something moving with lots of legs and drawn larger than life. Mother is recovering, tea in hand, and the scene is expressed almost like a drama. The blackbird (Figure 15) is drawn with a plump and well-fed look about it. Like the spider which moves, and the drawing of a guitar (Figure 5, in Chapter 3), there is no attempt to draw an exact perceptual illusion. The images we see are very advanced personal schema but still drawn in response to a knowledge of experiences.

From the age of around 6 to 9 years the schema change and become more elaborate. We can find drawings of girls (Figure 19) where a triangle forms the basis for the drawing, and we can see examples of the influence of other school activities on art. Often no real distinction is made between writing patterns and drawing (Figures 16 and 17). Another characteristic is 'X-ray' drawing, which we can see in the drawing of a house and garage (Figure 18) where there is no attempt to hide the car. The X-ray picture tells us what is known to be there so it follows that we can also see inside the house. Patterns are derived from the experience of filling in mathematics worksheets and writing. Number and drawing feature together if a child decides they will.

Awareness of space is often confused in young children's minds and they may solve problems by working all round their paper (Figure 19) so we have no firm idea of where the top and bottom of the room is. We must remember that at

*Figure 19*  All Around Dance. Age 6. 195 × 143 mm.

this age to teach perspective would be inappropriate as perception of space is unlikely to be as we experience it as adults. The circular expression of a dance is that particular child's way of solving the problem of coping with drawing three-dimensional space.

The age of 8 to 12 years is dominated by a greater concern for accuracy of detail and can broadly be called a stage of visual realism. No longer do we always see people drawn with both arms in view if they are standing sideways. One arm is allowed to disappear behind a person's body. For boys particularly, this is an age when they draw subject-matter like spaceships and helicopters, launches and battles. Not a detail is left to chance. There is some evidence that the organization of the design is carefully thought about, even the placing of the image on the paper is more critical than before. A whole tale can be told in some drawings where planes take off, engage an enemy, shoot, explode and dive, all within the same picture.

Such a concern is there for including detail that excellent opportunities present themselves for teachers to make use of this aspect of drawing. Older infants or primary children thrive on learning to develop detailed observation. Theirs is a world where drawing refuels their curiosity and lends itself to discovery. The stages they have been through – scribble, symbols, schema and visual realism – are each important experiences which a teacher could impede. Children must proceed at their own pace. Knowing the stages gives us the opportunity to match activities to what the children are capable of producing, and avoids forcing upon them those images for which they are not yet ready.

*Figure 20* Space Shuttle. Age 8. 340 × 300 mm.

The fixed blue line at the top of a painting and the green one at the bottom are sky and grass until the children are ready for it to be different. Faces are painted blue, green, or purple, until flesh colours seem important enough. Focusing their attention on the sky, or on flesh tones, but not demanding that sky meets ground, or that flesh is pink, encourages them to look and question what they see. The search must still be theirs, not ours.

Only experience gives us a true indication of what can be expected from children and without finding out for ourselves we could very easily over-direct them. The stages of development outlined here are a guide to expectations but no indication of what children can achieve for themselves. If we over-direct them or attempt to condition what they draw, we are misunderstanding the nature of art teaching and the minds of children. Then, they draw with only a fraction of their expressive power and energy. If we understand, encourage and direct their attention towards looking carefully, they draw with remarkable conviction and confidence.

# 5   Developing ideas

## Using themes

How difficult it is to resist finding an impressive piece of classroom art and repeating it as prescribed. Examples of 'things to do and make' are not hard to come by, but can lack a focus or context for learning. Linking ideas together in a theme can be more attractive than a set of recipes for art, but raises the obvious question 'How do I get from a theme to an art activity?' The question is a reasonable one. There is a great deal at stake in preparing, planning and teaching art, so a theme is not an activity. Either the activity follows from the development of ideas in a theme, or the theme is suggested by an ongoing series of activities. The excitement of working through themes is not knowing quite how well things will work out. By contrast, once outcomes become predictable, art is a very dull affair.

The UK National Curriculum and government schemes are full of learning objectives and pupil expectations. Learning objectives are essential to artistic learning, but not really the best starting point for creative planning. An obvious question is 'Where do I start?' because activities need to be specific and focused. Government documents in 2001 were full of answers to this in the form of units of study from the Qualifications and Standards Authority (QCA). Understandably teachers thought they provided answers because they gave step-by-step instructions. Studying the learning objectives in a government scheme is certainly one way of devising art activities. What studying objectives fails to do is show how skills and progression develop. Themes and learning objectives are partly symbiotic, learning objectives feeding off and giving back to a theme.

Understandably, some teachers feel more secure having lessons set out for them. Devising themes without knowing what learning will take place seems a risky way to proceed. Yet a set of unrelated art activities is no recipe for making progress. Chapter 6, alongside Chapters 16 and 17 shows ways to think about what might be achieved in art activities once a theme has been chosen. This chapter is strictly concerned with much broader ideas which then lead to worthwhile activities. The reality is that learning objectives often arise from the needs of the pupil, as well as from themes and schemes. There are needs such as developing the use of colour, improving skills in using a brush or widening the range of subjects in painting. There are also needs such as learning more about an artist's methods and ideas. If more than one activity is needed to do this, we have a theme of sorts.

A theme is something to generate excitement, investigation and interest. It is the catalyst to artistic development because it lies at the heart of invention and creativity. Even if thoughts occur such as 'We'll paint', 'We'll do this with collage' or 'They need to work on a larger scale', the theme is still the driving force. Themes are a legitimate creative indulgence because they spark ideas which can then be honed into art activities.

Developing children's ideas through themes is also educationally profitable. The one-off art activity has its place, but can fail to make contact with any other part of the curriculum and may not even fit easily into the rest of the art programme. Changing, adapting and adding to ideas can lead children in new directions. Disparate areas of the curriculum are threaded together and children make more of the original impetus to create. There may always be good reasons for providing the isolated short activity, one unrelated to any other context (shortage of a special material would be an example, children's brief attention span another). If a number of ideas do not quite constitute a theme, they can still encourage learning to take place across curricular boundaries (see Chapter 6 for a view of curriculum change, planning and development).

Themes are often focused around 'variety in materials' or 'developing a technique', but these are not long-term ways to create art activities. New materials, fascinating though they are to children, cannot be relied on to provide an endless source of ideas. Children enjoy discovering what various media will do and such exploratory activities characterize many art sessions. Important differences between one material and another cannot be denied, but if development is to take place, simply to confront children with a change of media is not enough. The development of their artistic ideas is a worthwhile activity and should concern us more than any new material.

Progression in art is possible if ideas, explored by the teacher with the children, are in a sequence. Crayon then paint? Draw a design, then choose the best medium to develop it? Look at a famous work of art and devise three art projects from it? Sometimes an apparent mish-mash of ideas is nothing of the sort because one skill in observing or drawing feeds into another as ideas flow. Recurring themes, such as 'Flight' are packed with possibilities ranging from close observation of birds to the science of keeping a kite in the air. Of course, ideas need to have a strong relationship one to another and this is evident in a theme which links to other areas of the curriculum.

Ideas and themes in themselves do not automatically suggest what opportunities for related learning will unfold. Choices have to be made and decisions taken in the light of what looks the most promising. For that reason, a theme needs to be sufficiently open to allow flexibility of purpose and the chance to cover an extensive area of interests. The popularity of themes like 'The Sea', or 'Animals', probably arises from their being sufficiently adaptable to a variety of possible outcomes. From the broadest of beginnings, material can be chosen, refined, put aside, or eliminated, as its educational potential becomes apparent.

## Themes as a resource

A useful strategy for developing ideas is to work the way many cartoonists do when they are in search of a punchline. They 'brainstorm' as many words on to paper as they can in connection with the cartoon. The technique is also used on Study Skills courses and at planning meetings. Some research evidence suggests that children brainstorming in pairs leads to better creative writing (Kenny, 2001). Once the paper is filled with word associations, and randomly placed ideas in connection with a theme, links can be made. Words can lead to other words, more words, reminders of any activity to be done, or new relationships between ideas. The resource is developed as a personal 'think-tank' and is quite unconditionally filled with anything which is triggered by the theme. One way of producing a good idea is to have lots of ideas and associations, then pick the best. Brainstorming words makes this a possibility.

Suppose we pick a theme, 'Animals', and begin. By free association of words we might arrive at ANIMALS, wild, domestic, camouflage, colour. These words could become themes in themselves or short-lived ideas for art activities. They also provide the beginning of a much larger resource which could evolve over a period of days or weeks. Imagine a sheet of A3 paper pinned up in the kitchen. It begins as shown in Chart 1 and develops more fully to produce a resource as shown in Chart 2.

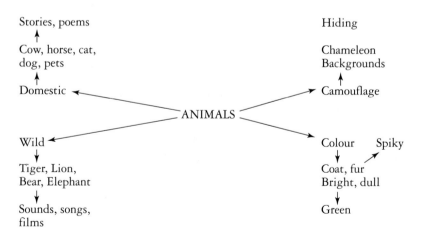

*Chart 1* Free Association on a Theme

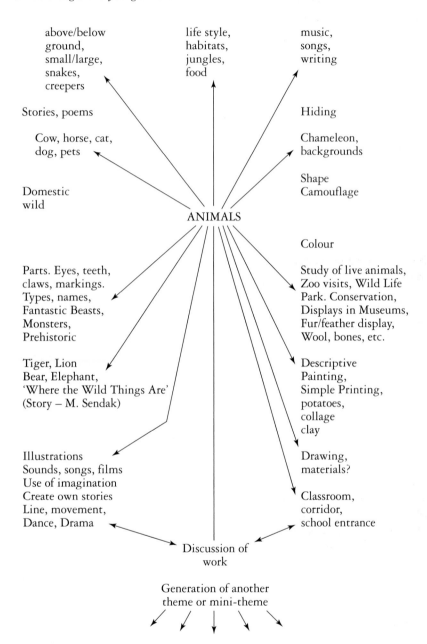

above/below
ground,
small/large,
snakes,
creepers

life style,
habitats,
jungles,
food

music,
songs,
writing

Stories, poems

Hiding

Cow, horse, cat,
dog, pets

Chameleon,
backgrounds

Domestic
wild

Shape
Camouflage

ANIMALS

Colour

Parts. Eyes, teeth,
claws, markings.
Types, names,
Fantastic Beasts,
Monsters,
Prehistoric

Study of live animals,
Zoo visits, Wild Life
Park. Conservation,
Displays in Museums,
Fur/feather display,
Wool, bones, etc.

Tiger, Lion
Bear, Elephant,
'Where the Wild Things Are'
(Story – M. Sendak)

Descriptive
Painting,
Simple Printing,
potatoes,
collage
clay

Illustrations
Sounds, songs, films
Use of imagination
Create own stories
Line, movement,
Dance, Drama

Drawing,
materials?

Classroom,
corridor,
school entrance

Discussion of
work

Generation of another
theme or mini-theme

*Chart 2*  A 'Brainstormed' Resource

## Some useful themes

There is some overlap possible with themes and these should be treated as if they were the beginning of a brainstorming chart.

| | | |
|---|---|---|
| Reflections | Holes | Gems |
| Growth | Fire | Old |
| Space | Spring | New |
| Fear | Summer | Churches |
| Dark | Autumn | Contrast |
| Flight | Winter | Biological |
| Magic | Work | Prehistoric |
| Night | Surprises | Machines |
| Mystery | Boats | Outer Space |
| Parks | Cars | Monsters |
| Shops | Lorries | Food |
| Buildings | Trains | Wood |
| Factories | Transport | Pattern |
| Uniforms | Stairways | Camouflage |
| Police | Underground | People |
| Milkman | The Sea | Jungles |
| People Who Help | Underwater | Carnival |
| Time | Animals | Fair |
| Spirals | Insects | Fantasy |
| Circles | Red, Yellow, etc. | Fish |
| Squares | Colour | Fungi |
| Triangles | Texture | Butterflies |
| Oblongs | Lines | Moths |
| Rectangles | Gardens | Fables |
| Trees | Playtime | Ponds |
| Leaves | Chimneys | Plants |
| Bark | Doors | Wild Flowers |
| Hedges | Lights | Costume |
| Farms | Birds | Earth |
| Surfaces | Faces | Travel |
| Insides | Masks | Stars |
| Inside/outside | Windows | Races |
| Habitats | Formal | Castles |
| Weather | Repeating | Walls |
| Skies | Abstract | Fences |
| Water | Form | Markets |
| Thin | Transparent | Smooth |
| Miniature | Giant | Liquids |
| Games | Light | Surfaces |
| Stripes | Metals | Vegetables |

| Wheels | Tracks | The Planets |
| Units | Tangles | Stones |

The two examples given in Charts 3 and 4 are taken from the list at random. To develop these it is sometimes a good idea to draw a circle round any word in the flow-chart and try making this a new theme.

## Making choices

We might think that a brainstormed flow-chart is enough to spark off a dozen ideas for activities. No doubt there are some teachers who find they can think of a whole variety of inspired ideas. But they still make choices and take decisions to structure and sequence activities, no matter how spontaneously they might feel they are working. These choices are common to all art activities. Decisions are taken about what stimulus to provide, what materials to make available, what technique to teach, what learning to emphasize and what problems to pose for children to think about themselves.

In choosing a theme such as 'Water' there are obviously resources to find and links to make. Artists such as Monet, Turner, Hokusai and Degas can provide knowledge about different ways artists have expressed ideas about water. Turner and Degas painted the sea quite differently and Monet's paintings of reflections in a lake are forceful images. Artistic progression may come through discussion, writing or using art media to create something. The learning objectives to achieve this come long after decisions about finding resources and developing ideas. In some instances, the resources generate the theme instead of the other way around. School trips to the coast are an obvious opportunity. Sea-washed twigs, tree roots, seaweed, rock-pools and pebbles are all visually interesting resource material.

## Development through ongoing work

In contrast to working through themes, development is also possible as children respond to what they are already doing. Quite outside any considerations of there being a theme, some visual ideas just take off as children make links with other forms of knowledge.

> We were looking at peacock feathers, some of the children using hand lenses to magnify. The purpose of it was to develop their skills in observation . . . one boy noticed that the pattern on a feather is rather like an eye . . . we discussed real eyes and things that looked like eyes. They looked at each other's eyes and compared shapes, lines and colours. When it came to doing some artwork, some did peacocks, some patterns based on feathers, others eyes and patterns based on eye shapes.
>
> (Primary teacher)

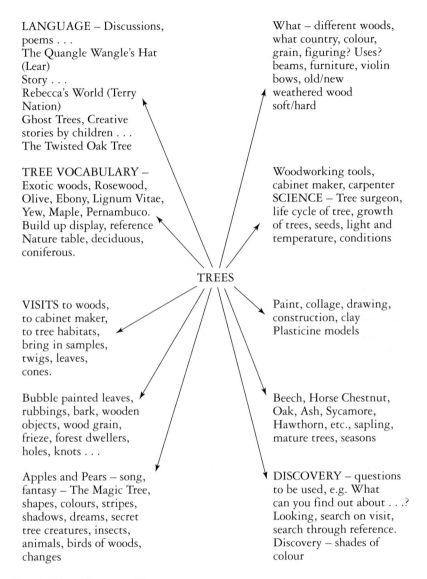

LANGUAGE – Discussions, poems . . .
The Quangle Wangle's Hat (Lear)
Story . . .
Rebecca's World (Terry Nation)
Ghost Trees, Creative stories by children . . .
The Twisted Oak Tree

TREE VOCABULARY – Exotic woods, Rosewood, Olive, Ebony, Lignum Vitae, Yew, Maple, Pernambuco. Build up display, reference Nature table, deciduous, coniferous.

VISITS to woods, to cabinet maker, to tree habitats, bring in samples, twigs, leaves, cones.

Bubble painted leaves, rubbings, bark, wooden objects, wood grain, frieze, forest dwellers, holes, knots . . .

Apples and Pears – song, fantasy – The Magic Tree, shapes, colours, stripes, shadows, dreams, secret tree creatures, insects, animals, birds of woods, changes

What – different woods, what country, colour, grain, figuring? Uses? beams, furniture, violin bows, old/new weathered wood soft/hard

Woodworking tools, cabinet maker, carpenter
SCIENCE – Tree surgeon, life cycle of tree, growth of trees, seeds, light and temperature, conditions

TREES

Paint, collage, drawing, construction, clay Plasticine models

Beech, Horse Chestnut, Oak, Ash, Sycamore, Hawthorn, etc., sapling, mature trees, seasons

DISCOVERY – questions to be used, e.g. What can you find out about . . .? Looking, search on visit, search through reference. Discovery – shades of colour

*Chart 3* 'Trees' Resource Chart

Once ideas like these develop to include a new subject, there are obvious opportunities for making further links with simple science, maths and language. Graphs of eye colouring within the class, stories, songs and discussion of how eyes function can prove valuable vehicles for learning. Unexpected events do not always destroy planning. On the contrary, they often enhance it.

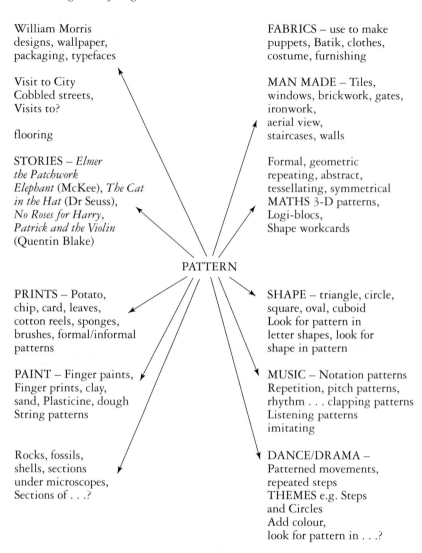

William Morris designs, wallpaper, packaging, typefaces

Visit to City Cobbled streets, Visits to?

flooring

STORIES – *Elmer the Patchwork Elephant* (McKee), *The Cat in the Hat* (Dr Seuss), *No Roses for Harry, Patrick and the Violin* (Quentin Blake)

PRINTS – Potato, chip, card, leaves, cotton reels, sponges, brushes, formal/informal patterns

PAINT – Finger paints, Finger prints, clay, sand, Plasticine, dough String patterns

Rocks, fossils, shells, sections under microscopes, Sections of . . .?

FABRICS – use to make puppets, Batik, clothes, costume, furnishing

MAN MADE – Tiles, windows, brickwork, gates, ironwork, aerial view, staircases, walls

Formal, geometric repeating, abstract, tessellating, symmetrical MATHS 3-D patterns, Logi-blocs, Shape workcards

PATTERN

SHAPE – triangle, circle, square, oval, cuboid Look for pattern in letter shapes, look for shape in pattern

MUSIC – Notation patterns Repetition, pitch patterns, rhythm . . . clapping patterns Listening patterns imitating

DANCE/DRAMA – Patterned movements, repeated steps THEMES e.g. Steps and Circles Add colour, look for pattern in . . .?

*Chart 4* 'Pattern' Resource Chart

My children were talking about a story we were reading which was all about Dutch children enticing storks back to their village. I got them drawing imaginary characters from the story and for that they had to think their way into being part of the action. We did some role play in drama and that led on to very simple mask-making. One girl had the idea we could draw a strip cartoon of the events in the story so we did. Then two of the boys wanted to make a shoebox 'peep' show and we enacted part of the story with them to help them get into the feel of what they wanted to include.

(Primary teacher)

Dramatic play is a superbly rich way of letting children feel from within in order to develop ideas for artwork. Using drama is not everybody's strength but for some teachers artwork borders on performance as they develop ideas with their children.

> I must confess it's difficult to dramatize tree-bark. If we did it in drama we'd do rough scratchy movements to try to 'feel' our way into the imagery . . . tree-ring movements . . . they internalize what they're doing . . . they experience fear, happiness, sadness . . . I remember we'd been working in art on a theme of 'Empty Things', objects which contain nothing. One boy drew the outlines of a rainbow which had been a theme in drama and song. I thought 'Oh dear, he hasn't understood.' I asked him why he'd drawn a rainbow in pencil. 'Well,' he said, 'it's an empty rainbow . . . no colours in it.' I thought that was very creative thinking.
>
> (Reception teacher)

## Games of the imagination

An intriguing device for developing ideas comes from Robert Eberle (1971), who in his children's book *Scamper* suggests a way of stretching the mind. The Scamper technique can be applied to drawings, session plans, writing and in fact anything which requires designing or planning. We can imagine it applied to ideas generated through themes, or we can think of it as a checklist to be used before ideas become too firmly fixed. Based on *Your Creative Power* by Alex Osborn (1948/72), Eberle suggests:

| | | |
|---|---|---|
| S | SUBSTITUTE | To have a person or thing act or serve in the place of another. |
| C | COMBINE | To bring together or unite. |
| A | ADAPT | To adjust for the purpose of suiting a condition or purpose. |
| M | MODIFY | To alter, change the form or quality. |
| | MAGNIFY | To enlarge, make greater in form or quality. |
| | MINIFY | To make smaller, lighter, slower, less frequent. |
| P | PUT TO OTHER USES | To be used for purposes other than originally intended. |
| E | ELIMINATE | To remove, omit, or get rid of, a quality, part, or whole. |
| R | REVERSE | To place opposite or contrary, to turn round. |
| | REARRANGE | To change the order, different plan, layout, or scheme. |

The Scamper technique can be used to play out five-minute games where children imagine what objects would be like bigger, smaller, combined, rearranged and so on. Or this mind-flexing idea can be applied to other areas of the curriculum so that questions arise:

S    Can you think of a new way of using this?
C    What do you think might happen if you try to put these together?
A    What else is like this?
M    Can you imagine this bigger? Smaller?
P    Do you think we might use this for . . .?
E    What might this be like if you got rid of . . .?
R    What happens if you turn it backwards . . . or upside down?

Artists, writers, composers and designers exercise many of these Scamper methods quite naturally as they create. 'Scamper' encapsulates a process which is true to the artist in one particularly important respect. When ideas are formulated they do not remain static and fixed for all time. The creative process is an unending, living, transforming one. Far from acting on one idea without modification, creative thinkers tend continually to reflect on the ideas they have evolved. They prefer to live with less certain outcomes and adapt solutions to different circumstances.

In practical terms the questions above, which as teachers we might ask of our children, are also those which apply to any planning we might do ourselves. A brainstormed resource can be adapted using 'Scamper', as can the art activities which are already under way. The more varied the development of ideas, the greater is the range of options open to children from which to make choices, take decisions and think independently. No idea is ever sacrosanct and nothing is really a final statement of intent. Even the so-called 'finished' artwork can change.

> A word my children love to learn is 'embellish'. It arose because I found my children tended to rush work and finish their art very quickly without taking much trouble over it. We discussed embellishment and decoration and now they very often embellish things with pattern . . . sometimes a design will go on for days as they leave it and come back to it, changing and adding to it.
>
> (Teacher of 7-year-olds)

Not content to leave ideas where they are, this teacher (see Plate 6) pushed the children further by giving a new direction to the work. In her judgement it was necessary to teach children that something else could be done. There would be other times when the best thing to do was move on to another idea entirely, because the work was complete enough in itself. For a teacher whose style was more geared to materials and techniques, work could develop in a different way.

> I know a lot grows out of the materials they use . . . I give them a choice . . . if they've done any simple printing with potatoes, I find they often want to print instead of draw or paint. There's quite a range of materials which they can go and get for themselves . . . I often keep one or two things

back, like a special paper or fur fabric, so I can introduce it later when they've got started . . . but I do want them to take decisions about the materials they use . . . a lot seems to come out of doing that. Sometimes they also need to see a technique demonstrated . . . we were doing a topic on 'Divers Under the Sea' and I decided to show them what could happen if the paper was flooded with water and colour added . . . when it was dry, they added collage and paint on top . . . some of them added pastel drawing as well.

(Teacher of 8-year-olds)

It is quite surprising how little encouragement some children need to think creatively. If a lot of artwork takes place around them they accept it as a normal way of thinking about ideas and the process becomes self-generating. Children make relationships between one idea and the next in a far more imaginative way than do many adults. To a child, there are all sorts of fantastic possibilities, and to encourage a developing idea, often all that is necessary is for the teacher to join in the fantasy. Acceptance of children's varied and bizarre ideas persuades them to develop much more in their artwork than if they only respond to suggestions their teacher makes. Too many suggestions from the teacher can elicit over-directed work and too few can result in little extension of their thinking.

Hitting the right balance requires a degree of judgement which is only possible as we gain experience and understanding of art. But there is no doubt that holding back our own suggestions, and trying to develop those ideas which are offered, is far better than making children dependent through over-direction. Whether we avoid this through developing themes with them, playing imaginative games, questioning, or stimulating their thinking, requires judgement. Perhaps the risk worth taking in art teaching is continuously to develop children's ideas and see what results. It is far more creative a teaching strategy than identifying some tangible end-product towards which we steer the children. Developing ideas demands sensitivity and a willingness to step back more than occasionally to allow children to take the initiatives. They will develop artistically provided they are allowed to follow their ideas through by themselves. To do so they need skilful guidance, rather than rigid direction, which is why no substitute has yet been found for high-quality teachers.

Anyone who has the courage to develop themes will probably be surprised to find ideas for art activities occur anyway. Themes and ideas are not subject to a formula that says 'Do this first, then this, then this.' We think in a variety of ways. For example, here are the thoughts of two teachers. Some thoughts are the same, but the differences are going to be important in developing the theme.

I thought we might do something about hedges. I immediately thought of hedges full of gaps and holes. I see these on the way home. Then I thought of light and dark brushstrokes on a green base, rather like a Leylandii hedge. Elder in flower and poppies by a roadside hedge took me on to thinking about birds' nests, garden hedges and the science of growth. None of these ideas really triggered an order or a starting point. I could think of food chains, the history of hedges from the sheep farming after the 'Black Death' and the way they are being replanted in this new century. We do need some green paint though! Could we look at leaves? Is this suggesting murals or collage? Have I a burning need to improve their handling of paint or is it something to do with close observation of Hawthorn walking sticks? Art is a bit like that isn't it? You have to cast yourself adrift for a while before the really interesting ideas spring to mind.

Hedges, to me, are boundaries. They surround a garden or a field, a playground or a park. They give privacy so nobody sees you sunbathing, but they have gaps and you can even creep through these. Hedges can be very old. Actually, the more species of plants you can find in a hedgerow, the older the hedge will be. They shelter lots of small creatures and they change from winter to summer. They've got bare twigs, blossom, green and berries. What can the children learn about a hedge? What patterns do the boundaries make and is there a pattern we can find? Formal hedges in a maze or knot-garden are fascinating, but an aerial photograph of fields is something quite different, with a different history. In art I'd look at a changing hedge, so that would be an ongoing theme. I would look at what you could see through a gap, not the hedge itself but a 'peephole' of the world because there are patterns of twig growth and leaf shapes which might be useful for printing. I'd probably want to do formal tessellations in printing using hedges as a starting point. Using the colours of crops in aerial photographs, I'd do patchworking areas with collage or fabric. I might do some weaving, looking at pleached hedges. In fact I could use real twigs as part of a weaving.

Themes are art in the melting-pot, and the risk of not knowing what will happen is the excitement of wondering about what could boil over. A rewarding experience for teachers can be the surprise of seeing how well children develop and respond to the unexpected. Children think differently from adults and have a curious logic. As one young child put it,

Rainbows are just to look at, not to really understand.

# 6 Activities, curriculum and progression

In the year 2001 the 'Tate Modern' gallery became the most visited gallery in the world. Its contents are not always understood as art continually redefines itself. Whatever can be said of art can be both true and false. Consider these assumptions: Art is painting on canvas. Art is whatever we want it to be. Paintings are all about light and colour. Sculpture is chipped away from a marble block. The digital image is an art form.

Few propositions about the nature of art education stand the test of time because art reflects the society in which it is created. Two key school examinations in the early 1900s were in drawing and knowledge of the Bible. The drawing examination was a test of hand and eye coordination, not of creativity or the aesthetic quality we have more recently come to expect of it. Before the nineteenth century, most art could be found in churches because creating a work of art for an exhibition was not how artists made their living. They were decorators of buildings, craftspeople and guild workers. There were few, if any, collectors of art. The idea that art could be a temporary 'installation' would have been unthinkable, and sculpture was mainly of wood, stone or bronze. Displaying art in a gallery was a late innovation in the history of art. Drawing took place in schools, and books were produced showing how to hold chalk and how to draw with both hands at the same time. Certificates in 'Chalk Drawing' were given alongside those for 'Freehand Drawing of an Ornament in Outline', 'Perspective' and 'Drawing from a Plaster Cast'.

Formal UK schooling is a product of the 1870s and exactly what children should learn in art has changed rapidly. After a child-centred 1950s and 1960s where educators such as Marion Richardson dominated, the years of Margaret Thatcher's 1980s government saw a brief swing towards Design Education. This was an initiative which slowed to a halt in the late 1990s when literacy and numeracy strategies held sway. Now, not only is art and design part of a nationally agreed curriculum, but in the year 2001 the UK Qualifications and Curriculum Authority (QCA) published units of study in art. The quality of this varied. The activities suggested assumed a certain level of skill on the part of both teacher and children, who were expected to design murals, print, paint, weave and draw the human figure. Some of the discussion questions suggested would defeat practising artists, but the units were a useful resource for a teacher prepared to adapt them rather than slavishly follow the prescriptions. Questions suggested, such as 'Ask children to think of a purpose for their work', 'How can they use techniques of gathering, scrunching, pleating, folding?', 'What have they included in the portrait and why?', assume analytical and practical skills which children may not have.

Any art curriculum, when published as a summary of principles and practice, tends to deal in generalised statements, themes and units of study. Phrases such as 'Provide opportunities for children to discuss their plans and think through the ideas they would like to convey' are not tied to quality or specifics unless a teacher is skilful in handling discussion. Teachers deal in specifics, but the problem for policy-makers is that specifics can quickly date, suit one teacher rather than another, and appear prescriptive. The age-old response of teachers to the generalities of a newly published curriculum is not surprisingly 'We already do that don't we?' In art and design education, creativity can of course be stifled by prescriptions for doing activities. Even so, generalities need to trigger specifics if they are going to be of any use. Some suggested activities require organization such as 'Arrange a visit to a park, wood, forest, rocky place, coast or scrubland. Ask the children to work in pairs and look for "natural" sculptures'. Whatever the specifics, a directive to 'record visual and other information' is a generality which assumes that children or their teacher actually know how to go about this. In one example from the 2001 Qualifications and Curriculum Authority (QCA) scheme, there are suggested examples of art, craft and design. These include looking at 'good and bad composition' which again assumes the teacher or child knows what this means. Any art scheme will need to be adapted and modified however useful it first seems.

What are schools likely to provide? Very young children need to paint or draw their 'stories' of life in symbols and are less concerned with techniques, skills and investigation. For them, art is a language and only later do concerns about colour-mixing and patterns begin to dominate. The timeless elements of a school art curriculum are those conditioned by available materials and costs, as well as tradition. Pupils will inevitably use crayons, pencils and paints. Collage techniques will be on the menu too. Some children will model in dough, Plasticine and clay, cut and fold card. They will less frequently or rarely use complex, expensive materials, such as digital cameras or hot melted wax used for a Batik. The art curriculum is not a pick and mix of everything an artist might do. Welded steel sculpture is never going to be an option for the younger age range. A good art curriculum is an introduction to visual art and a way of knowing the world other than through words. It comprises activities designed to develop interest and skill in investigating, making and understanding the visual world.

## Four areas of activity

Whatever might be the prevailing art curriculum, whatever the chosen theme, teaching an art session is about where to start and what to emphasise. This is ultimately true of every other subject on the curriculum too. Looking at published curricula and schemes in this way does not actually deny their value. Teachers inevitably have to make decisions, despite anything they have found in someone else's scheme of work. In art and design, four areas prevail.

1  Something SEEN, HEARD, FELT or TOUCHED (children actually look at something, feel it or hear it and respond to the sensory stimulus).
2  MEMORY and IMAGINATION (children build up images in their 'mind's eye' and work from these).
3  MATERIALS (children explore a particular material or medium and see what they can do with it).
4  TECHNIQUE (a particular technique is demonstrated or, if already learned, used as a way of starting).

| Example Area 1 | Provision of a display 'Trees' table – tree bark, twigs, photographs, visual aids, diagrams, reference books, wood samples, paper, furniture, seeds. Fruits, blossom, leaves. Discuss, sort, examine, similarities/differences, features. |
|---|---|

| Example Area 2 | Imaginative stories about trees, memory, magic trees (fantasy), moving trees, golden tree. Brightly coloured imagined trees, animals, insects, tree dwellers (fantasy), forest dwellers (fantasy), e.g. 'Grumbly the Worst Wizard', poems about trees, songs, drama (fantasy), music (*No looking at all*). |
|---|---|

| Example Area 3 | Provision of collage materials, glue, scissors, paper, drawing materials, as a stimulus for discussion on trees. |
|---|---|

| Example Area 4 | Demonstration of a technique for creating tree bark patterns in clay or Plasticine. (Technique demonstrated but bark pattern not used in demonstration). |
|---|---|

*Chart 5*  Areas of Stiumulus and Emphasis

Whichever area we choose to start, we will touch on the other three areas quite quickly. Once children make a mark with paint, they are looking. Their imagination inevitably comes into play and they use materials and techniques.

If we want to create art by investigating a theme such as 'growth', then looking at these four areas has advantages. We can vary the way we start an art activity and emphasize artistic learning once it is under way. In practice, there are not enough different materials and techniques to ring the four changes in sequence, so 'Something SEEN, HEARD, FELT or TOUCHED' and

'MEMORY and IMAGINATION' will be the most obvious starting points. There is no way that taking each area in turn to start is going to produce a balanced diet of art activity. A pitfall of designing an art programme based on variety in materials and techniques is that the teacher creates a demand which cannot be satisfied. Children expect a new material or technique to be on offer the next time. Some schools seem to promote a carousel of painting, printing, model-making, Batik, wax-resist, rubbings, weaving, tissue collage and clay-work. The value of these media cannot be denied, but the idea that each week the teacher presents a new technique or medium is thoroughly flawed. Coverage is at the expense of familiarity. Such an art curriculum is bound to rule out development and progression in using a technique or material more than once. The notion of refinement and further development of skill is absent from a cursory encounter with some new material.

Sometimes children need to learn a new technique, sometimes they need to develop and refine one they already know. Sometimes a rich variety of media is needed. Sometimes pencil and paper is more appropriate. Asking the questions 'Where shall I start?' and 'What will I emphasize?' hones ideas and can give purpose to the often generalized activities already in a scheme. It is all very well to say 'children will learn that familiar geometric shapes can be found in the built environment', or 'children will learn how to choose materials'. These are meaningless without some element of progression from ignorance to relative expertise. Children do not really learn to choose media by chance. They learn why one material does something another will not and then they have a reason to choose it.

Good starts are important, so deciding which of the four areas is going to provide the most useful introduction conditions what follows. Attention to TECHNIQUE and MATERIALS becomes far more important once work has begun, even if this is a matter of frequent reminders about how to mix colours and use a brush. Each of these four areas act together at various stages of art work. In using a technique, marks may be made and the artist responds by looking and imagining changes. There is a continual cycle of activity whatever the starting point. The teacher, however, may still want to emphasize one area more than another and base learning objectives around this. It would be a poor learning objective which stated 'to introduce pupils to watercolour wash' and a better one that stated 'to teach the technique of applying watercolour wash and use this as a way of creating smooth changes of colour'.

## Examples of progression

Suppose a theme of 'Where We Live' began by children looking at doors, garden gates and chimneys, making comparisons of shape. Pupils might make drawings and compare the shapes and patterns they found. The stimulus would be something SEEN, HEARD, FELT as in area one of the four areas. Gathering ideas, making drawings and designs is likely to produce learning objectives such as 'learning how to look for shapes in buildings', or 'comparing the different shapes of gates in the locality'. This activity could encourage children to look at aspects of the built environment in the city, town or village.

The learning objective for an art activity, however, might be one of teaching a TECHNIQUE such as shading or brush drawing. If the emphasis switched to IMAGINATION and MEMORY, children might mainly design imaginary doors, gates and chimneys. More ambitiously, the stimulus for further work could be to look at the ways artists such as Turner, Lowry or Van Gogh painted the places in which they lived. This would emphasise something SEEN and knowledge about the very different TECHNIQUES used by these artists to paint pictures.

Although we might have a very interesting project on our hands, it would not necessarily lead to progression in art. 'Where We Live' could be absolutely anything we wanted, including links with history, literacy and numeracy. Progression needs at least two art activities where learning is sequential, even if these activities are divided by time and lack of opportunity. It also needs these activities to be planned in the right order for objectives to be achieved. Too often, the logic of developing ideas, trying them out in an art medium and evaluating the result is seen to be enough. It is not too difficult to achieve variety in art, but hard to make sense of this in a sequence of activities aimed to ensure progress. If progress is to be made, then children need to do things better, more efficiently or with greater understanding than they previously did. There is something to be said for working through themes and topics because they can be so memorable. How, though, do we step back a little and look at progression in a theme like 'Where We Live'?

Logically children might look at their environment, maybe through card viewfinders or by sketching the shape of doors, gates and chimneys. A skilful teacher could steer discussion of this so that children were poised to decide which shapes they want to use in a painting, a collage or piece of craftwork. The stimulus of looking would already have primed them for choice and made them look more carefully than ever before. If children already have enough technical skill to mix colours or handle collage this is a start. But the real emphasis of the activity might be on developing further expertise in using media, or in developing expertise in planning, reviewing and changing work in progress. The emphasis on learning is most often the teacher's choice.

Here are two versions of the same activity after looking at and recording the shapes of doors, gates and chimneys.

### Version 1

**Learning objectives:** To develop control over the technique of sponge printing and to discover how card can be used as a stencil.

**Activity:** A variety of paint colours and shades is provided. Children cut card shapes based on their observation of chimneys/gates/doors. Teacher demonstrates 'sponge printing' around the edges of similar shapes. Some children are able to cut shapes out of card, making more than one chimney stencil (differentiation). Teacher discusses changes to the darkness or lightness of paint being used. When dry, some children add crayon detail to some of the shapes. Discussion of similarities, differences, techniques and future projects takes place.

**Analysis:** Area 4, TECHNIQUE has been the emphasis for the actual work. This has shifted part way to MATERIALS and back to TECHNIQUE in refining the paint mixtures used. MATERIALS have further been emphasized in the completion of work. Discussion covers looking, decision-making, techniques, materials and future projects.

### *Version 2*

**Learning objectives:** To develop some further skill in colour-mixing and in creating pattern from shapes which have been observed.

**Activity:** Paint is in powder rather than ready-mixed form. Children draw broad overlapping outlines of chimneys on grey sugar-paper using a thin brush and different coloured lines of opaque paint they mixed. They treat these like a pattern rather than representing a chimney. They attempt to mix different shades of imagined brickwork colours using white and black as well as other colours. They paint these and some children add other features to their work such as sky and clouds. Some children repeat chimney shapes in a pattern which they decorate in colours of their choice, attempting to vary shades as much as they can. Other children choose to do the same activity using pencil-crayon on white paper adding pattern within individual bricks and chimney features. Discussion of similarities, differences, techniques and future projects takes place. Teacher brings points to children's notice concerning learning about technique and materials, effects of crayon and paint.

**Analysis:** Areas 1 and 2, SOMETHING SEEN (effects of drawing in paint) and IMAGINATION or MEMORY, are the stimulus in almost equal measure. There is a shift to area 4, TECHNIQUE, and discussion compares both MATERIALS and TECHNIQUE. Children learn, for example, that drawing using a brush produces different effects from drawing using a pencil-crayon. They learn that it can be easier to decorate bricks with pencil-crayon detail than when using paint brushes. They learn that opaque paint on grey paper produces different effects from pencil-crayon on white paper.

   In providing an art curriculum, there is plenty on which to build for progression in another lesson. Examples are:

- Applying the same technique to a new theme or topic (e.g. sponge printing, collage).
- Learning to refine the use of a technique during the art activity (e.g. learning to improve cutting and sticking).

- Using a familiar medium in an unfamiliar way (e.g. blending different coloured pencil-crayons on white, yellow and green paper).
- Discovering that different types of paint need different techniques (i.e. powder colour, opaque poster paint, watercolour).
- Learning to draw an object from different angles (from above, back and side).
- Learning to combine more than one medium (e.g. collage and paint).
- Learning to choose colours and media, rather than trying to use everything possible (e.g. selecting a wide range of green and blue paint shades for a picture).
- Learning to adapt the technique to the scale/size of a piece of work (e.g. mural and miniature) .
- Learning to draw in preparation for another piece of work (e.g. drawing doors and windows before designing a palace fit for a king).
- Learning to review previous work and make use of successful techniques.

Since there could be several reasons why a particular session is taking place, purpose is not confined to a single objective. But there are various aspects of artistic learning which might be included. For example, we can choose to emphasize:

- learning about line
- learning about colour
- learning about shape
- learning about pattern
- learning about design
- learning about the medium
- learning a particular technique
- learning about texture.

All these form the basis of rather formal elements of art. The purpose of our sessions is far wider and can include

- stimulating an imaginative response to . . .
- encouraging colour-mixing in . . .
- developing new skills in . . .
- increasing awareness of . . .
- consolidating work in . . .
- exploring the qualities of . . .
- expressing the movement in . . .
- expressing feelings of . . .
- trying out/combining . . .

The objectives of any session should never be contrived simply to reassure ourselves that we are actually teaching. Good practice usually includes taking

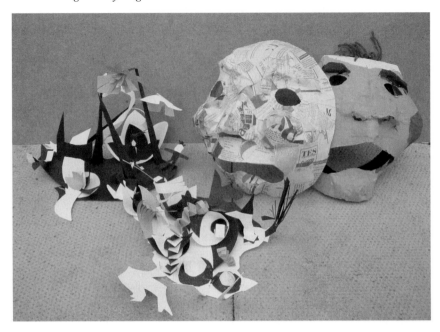

*Figure 21* Fantasy Landscape and Masks. Age 9.

advantage of the unexpected and learning from it. Inevitably, art is meant to develop awareness of 'something'. But to find out what that might be raises art above the superficial level of its being for entertainment or recreation. Within the theme 'Where We Live' transferable techniques and approaches could be developed for a quite different topic, such as 'self-portraits'. Children would already have some experience of a wider range of drawing technique than simply using a pencil. It is not too difficult to imagine discussing with children the materials and techniques they have already used and building in refinements and improvements. An example of transferable skill can be seen in Figure 21 (and Plate 33) where the 'Fantasy Landscapes' were produced to develop techniques for future mask-making using paper and card.

### Fantasy landscapes – a prelude to mask-making

**Learning objectives:** To use the imagination or memory to create a 3-D landscape in cut and folded paper. To develop some skill in cutting, folding and sticking paper. Drawing, choosing colours and decorating shapes which have been invented or memorized.

**Activity:** Children begin by trying to imagine or remember the shapes of hills, trees and buildings in a landscape. They cut irregular and circular paper shapes. They cut a slit across the shape to form a 3-D shape. Further cuts are made to form tabs for sticking these shapes to a background. Folds, trees and additional surface mounds are created by cutting, sticking and decorating paper. In some instances materials are restricted to black and white to encourage the use of contrast in the work.

**Analysis:** Area 2, IMAGINATION or MEMORY, is the stimulus and the TECHNIQUE is a means of expressing imagined ideas. The cutting and sticking technique characterizes the way the imagination is used and the progress of the work is evaluated for ways to improve it. Children learn a technique of creating shallow curves and building these into a coherent whole. They learn to embellish shapes and to cut tabs for sticking to a background surface.

**Teaching points:** Unless previous experience of using glue is well established, children will need to be shown how to use very little glue to the best effect. PVA glue easily buckles paper if it is used thickly. The idea that more glue is better has to be eradicated from the art process if good technique is going to be established. This involves very close monitoring of what 'a small coating' actually means. Children may also need to decorate some of the shapes before they are stuck, rather than afterwards.

The transfer to mask-making included drama, fitness for purpose and invention in the characterization and decoration of the mask.

## Progression and achievement

An art curriculum is not in itself an indication of essential standards or benchmarks of progress. There are several indicators of achievement, both technical developments and perceptual ones. The perceptual ones depend on age as well as ability and are indicators of growth rather than artistic learning. For example, it is no benchmark of achievement when a child discards the symbol of the sun from drawings or the blue line at the top which represents the sky. It simply means they reached a stage where they were no longer satisfied with the symbolic method of describing sky and ground. Two summaries of making progress are given:

### Progression in looking and perceiving

Children, up to the age of around 6, 7 or more will rarely overlap shapes so that only part of a person is seen behind someone else. Each object or person tends to exist in its own right (as far as it is possible to generalize). Pre-school and up to the age of 6, children are storytellers. A significant later indication of perceptual progress is when children can draw from objects and place them within the illusion of space. A further indicator is when children can draw objects from more than one angle or viewpoint. Long before this, children find it difficult to determine the shape of things accurately, so progress in drawing people with necks, a head that is not simply a circle and a skirt which is not a triangle, shows a developing ability to look. Shading is a much more sophisticated perception. It is a very advanced 9-year-old who can (accurately) show reflections, shadows thrown by other objects and light falling across a group of objects. It is also sophisticated to be able to notice how an artist uses shading, brushstrokes and colours in a drawing or painting.

### Progression in practical skills and techniques

In the use of a medium such as paint, very young children load a brush and get on with the job. Considerable progress is made when they are able to control how much (or how little) paint to put on a brush before it lands on paper. Colour-mixing is almost impossible until there is some ability to organize a brush, water and workspace. Mixing dry colours with water is a longer-term achievement needing practice. So is knowing and understanding the difference between the effects of opaque and translucent paint. Knowing the best paper to use for each is initially the responsibility of a teacher or classroom assistant, but informing children of why increases their ability to understand and choose for themselves. There are brush techniques to discover, and informed choices to make about organizing colour on paper. Being able to emulate the characteristic brushstrokes of a famous painter, for example, requires both perception and practical skill. Other progressive skills include improving joining clay, improving the ability to cut, fold and stick things.

Given the difficulties some children have with drawing, it is no surprise that schemes of work include activities which avoid some of the problems of shape and space. Children can design or draw almost anything which is flat. They consequently can create designs for a pizza, or fantasy fish seen from a side view. Birds of paradise, patterns for the sake of pattern, a section through a red cabbage, designs for kitchen tiles, fabric designs and wrapping paper all emphasize the flat image. Even a drawing of a bicycle is essentially a flat pattern if it is seen in side view. Imaginative drawing has no boundaries so designing a new fantasy flying machine cannot easily be criticized for inaccuracies. True progress in drawing comes in facing the difficulties of tackling something with a little more accuracy and placing in space. Symmetrical objects, such as bottles are an easier starting point than drawing a three-quarter view of the human figure. Sooner or later, more ambitious drawings of people, natural forms, trees, plants, rocks and the landscape need a developed perception and technique to draw them.

Although many good art lessons fit a learning objective decided in advance, this is not always an easy way to plan for progression. It is often far easier to decide on a theme of investigation or imagination (mini-beasts, gardens, our street) then think what emphasis and learning objective is the most useful. 'I want them to draw and paint mini-beasts such as snails, caterpillars, bees and spiders' again begs the questions 'How will you start?' and 'What will you emphasize?' Children will look or invent, but the learning objectives might be some of these:

- To choose three main colours and demonstrate that these can be mixed to make other colours.
- To make full use of the size of paper provided and attend to accuracy in drawing.
- To create mini-beasts from coloured tissue, glued to white paper (technique demonstrated).
- To introduce children to making wax crayon rubbings prior to creating a collage (vocabulary, texture, colour).
- To make detailed drawings prior to using collage as a medium (drawing for another medium).
- To develop variety in the use of a pencil line.
- To be able to show surface markings and patterns on mini-beasts.

A perfectly reasonable and recurrent teaching aim is to improve children's ability to use a medium like paint. This can almost always be improved and developed. There is a sense of self-preservation involved here, since ideally we would like pupils to be able to manage the use of paint from start to finish, getting it out of storage and putting it back. Some teachers achieve this and can concentrate far more on the content of their art curriculum than the practical organization of materials. Organizing workspace and developing skill in handling media are aims alongside the content of an art lesson. This can apply just as readily to a project such as designing a treasure map as it can to drawing mini-beasts.

The UK National Curriculum in 2001, and layout of QCA schemes followed the time-worn tradition of plan, do and review. Translated into the language of art expertise, these became 'Exploring and Developing Ideas', 'Investigating and Making' and 'Evaluating and Developing Work'. This is by no means a cynical view of the National Curriculum but a logical outcome of creating any workable art scheme. Where the four areas of SEEN, IMAGINED, MATERIALS and TECHNIQUE help to turn an inspiring theme into realistic art activities is in sharpening the learning outcomes. Learning objectives like the QCA 'to record from first-hand observation' become more focused if we know whether the emphasis is mainly on comparing shapes or focuses more on how to shade with a pencil. Knowing where the emphasis lies makes evaluating the outcomes much easier. In summary, the objectives are sharpened by taking five steps.

1  Find an interesting theme
2  Think about what materials are available
3  Think about what to emphasize (chosen from the four areas)
4  Think about how best to start (chosen from the four areas)
5  Think about the organization of materials needed.

The four areas so far mentioned are no more than useful pegs on which to hang ideas. They are easy to keep in mind as work progresses and they can stimulate new ideas. Sometimes all that is necessary is to ask 'What might this look like in a different medium such as clay?', 'What happens if we use smaller brushes?' or 'What might this be like as a collage?'

Linking art with other areas of the curriculum is a natural consequence of learning. A curriculum is not just a collection of subject-based activities, but has coherence when purposeful links are made. The point has already been made in other chapters that history projects are not always useful for developing art and design education. Science and geography, however, sometimes prove to be more useful because they are concerned with investigating the natural world. Food-chains, rivers, mountains, rocks and the weather all have visually interesting features children can portray and discuss. A theme like 'Look at how things are made' embraces science, art, literacy and other areas of the curriculum. The role of an art coordinator needs to take account of these ongoing themes and activities within other subjects. Too often, incompatible links are forged when there is no reason to do so. Three criteria for making cross-curricular links are suggested.

- That the cross-curricular link benefits each subject.
- The link develops the core concerns of each subject.
- The link gives coherence to an otherwise fragmented curriculum.

Links between mask-making or puppetry and drama are obvious ones. It is disappointing sometimes if art is used as a strong visual aid for a story, rather than an exploration of ideas. In the hands of a skilful teacher, almost any art activity can be made worthwhile, but there is no point making curricular links where no obvious ones exist. Mathematics, for example, tends to require its own teaching methods despite links to be made with ratio and proportions. Try linking fractions with art. The artwork may be diminished by the constraint of shapes representing fractions because they are abstract. Designing a pizza and cutting it into fractions may not be a good link if there are better ways to teach children art and maths.

## The role of the art coordinator

Being an art coordinator is not the same as doing all the art teaching in the school. A coordinator involves staff in decisions and tries to meet preferences for materials and ideas as far as is reasonable. A coordinator does not simply provide a scheme of lessons from a website or a published set of suggestions. There are developments to be made within the school and questions to address:

- How can children become more skilful in their use of media?
- What variety of media is needed and which year groups will use them?

- What paint is it best to buy? (Non-runny, two reds, two blues, two yellows, black and white as a minimum – see Chapters 9 and 16.)
- What storage and resource management facilities are there?
- What can best be made of government schemes without slavishly following them?
- What useful programme of activities might be attempted across the years?
- What might each year group be expected to achieve in terms of technique and experience?
- What professional development sessions are needed?
- How can links be made with the rest of the curriculum without destroying programmes in art and design?

Part of the role of art coordinator is to suggest resources and provide some of these. Some resources are art materials, but others are items such as posters, reproductions of great works of art, books, natural forms like stones, twigs, shells and plants are also necessary. Visits to galleries may need to be organized. Spending the art budget wisely means buying a range of papers, paints and more specialist equipment, but ensuring these materials are well used. Naturally enough, staff may want quick solutions and trouble-free painting techniques. The reality is that staff often need to understand that teaching children to use paint well is all part of a good art education. The art coordinator may need to map out the options for using paint (which are several, see Chapter 9). The great fear any art coordinator has is probably of running out of materials. A programme of staff development includes a strong element of skill development (Chapter 16). Otherwise, children and staff use vast quantities of art materials very quickly indeed. The economics of art materials are driven by their careful use and time spent teaching children to think about skills is never wasted. Staff development will also include something about classroom displays.

Finally, an art coordinator needs to be a curriculum leader who is familiar with art techniques, art vocabulary and the prevailing documents and schemes. No teacher commits everything in a nationally agreed curriculum to memory, but there is some expectation that guidelines will be given for implementing it. The school scheme may be published and a programme year by year mapped out. Coordinating, persuading and inspiring staff to develop children's art means taking them beyond a grind through a thousand things to do and make. Quick solutions and prescriptions for success may seem attractive, but they can become the teacher's personal hell when they show themselves for what they are. An art coordinator's long-term aim is often to convince staff that developing skill is quite different from following a recipe for producing art. If the recipe fails, the finger is often pointed at the art coordinator who suggested using it.

# 7 Classroom organization

A feature of work with very young children is that they often work in groups for much of the day. Further up the age range, more whole-class teaching may be usual, with creative artwork being taught to the whole class. Whether to put children in groups or not is a matter of choice, and the outcome reflects the educational philosophy of the school or teacher. The issue is one left open for debate. What is best is what organization is appropriate at the time, not simply what we happen to believe in, though personal teaching style naturally has an influence. There are enough opportunities for formal class teaching later on in children's lives without introducing it too soon. Teaching in the early years usually demands far more flexible ways of looking at classroom organization if the best is to be gained from it.

However brilliant the ideas for producing wonderful artwork, without a firm grasp of how organization can be effective, success is doubtful. There is little reason to think that children will work independently in art without first having learned skills and strategies necessary for coping. Of course, a price must be paid for good organization. It is demanding and even complex, especially if the school operates an integrated curriculum. Yet it is necessary because the alternatives to a well-run classroom lead to mediocre, not to say unprofessional, teaching. A well-organized class commands the respect of other members of staff and is one of the indicators of an ability to manage groups, the whole class and all the hardware in terms of practical materials and equipment.

> I don't always teach groups. Sometimes I have one group and the rest of the class doing something else, sometimes I teach the whole class, other times I divide up the class into as many as four groups – it depends what we're doing.
>
> (Teacher of 6-year-olds)

> I never have all my groups doing completely different activities. There's usually something in the curriculum I want to emphasize with more than one group.
>
> (First school deputy headteacher)

## Organizing groups

Suppose the policy was to teach children in groups. There could be several ways of organizing this to the best advantage, and here we cannot limit strategies to art, because group organization obviously affects all areas of learning.

If a class is divided into groups, then to free the teacher to teach one group, it follows that the other groups must do tasks with which they are already familiar. It is surprising how many student teachers think they can deal with each group by dashing round from one to the other. In practice this is not very effective but an understandable response to a difficult problem. The results can often be to increase wear and tear on the nerves and eventually invite the possibility of becoming physically and mentally drained. A more effective strategy might be to choose one group we intend to teach art and involve the other groups in revision or practice tasks, something which they are used to doing. (In a reception class, for example, this could include structured play activities and with older children good-quality workcards, board games, pattern-making, or possibly practice in handwriting.)

Given that we cannot teach all of the children all of the time, it is only reasonable to recognize that to use these practice tasks is a somewhat imperfect solution to an intractable problem. A vital element in organizing groups, however, is delegation. Children need, for instance, to find their own scissors, and can do this from habit if they know where they are kept and that they are expected to do so. This is not to say they always will, but a good organizational policy is to teach as if they will for some of the time. Then they can learn to cope with simple practice tasks in a more independent way.

The quality of those tasks need not necessarily be poor, neither need they be dull or boring. But like most teaching methods where children are meant to work unaided, children's skills in working independently are only gradually built up. The less worthwhile task, which we might use with an inexperienced group, can gradually be replaced with a more demanding one as learning and resourcefulness develop.

If the decision is to teach a small group, then the aim is to try to buy time for working with little interruption. As far as the other children are concerned, the promise of better things to come is sometimes the best we can hope for. Our attention can then turn to the group which really demands it, the one we are teaching. In practice, moving quickly from group to group may appear to be effective, but we should ask what children learn from such a brief contact with us. Contact with the teaching group does not, after all, rule out work with other groups.

The UK Numeracy Strategy of 2000 has had its impact on organization, but as one teacher points out, there are other ways to consider.

> When I'm teaching maths I have three groups . . . a 'teaching' group, a 'revision' group and a 'practice' group. I tend to move from my teaching group to my revision group (who are usually consolidating work they

started the previous day), to my practice group. Next session they change round.

(Teacher)

If the teaching group is taught with future practice tasks in mind, we can more easily move on to another group and work with them. Individuals within a group never finish work at the same time, so built in to the teaching of most subjects there is a need to set further tasks which the children can do when they have completed their work. It is a pity if the extra task is always to draw a picture, though it cannot be denied this is a legitimate practice task. The trouble is that drawing a picture does not always practise what the children are being taught at that moment. Often it relies on a quite different area of thought.

A familiar trap to avoid is one of describing what we personally value in the rest of the curriculum as being *work* and anything else as *play*. How, for example, would we describe structured learning through play? Is it work? Or is it play? Why should we think of making the distinction? Is it because we want to convince children that they should endure a certain misery and difficulty in work? Or is it, perhaps, that the artwork we do is not taken seriously enough and therefore mistakenly associated with enjoyment or recreation? The point is made here because the way we view art activities clearly influences the way groups work. It would be a great pity if there were work groups and, in contrast, groups we described as recreation groups operating in the same room.

Although mathematics has been mentioned as one example of group organization, there is no reason why the same approach should not apply to art. Children need to build up independent thinking skills for considering what they do with art materials. We could have four art groups, but more likely art and language, or art and mathematics groups working. Alternatively, three or four art groups could take it in turns to work throughout the day. Whatever the style, the teaching group in art needs to be treated exactly as we would any other subject.

Variations of these combinations can be tried to find out how effectively the teaching group can be managed. Effective group management is crucial to learning, but it would be easy to confuse it with effective teaching. In many instances, the ability to manage groups has little relationship with a session's content or aims. In theory, an art group could be managed well without ever having its attention drawn to anything particularly worthwhile. In practice, it would learn little except perhaps what was picked up by chance. When, for example, children become adept at finding pattern in everyday surroundings, this is often the result of careful work done when they were in a teaching group. In the whole class they can still learn through discussion and observation, but it is in the small group that ability can really be extended. Not only is the teaching group crucial to learning, but in art there are similarities with mathematics. We quite rightly assume that if mathematics is not understood then further time and practice is necessary. So it is with artistic learning, which (Chapter 2) can need repeated experience for ability to develop.

Very often we may feel like giving up the effort just at the point where children are about to make a breakthrough in skill acquisition or artistic awareness. To be surrounded by children's artistic disasters, accept them and believe things really are about to get better, is a necessary ingredient for working with this age range. Children do improve and learn to cope with very difficult problems in their artwork. But it cannot be emphasized too strongly that it does take time. In a group they can learn a great deal from one another providing a deliberate effort to find time to teach them is made.

Finding the best time to discuss an art project with children is sometimes difficult. There are, however, a number of ways of coping with this and they are all worth trying. If they ring familiar bells well and good. The alternatives suggested here are practical solutions which some teachers have found work for them.

1   At the end of the morning, clear up for lunch, gather all the children round and explain what the afternoon art activity will be about. (With luck this gives some of them a chance to think about it over the lunch-hour.) Not all children may do art, some will follow this up the next day.

2   Set one group, the teaching group, new work (simple potato printing, for example). The other group practises tasks like colour-mixing, drawing, or pattern-making. Then the groups change over halfway through the session. Next day they finish off work as one large group, or continue as two groups, or finish off work as individuals.

3   Set one group the task of using the book corner, or reference library, to try a 'finding-out' game. For example, 'See how many round shapes you can find and write down the page numbers . . . see how many different blues . . . see how many different creatures you can find that have two legs.' (Builds up awareness of shape.)

4   Let one group cut up pieces of coloured paper in preparation for working with collage materials. They need to create a reasonably useful pile of pieces. (Practice in using scissors – even measuring.) This should be a short activity as it can be uninteresting, but it does buy enough time to start off another group activity (which may not be art). It is then possible to return to the paper-cutting group to begin a collage and explain much more to them.

5   Take one group which learned how to work with a different material yesterday and rearrange groups so that children work in pairs, one child showing the other how to use the new material.

6   Explain an idea to three groups at the same time (for example, a drawing and painting project). Then change the rules for each group so that there are limitations on how each group uses materials. For example, one group might use only blacks, whites and greys. Another group might be told to choose one colour to emphasize rather than any other, another group might not in the end use paints but take the same idea using pencil-crayons. The purpose of this would be to use the results for further discussion on art and compare the different responses each group had.

7　Introduce a new skill to the whole class rather than one group. Then when they come to do the group activity they already know something about it. They will need reminders, development and adjustment to the new skill, but this can be more profitable than explaining the same thing five times over, once for each group.

## The whole class and the group

Some teachers prefer to organize art for the whole class, which does not mean that they do exactly the same activity with every child, but that only art takes place within the classroom. This is not without its advantages because the focus can be very powerful as the children see what one another have done and the teacher draws attention to what has happened. There are, as we might expect, serious limitations regarding space available and the kind of materials which can be used. Sometimes it is possible to arrange with a colleague to take a small group (a live-now-pay-later approach where we agree to take a very large group in return for having had a small one with which to work). There may be opportunities for a large group to work in the hall, or extend to the corridor, depending on the self-discipline of the children involved. Even so, children will inevitably need to share materials so that in effect the whole class will still find itself working in smaller groups. The focus of all the children is towards art and there may be greater opportunities for the development of social skills through sharing, tidying away, helping each other and learning to use space wisely.

The kind of larger group project which proves worthwhile is one where it is possible to make use of children's differing abilities. For example, in language children might make a class newspaper where the written or drawn contributions are of different size and complexity according to the contributors. The final product is a 'scissors and glue' assemblage and depends for its success on involving each child in an individual way. The outcome is then greater than the sum of its parts. In art, it is likely that only a few things lend themselves exactly to this approach. For there to be entirely individual contributions each child needs to work on a small part which finally pieces together to form the whole. If we contrast this with a frieze, someone has to design and cover the background on which are stuck the various contributions. Decisions are taken about where things are placed, and at that point it is very difficult for a teacher not to offer advice or interfere.

Despite this problem, a large-scale work (see Plate 12 and Plates 13 and 14) captures the attention and periodically provides a memorable experience for the participating children. Subjects commonly attempted are things like 'The Magic Garden', where each child contributes an imaginary exotic flower and where materials like tinsel, foil, bottle tops and objects can be stuck to a background. This is a useful experience for children to have, but how could such a project be developed further?

One interesting way is to use the exotic background which has been finished and gradually build out from it to make a garden on a table in front. Piece by piece the garden can grow to include junk models, Plasticine or claywork, paths, hedges and fences. Much depends on how a creative idea like this is used. For instance, there are a number of worthwhile discoveries to be made using either hedges or fences as a sub-theme. Children can design their own fences, look for differently shaped fences in the environment, or find out about the creatures and plant life which inhabit the hedgerows.

Organizing a mural where abstract pattern is used is slightly different. The children each have the opportunity to produce a unit, such as a tile-sized piece of work, which forms part of the final product. There are interesting choices to be made about colours and materials, and the source of the patterns can be very varied. In fact a pattern may grow from a previous mural idea so that development takes place from one large-scale piece to the next. The work may be three-dimensional but still using a unit as the basic form. As with all group projects, the children may need to be made aware before the start of where their own unit fits in with the final product. Ideal projects are those in which each piece of contributory work is a variation on a theme. A simple example of this would be a theme of circles or stripes, where each child finds something which can be a stimulus for their part of the whole.

Since children frequently work on the same-sized paper, it is likely that occasionally they produce work which can later be assembled into a mural, even if that was never the original intention. On the other hand, it might be necessary to organize the class into groups for discussion and pool ideas before planning a mural. The children might work on scraps of paper planning out their individual designs. Alternatively, an appropriate time to organize discussion groups could be at the assembling stage, where various arrangements for the final form could be tried out.

In contrast to a whole-class project, which is put together as a group effort, pupils can work on murals in small groups. Sometimes large paintings or collages using sheets of brown wrapping paper are appropriate projects. However, there is no ideal fixed number of children to have working this way, though there are some combinations which do not seem to be successful. Four children working cooperatively works well, as does two. But six or more children all trying to do a frieze tends to produce group leaders and passengers. This can still provide good learning experiences though the social learning may outweigh the artistic development. Naturally, what determines decisions about group size is the nature of the project, the children there to do it, and the constraints in terms of space and organization of materials.

## Organizing materials

Although organizing materials involves personal preferences there are some ideas worth examining. Sinks, for example, are too often well away from the classroom and the design of many schools can stretch the ingenuity of teachers to the limit.

The nearest sink is at the bottom of the corridor through a Fire Door which has a strong spring to keep it shut. I cannot possibly send a child to empty a bucket of water, and for me to send children all that way to clean palettes is out of the question. We manage with two buckets and a lot of kitchen rolls . . . painting . . . yes it's messy but we do a lot of it and they learn to cope.

(Deputy headteacher)

This particular teacher produced remarkable paintings from her children and her organization contributed substantially towards the success of her sessions. She was unable to do much colour-mixing on palettes but still managed some with small groups rather than none at all. When mixing colours was impossible, she provided up to eighteen different mixtures of colour in non-spill containers. At any one time there were about twelve colours being used and the children took these pots of colour from a trolley which had been wheeled into the centre of the room. There were various brushes of different sizes provided, one for each paint pot.

They ask each other 'Have you got a thick blue?' by which they mean 'Is there a pot of blue with a thick brush in it?' They refer to thin yellows, thick yellows and so on according to the size of brush . . . obviously there's a lot of sharing but it works. I sometimes have to keep returning pots to the trolley because the children forget but I don't mind that.

The same teacher often took all the chairs out of the room, even the tables, for a whole afternoon's painting. If the tables were still there, the children worked standing up and if the tables went, the floor was used. On her trolley was a shelf for a basket of brushes, some chalks, pencils, rubbers, glue with spreaders and a stack of palettes. Other materials were in boxes or racks and there was a bin which had wheels and contained bits and pieces for collage and junk modelling. A bench was full of materials, including felt-tipped pens, dyes with screw-top lids and oddments of paper.

A well-organized room which looks tidy and neat is by no means the best classroom. It may be so clean and tidy that it dissuades a teacher from using paint, thereby restricting what the children are allowed to do. But an untidy and disorganized classroom is certainly the worst. Materials are soon lost, damaged, or wasted, and the room reflects a poor standard of care. Children enjoy some form of social training in looking after their classroom and it is worthwhile teaching them to look after paints, brushes and similar equipment. The general emphasis on care affects other pieces of equipment throughout the school, such as musical instruments or maths materials. Where educational funding is unduly restricted, taking care is obviously important and affects the economy of the school.

The school day is punctuated by minor irritations which are connected with organization. Trivial details like counting scissors or pens can be made easier by making (or persuading someone else to make) racks for everything possible. Some teachers like children to practise their counting, but if that is not a priority, racks save a considerable amount of time and effort expended in needless counting.

Where water is being used it is dangerous practice to use glass jam jars. (This might seem obvious, but it is surprising how the practice still continues to be found.) It is not worth the agony of searching for splinters of glass if they do break, let alone the risk of accidents to children's eyes. There are plenty of non-spill water pots on the market, some of them designed to be extremely stable when knocked. Trays, trolleys, shelves, containers and racks are worth some experiment to find out what works best. The effort needed to do this is amply repaid in terms of energy saved over the term.

A popular idea is to create an 'art corner', or a 'maths bay', which can be useful as a way of tempting children to try out materials which are already there. It can be a space-saver which cuts down unnecessary movement around the classroom. A better description of it might be an 'art resource area', an idea which conjures up the feeling that much more should be available than art materials. Twigs, plants, wall displays and organized materials make up an interesting corner to investigate. This kind of organization is attractive and makes children feel secure, but it can also lead to inflexible arrangements of space. A handful of teachers become obsessed with the unchangeable arrangement of their room and would never dream of moving things around. Their art corners and mathematics bays hardly ever change. The 'art corner' is a good idea, so long as other arrangements are also tried out. Then it really is a resource, and not a regular dumping-ground for children who have finished something else and are at a loose end.

## Organizing space and time

A balancing act is often needed to judge between scale of work, space available and the time taken to complete artwork. These affect each other. It does not take long to work out that large sheets of paper, which occupy a great deal of space, obviously take longer to cover with paint or collage materials. But more relevant is the way in which time is organized according to the specific activity being done. Whilst this kind of organization requires some experience and a few good guesses, there is no doubt that devising short activities which are like games is a useful way of balancing up the different work rates of individuals. Making art workcards about pattern, for example, or using up scraps of paper for drawing fantasy pictures (such as 'A Dancing Jelly', or 'A Melted Piano') is another way of making the sessions more flexible. The need to organize time should cause us to try out different approaches, none of which should become a fixed habit or ritual. Here are some further examples.

8  Try to contrast detailed and lengthy discussion with giving a very short introduction, followed by artwork, followed by stopping the class or group

in order to discuss details at much greater length, followed by further work.

9  Try three short practice activities like (a) a two-minute drawing, (b) trying out different pencils, (c) making ruler and pen patterns, followed by an extensive piece of work which uses all three practices.

10  Stimulate two activities at the same time and allow the children to decide how much time to spend on each. For instance, children might draw a collection of fruit and also make Plasticine models of it at the same session. They would be thinking in two and three dimensions, leaving one, coming back to the other. (They must eventually finish both.)

11  Give children a piece of paper which they are told has to last three days, be drawn on, added to, embellished and altered with a variety of materials including white paint or chalk. (This is one way of helping children to understand that artwork can change and develop.)

12  Stop an art activity halfway through to play an observation game, then return to the activity. (This allows for children to take a mental break from their task and with luck come back to it with new energy.)

Space in the classroom and on work surfaces can be organized differently depending on the activity. The example of having a central trolley of materials has already been mentioned. But there are other ways of sharing out space so that materials are used to the best advantage. Children who are used to a formal arrangement of desks or tables take time to adjust to having their room reorganized. Yet they do benefit from trying different groupings of work surface. They might be working on a frieze where two long rows of desks put together is the answer. They might be doing a continuous pattern where each piece of paper joins on to its neighbour. A circle of joined tables might work best or a group of children using the full length of the corridor.

An experienced teacher develops a sense of organization which foresees most of the likely problems children will encounter. Despite this, children can still be seen trying to work on paper whilst placing paint pots, water pots or palettes on top of the work they are doing. They do not seem to have any natural inclination to use space well and often need to be shown how. It is staggering what they will endure even though it seriously restricts their ability to cope. It is worth working out what the likely movements of children will be to see if the best arrangement of tables has been arrived at. Can some children work better standing up at easels? Would it be better to put some tables against the wall to leave more space for movement around the room? Is it worth having some folding tables which are used for art, possibly shared between classes?

> I'll have one group working in the corridor, with these large pieces of paper and chalk, drawing their pictures . . . another group might be painting, and another group might be chalking on top of their finished pictures.
>
> (Deputy headteacher)

Organizing the rationing of time throughout the week is more awkward to envisage. The example which follows is not a curriculum model, simply a way of thinking about time in relation to subject areas. An interesting way to think of the week is one where at least *something* is pulled into the foreground.

> I organize what I call my 'thick sandwich' week. I like to think that each area of the curriculum is covered during the week . . . that's the bread. The filling is what I particularly want to do that week . . . one week we'll do a lot of science . . . another week it's extra art, or maths, or language.
>
> (Deputy headteacher)

There are other ways of organizing time across a term, like running a two-week project, or a longer one still. They affect the available space for doing other things. Organizing a long-term project can have similar constraints on time and space as using the school hall, or the dining-room, might have. A project which takes up space and time usually displaces other activities. This and other variables need to be considered carefully even if some of them seem at first sight to be unimportant.

## Organizing wall space

A feature of organizing a classroom is how wall space is used, not only for display, but for siting various pieces of equipment. Although electric points can condition some of the organization, the classroom may be made far more workable and attractive if the siting of equipment is rethought. A natural tendency is to use equipment in the place it has always been available. But children's needs change and an occasional rethink is necessary. Apart from this, the appearance of the wall displays can be made to look very professional. In this respect there are one or two pointers to success. These also apply to exhibition space but are included here as simple guidelines to be tried out. At the end of this chapter is a diagram showing how work can be aligned easily for display.

- Where possible, work should be mounted (e.g. on black paper) creating a margin around the work of not less than 10 mm. Use a trimmer or guillotine which cuts at right angles or the work may look square but prove not to be when the display has been assembled.
- Wallpaper used as a backing, especially if it has a strong colour or pattern, tends to detract from the display.
- Some attempt can be made when placing work on display to level the top edges of various pieces so they create a level top line to the whole display. Similarly the bottom edges of display boards can have work aligned.
- An alternative to this is to make up a symmetrical pattern with the pieces of work. The pattern should be spaced and balanced with a good margin around each piece of work. Avoid placing work at angles.
- A minimum space of 50 mm should be left around each piece of work to

avoid overcrowding it. No work should hang over the edge of a display area.

- Titles or headings need only be few in number but should be well lettered. Using questions on displays often makes them far more useful, especially if they include visual aids and teaching resources, as well as children's work. Try any lettering aid you can find, including computer-generated labels and headings. Paper can always be trimmed off later to leave a generous margin all round.

Sometimes good organization comes through the headteacher of the school. There are, despite traditional criticisms, excellent heads in each authority and many staff learn their organizational skills from them. Last-minute organization is inevitable during a busy working week. But there are many routine reorganizations of groups, space, time, wall space, equipment and materials which are well worth experiment. Viewed individually these organizational details do not loom large. Collectively they permeate the whole ethos of the classroom and school, contributing to its smooth running, encouraging better discipline and ultimately enabling more efficient teaching to take place.

Displays which include the original source material as well as the work from which it has grown have considerable impact. An example would be a disused wasp's nest or a honeycomb and the models and drawings made around that topic. We can see what the inspiration was and how inventive the outcomes were.

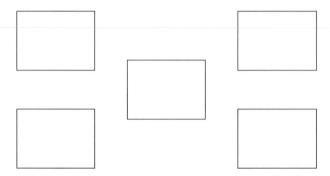

*Chart 6* Symmetry

Charts 6 and 7 show two simple ways to arrange work. The easier of the two methods is that shown in Chart 7.

One final helpful idea is to leave captions until the display is all but finished. That way, any empty spaces can be used and the caption size varied according to space available. Tastes vary, but teachers are not alone in thinking that the child's work is valued more when a caption is *not* stuck to the work itself. Name captions within the child's work destroy the rectangle in which the artwork was done. It is a pity if there are so many bits and pieces stuck together that the display board looks more like a flea-market than an exhibition.

**Plate 1**   My Mum. Age 4 yrs 6 mths. 620 x 425 mm
Princess. Age 5. 620 x 480 mm

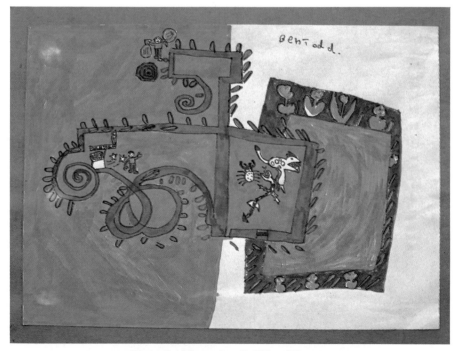

**Plate 2**   Maze. Age 6. 300 x 210 mm

**Plate 3**　An Angry Face. Age 7. 500 x 400 mm

**Plate 4**　Elephant. Age 5. 580 x 420 mm

**Plate 5** Lost Your Mum? − poster. Age 7/8. 280 x 400 mm

**Plate 6**  Patternwork. Age 7. 330 x 270 mm

A furious dilemma.

**Plate 7**  From *James and the Giant Peach* – story.
Age 6. 750 x 480 mm

**Plate 8** From *James and the Giant Peach* − story.
Age 6. 750 x 480 mm

**Plate 9** Tiger. Age 6. 280 x 205 mm

**Plate 10**   Violins. Ages 6, 7, 5.

**Plate 11**   Feathers − drawing. Age 8. 280 x 330 mm

**Plate 12** Fairground – group picture. Age 7/8. 2000 x 1500 mm

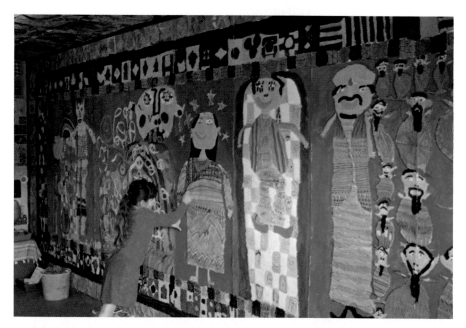

**Plates 13, 14** A Thousand and One Nights. Ali Baba — group mural. Age 7/8.

**Plate 15**  Lowry Pictures. Age 7/8.

**Plate 16**  Looking at the Crust of a Loaf. Age 8. 180 x 137 mm

**Plate 17**   Multi-Coloured Spaghetti. Age 8. 450 x 380 mm

**Plate 18**   Inside a Sprout. Age 7. 265 x 232 mm

**Plate 19**   Package Design — study. Age 7. 210 x 300 mm

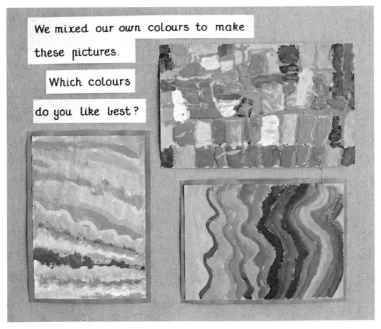

We mixed our own colours to make these pictures.

Which colours do you like best?

**Plate 20**   Colour-Mixing. Age 7.

**Plate 21**   Bee Collage. Age 7. 500 x 300 mm

**Plate 22**   Castle – potato print. Age 7. 430 x 320 mm

**Plate 23**  Dragon – potato print. Age 6. 420 x 290 mm

**Plate 24**  Peacock – print. Age 7. 450 x 340 mm

**Plate 25** Pheasant – claywork. Age 6. 190 x 75 mm

**Plate 26** Spiky Clay Monsters. Age 7

**Plate 27**   Fabric Collage. Age 7/8. 301 x 245 mm

**Plate 28**   Diving into a Pool. Age 7. 230 x 290 mm

**Plate 29**   On the Beach. Age 7/8. 450 x 320 mm

**Plate 30**   Dinosaur. Age 7. 530 x 330 mm

*Plate 31* Fox by Moonlight. Age 9. 310 x 250 mm.

*Plate 32* Popups. Age 9.

*Plate 33* Fantasy Landscape. Age 8.

*Plate 34* Miss Cranston's Tea-Rooms. Age 9. 200 x 150 mm.

*Plate 35* Overlaying Colour. 450 x 350 mm.

*Plate 36* Van Gogh Church. Age 7. 510 x 320 mm.

*Plate 37* Van Gogh, Peach Blossom in the Crau, 1889. 810 x 650 mm.

*Plate 38* Claude Monet, Japanese Bridge, 1923. 1,160 x 890 mm.

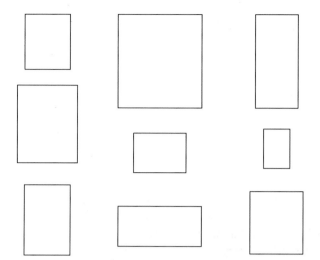

*Chart* 7  Vertical Columns

# 8 More activities for young children

We live in a throw-away society where two years in the life of a home computer labels it old, or even obsolete. Children's individual need for a wide range of activities is insatiable and in the classroom they sometimes expect that what they did in art sessions yesterday should not be repeated.

To repeat the experience would be instant boredom. Consequently, trying to persuade them that by doing things more than once they will develop artistically can be an uphill struggle. That is, of course, if we have unwittingly taught them to expect novelty to be the keynote of their artistic learning. Some semblance of continuity of thought and learning is not only desirable but sensible, given the complexities of an average school day. Extending ideas through themes, and making links with the rest of the curriculum, has too great a learning potential to be missed (Chapter 5). In practice, young children most frequently draw, crayon and paint in response to the things they see (Plate 16), or their imagination and memory (Plates 7, 8). Yet both of these areas are not difficult to weave into ongoing themes, and it can be expected that children will benefit from linking one idea and another. Of course, there are occasions when using a new material is very stimulating. Even so, the specially different materials are best brought out of the cupboard when they are suited to an appropriate idea.

## Ingredients

We can think of devising art activities as being like making a creative cake. We can change the ingredients and even the recipe to make a better cake, and if everything is skilfully blended, the result will be tasty and look delicious. In Chapter 6 (Chart 5) it was pointed out that activities have a starting point and emphasis. The art activities suggested here will all work in the classroom. But structure, sequencing, discussion and the learning principles so far mentioned must be considered and implemented. Otherwise, the worst imaginable, tasteless and superficial artwork may be produced despite the very best of ingredients. There really is no such thing as a foolproof recipe for success.

At the reception age, 'structured play' activities include art and design. Children may think they are playing but that is to underestimate the development that takes place. We may feel 5-year-olds are playing with art materials, but the resulting drawings and paintings are an important reflection of their interests and egocentric selves. Periodically there are signs of development in images, in ability to use materials and in awareness of space on the paper. Beyond this 'play' stage of activity, as children become less egocentric, the subject-matter of their artwork is more diverse. To produce the very best artwork we still need to let them begin with play and, more important still, observe and listen to their response to their own world.

It may come as no surprise that playing with colours, playing with lines, playing with shapes and playing with paints are also the games of most adult artists. In any creative learning activity, we never quite stop playing, especially when materials are new. Most things are new to children and they need to learn through play long before they can develop any skills. In the 'Me' world (Chapter 4) of the 5-year-old, activities such as playing with art materials can typically absorb children in subjects like 'Me at School', 'Me in the Car', 'My Lunchtime', 'My Bedtime', 'My House', 'My Mum', 'My Dad', or 'My Dog'.

Whether or not activities are suited to a particular age-group depends on children's interests and their ability to cope. An understandable example is that of finger painting, which is often a 3-year-old's first opportunity to paint. Here the determining factors as to suitability are undeveloped skill in controlling paint, and a toddler's need to explore new materials in a tactile way. Very young children enjoy finding out through touch as much as sight. They will often place things against their cheek to feel them, or examine them by mouth and by exploration in their hands.

As adults we are inclined to take the sense of touch for granted. Yet we know that anyone who is blind can describe the most complicated of forms through their own tactile experience of them. For young children, activities which include the experience of working with dough, clay, Plasticine and tactile objects are vital to their development. They delight in discovering that clay is malleable and can be enjoyed for its own sake. They twist, roll, thump and push dough about to feel what happens. They enjoy playing games where objects are hidden in a 'feely-box', where they have to discover what the object is by touch.

Tactile experiences, play and exploration of materials new to children feature very strongly as characteristics of the 3- to 5-year-olds' art activity. Their attention span is very short and it is entirely justifiable to organize artwork so that there is a good measure of freedom in their artistic play. But that does not mean they do as they please. Each activity should be designed with learning in mind, even if practice in using materials is the sole objective. Inevitably, apart from artistic learning, language development can evolve as different subject-matter begins to appear in the artwork.

Beyond exploratory play, the search for interesting subject content can always begin with the children themselves. One well-known way is to bring something into the classroom and generate a response as they touch it, look at it, discuss it and draw it. Traditionally, this might be anything from a wild plant, animal, natural form, museum specimen, clay model, to a piece of household equipment. The important activity is that of looking and responding. Another well-tried approach is to exercise children's imagination through stories (Plates 13, 14), but there are intriguing activities which are alternatives to these well-known ones.

## Finding-out activities

These examples are designed to encourage looking and imagining. There is no final artwork involved and they may be used as games or could be developed into longer-term projects. Much depends on how well they are presented to children. Some of them should be of very short duration if they are to be interesting, otherwise they need to be developed into specific art projects or changed to fit other areas of the curriculum.

### *Example 1 finding out from photographs*

**Learning potential:** Develops discrimination of shape. Exercises children's observation skills. Has potential of extending to observation (and development of visual memory) of the outside world.

**Materials:** Old colour supplements, newspapers, ballpoint pen, strong dark pencil or felt-tipped pen, scissors (optional).

**Activity:** Children choose photographs from the magazines or newspapers. They cut them out (as carefully as they can), search for circles, triangles, squares and rectangles. With felt-tip or ballpoint, they outline these on the photographs.

**Development for art sessions:** Children exchange their findings with other children for checking or discussion/comparison. Found shapes are filled in to make them more obvious. Children draw a diagram copied from their outlines drawn on the photographs. Search for shapes is extended to the room, school, people. Quick drawings made, temporary displays, discussion by the teacher with her class.

### *Example 2 looking for lines*

**Learning potential:** Fosters awareness of line directions, thicknesses, complexity, angles and edges.

**Materials:** Plain notepaper and pencil, pen.

**Activity:** Depending on age and ability, children count the number of objects in the classroom which they can see have lines. Stripes, straight lines (edges of tables, books, window frames, doors, switches). Curved lines (chair backs?), printed or drawn lines, string, wire. Or they write down the names of objects which they think have lines. Or they look in their wordbooks (personal vocabulary books) to see how many things might have lines, stripes, or edges. They make a list from these words (no extra words needed).

**Development for art sessions:** Extend to other parts of the school. Make drawings using lines they can find. Try out different line-making tools, pens, pencils, crayons. Look for lines as decoration and pattern. Create patterns with lines. Look specifically for stripes. Extend to 'Stripes' as a theme rather than a short activity (Chapter 5).

### Example 3  colour-matching activity

**Learning potential:** Discrimination of colour. Awareness of shades and specific colour qualities.

**Materials:** Scraps of coloured paper or cloth. These should be differing shades, like the kind best found in decorators' shade cards, materials catalogues, or objects brought in by the teacher. Pencil, paper.

**Activity:** Children try to match the sample piece of colour they are given. They compare parts of book illustrations, scraps from magazines, each other's clothing, maths equipment, objects in the room. They note down (depending on ability) page numbers, the number of matches they find, names of objects, or make collections if practicable. Discussion of colour qualities, comparison in accuracy of matching.

**Development for art sessions:** Extend to sorting shades into groups (e.g. three collections of different blues). Collected paper used for collage, mosaics. Children make a display of each collection. School or class embark on a 'colour' project.

### Example 4  surfaces

**Learning potential:** Awareness of pattern qualities, surface colour, surface textures.

**Materials:** Paper, large black or brown wax-crayon, notepaper, pencil.

**Activity:** Children list names of objects in the classroom which have same surface, e.g. using words like shiny, smooth, undulating. (Or describe if they are unable to make a list.) Make rubbings.

**Development for art sessions:** Children make small scrap-paper drawings of markings on surfaces, look in books for animals/birds, which have special markings on their coat, skin, or feathers. Create their own surface patterns based on the rubbings they make. Flood the rubbings with dye or light-toned ink (wax-resist technique). Make displays, use rubbings as collage material.

### Example 5   *what happens to shadows?*

**Learning potential:** Understanding of light and shadow. Awareness of change in appearances. Science of light.

**Materials:** Pencil, paper. Light source alternative to the sun (e.g. slide projector).

**Activity:** If the sun shines, children observe, discuss, draw effect of changes to objects which remain in the same position (e.g. things on the window ledge). Alternatively, teacher moves light source around objects so children observe shadow changes. Observation, discussion of effect of shadow which crosses wall and floor.

**Development for art sessions:** Children make a chart showing changes to shadow lengths, directions. Shadows idea becomes a project for class. Drawings, paintings, collages of shadow effects (sometimes without the objects needing to be drawn, i.e. shadows only). Work with black paper cut-outs representing shadows. Overhead projector? Shadow puppets? New theme: 'What Happens to Reflections?'

Variations of most of these 'finding-out activities' are not difficult to imagine. Matching shades of colour, possibly a five-minute game, can alternatively be translated into matching of shapes. For example, children can match clothing colours and patterns as they are waiting to go out of the classroom. Such useful exercises in discrimination of colour pay dividends as they permeate the children's artwork, and when art projects are under way, these games, exercises and activities can usefully be recalled. They provide teachers with the opportunity to remind children of the matching, sorting and comparing activities they have done. By this means the children's visual memory is jogged into action, making these short activities a valuable working resource.

Sometimes, with hindsight, an experienced teacher knows that valuable teaching ideas have been thrown away. A common enough experience, especially when first becoming a teacher, is to have planned ideas well but not exploited them to the full. There is no substitute for experience, and a skill worth developing is that of presenting ideas for art activities so that they have the maximum impact. Not giving children too many different new things to think about at once is an obvious help, but would it be better sometimes to hold back part of the more complex explanation and introduce it later? Sequencing the stimulus to the activity is important if detailed explanation is necessary. Otherwise the children hear only a fraction of what we would like them to and often rush ahead without thinking. A question to consider is whether or not the children need to try things out on scraps of paper first, as a warm-up to the main activity.

Alternatively, we may need to devise practice activities which are a prelude to a more ambitious project.

The following activities will need presenting with care so that children become very involved in and interested by them. No activity is absolutely perfect for every known group of children. Each activity needs adapting to fit the circumstances of the session. The structure used here includes a few alternatives from which to choose, which is no more than we would ask of the children we expected to do them.

## Extended activities

### Example 6 mazes (figure 2, plate 2)

**Concepts:** Line, pattern, shape, function.

**Learning potential:** Problem-solving, design, use of imagination, discrimination of shape, language development.

**Skills:** Drawing, fine motor skills.

**Stimulus:** Begins in drama. Teacher discusses with children to see what knowledge they already have. Children act out themes on the 'maze' topic, mythical beasts, being trapped or lost, finding gold, treasure.

Discussion before using art materials. What is it like to see a maze from inside it, from a helicopter looking down, from the maze entrance? Meeting nasties along the route, finding treasure? Discussion about walled mazes, hedges, a playground maze – detailed descriptions from children about brickwork, hedges, colour. Ghost mazes, computer mazes, puzzles in books. Amazing mazes.

**Options:** Trial drawings of mazes that function in plan – scraps of paper. Choice of viewpoint, choice of materials. Decisions about size, scale, content (how big?). Could it be in a garden? a city? a large estate? a funfair? Narrow, wide pathways? Movement, e.g. spiral?

**Materials:** Choose from coloured felt-tips, paint, crayons, card, scissors, scraps of paper.

**Practical session:** Working from the stimulus, children make decisions about materials they should use, consider options available and use their imagination to produce a whole variety of personal mazes. Experience shows that ideas associated with this project can emerge spontaneously in other areas of the curriculum.

**Development:** Children gather round to make a combined maze using a large sheet of paper placed on the floor. Children add strips of black paper to make a route for the maze. Each child has only two strips of paper. Some children have the task of making false trails. Finished maze is glued and displayed. Work then moves to writing, further drama. Solve a riddle to find your way? Children make their own black and white paper collage mazes. Maps? Displayed. Drama: with partners (one blindfolded), one giving descriptions and directions for a path through a maze, in hail, open space.

### Example 7 'multi-coloured' colour-mixing (plate 17)

Note: depends on previous colour-mixing experiences.

**Concepts:** Awareness of colour and shades of colour.

**Learning potential:** Discrimination of colour, use of imagination, memory, control of medium. Comparisons of tone (dark and light).

**Skills:** Mixing, drawing, painting. Control of clean water/paint.

**Stimulus:** Begins in fantasy. Imagine a plateful of multi-coloured spaghetti? Imagine multi-coloured knitting? Imagine a sweet jar of multi-coloured jelly beans? Imagine a magic multi-coloured carpet?

Discussion with children to try to get them to think of multi-coloured fantasies. What might it look like? Can you remember objects which are different reds? Can you think of objects which are different greens? Greys? Muddy browns? How big on your paper? Try to elicit ideas from children, explore and develop their artistic vocabulary.

**Options:** Try mixing on newspaper or scraps first. Limit colours, then gradually introduce more. Try different-sized brushes. Try short strokes/long strokes. Encourage mixing different dabs of colour. Encourage blending colours (using brushes, fingers, rubbing). Dots of colour.

**Materials:** Paints, newspaper, coloured papers, crayons, pencils, brushes, mixing trays or plates/biscuit-tin lids, water pots.

**Practical session:** The children experiment and explore colour-mixing, depending on previous experience the teacher may need to help with basic skills/mixing colour thickly enough.

**Development:** Children sort through paint manufacturers' colour charts. Use for mosaics. Evolve 'colour' displays, tables, rainbows, writing, music (e.g. 'The Multi-Coloured Music Bus'). Reawaken fantasy (e.g. 'Spotty Multi-Coloured Monsters').

*Example 8  colour on black*

Note: a development from Example 7.

**Concepts:** Colour awareness in relation to black. Awareness of tone (light/dark) in relation to black.

**Learning potential:** Discrimination of tones and colours. Learning to handle white as an important colour. Comparison of colour on different toned surfaces.

**Skills:** Mixing (much more difficult to control mixtures of white on black). Keeping water pots clean enough to mix light colours. Mixing paints thickly enough for colour to be seen against black paper. Organizing mixing trays/dishes. Drawing.

**Stimulus:** Children imagine dark settings, skies at night? Outer space? Darkened caverns, rooms? Colour which is light enough to be seen is discussed, e.g. fireworks, lights, spaceships, planets, jewels? Discuss with children how it feels to be in a dark place – evoke memories, dreams.

**Options:** Try small pieces of black practice-sized paper. Use dark brown, dark grey, dark green, dark blue, instead of black. Deliberately try out colour which is too thin/too dark/badly mixed. Encourage children to develop own brush-stroke styles.

**Materials:** Paints, palettes, brushes, water pots, black paper and chalk.

**Practical session:** Children could work individually, or in pairs, or in small groups. This would involve discussion, joint decision-making and problem-solving.

**Development:** Extend to drama, building environments, imaginary dark places. Introduce 'simple science' of light, colour? Write stories? Sing, play? Read? Imagine? Try out same colours against different backgrounds? Topics – e.g. 'People Who Lived in Caves'. Underground caverns, stalagmites? 'The Bottom of the Ocean'.

*Example 9  packages (plate 19)*

**Concepts:** Design development and organization of space/surfaces. Awareness of two- and three-dimensional shapes.

**Learning potential:** Translation of three-dimensional package into two-dimensional form. Understanding of design concepts in commercial products. Decision-making over drawing media, organization of space.

**Skills:** Drawing of letter shapes in specific styles. Control of colouring media. Organization and placing on paper.

**Stimulus:** Begins by looking at household products – breakfast cereal packets, soap boxes, shampoo boxes or plastic containers. Consider shapes, colours, backgrounds, lettering, size, organization of designs on folded and unfolded card packages.

**Options:** Children can collect these packages, teacher may provide. Children may choose to draw in pencil, crayon, felt-tips, pen. Paper size may vary according to packages or cartons used.

**Materials:** Cartons, packages, glue, glue spreaders, scissors, felt-tips, crayons, coloured pencils, pens, assorted papers.

**Practical session:** Children make drawings of chosen package, container, or carton, carefully noting style, lettering, etc. This is then mounted together with the original package on a backing paper or displayed on the wall. Children are able to choose drawing materials.

**Development:** Children design their own carton or package to advertise an imaginary product, e.g. Whizzo Washing Powder, Non-Spill Unbreakable Milk Bottles, Instant Beefburger Maker, Everlasting Ice-Creams. Children design posters using lettering from packages to advertise, e.g. Jumbo Jelly Factory, Amazing Beans Ltd. Advertise school meals? Class assemblies? Discuss television adverts?

### Example 10  *black and white project*

**Concepts:** Pattern, shape, awareness of tone (dark and light).

**Learning potential:** Problem-solving, increasing visual perception, shape discrimination, comparison of tone.

**Skills:** Sticking, paint-mixing. Control of clean water (important when using black paint). Control of paint.

**Stimulus:** Pictures, stories of 'Black and White', stripes, spots, patterns, e.g. *Black Bear, White Bear* by T. Harriott and L. Kopper. Books with illustrations entirely in black and white, direction of stripes? Create a mind-picture of a black and white fantasy creature? More black than white? More white than black? Dalmatians? Zebras? Zebra crossings? White snowflakes on tarmac. Newspapers. Coal/snow. Lights, holes.

**Options:** Choice of materials, choice of shapes: making patterns with shapes. Limit choice to two shapes? Three? Ready-cut shapes? Children cut?

**Materials:** Choose from black and white papers, card, scissors, glue, mixing trays, water, brushes, water pots, paints.

**Practical session:** Working from the stimulus, children discuss with their teacher what materials are appropriate and consider the options available. Using imagination, children create patterns (using paints or sticking paper). Children draw with a brush or arrange shapes freely on paper. The goal is to try to create a pattern which leaves half the paper showing.

**Development:** Patterns where three-quarters of paper is covered. Construction of fantasy creatures, recalling stories. 'Black and White in Everyday Life': e.g. sweets, humbugs, Liquorice Allsorts – sorting according to pattern. 'Night and Day.' Collages using different kinds of blacks, whites (these vary slightly according to what kind of paper and paint is chosen). Children make collections of different black and white objects.

*Example 11  magic-spell patterns*

**Concepts:** Pattern, line, colour.

**Learning potential:** Imagination development, pattern invention, control of pattern, line, colour.

**Skills:** Drawing, colouring.

**Stimulus:** Magic 'pattern' spell reading. Teacher reads, children read:

> Frog of eye and Bat of wings,
> Change round all the usual things,
> Pocus-Hocus patterns grow,
> Cover all the things I know.

**Options:** Choice of drawing, colouring, painting, collage materials. Children can transfer patterns they know from one object to another, or invent new patterns entirely.

**Materials:** Pens, pencils, chalks, paper, paints, collage materials, scissors, glue. Pattern samples, wallpaper, fabrics.

**Practical session:** Teacher reads; children read, spell and imagine everyday objects, the classroom, themselves turned to patterns. Some bright, some dull, some big, some small. Imagination can be stretched to ideas beyond themselves and the classroom, e.g. animals, buildings, forests. Children choose to draw, paint, etc., images from imagination. Colour? Size? Shape? Keynote is organization and control of patterns (e.g. 'How might you do this without all the patterns getting mixed up?').

**Development:** Invention of their own magic pattern/colour spells – language extension, poetry. Function of spell? What changes? Develop using old magazines for pattern sources. Apply to music (magic music spell?). Drama, plus a combination of art and music. Make masks, objects for the spell, dressing-up materials?

*Example 12  brickwork*

**Concepts:** Colour, pattern, shape.

**Learning potential:** Increases awareness of subtle colour-mixes, irregular pattern qualities, shape. Develops colour-mixing and control of medium.

**Skills:** Drawing, colour-mixing, painting.

**Stimulus:** Brickwork outside the school, pictures of brickwork. Discussions, comparisons of colour, shape and pattern.

**Options:** Children find other sources of reference near their homes, prior to session. Teacher brings in old bricks, new bricks. Choice of drawing, painting, or colouring materials.

**Materials:** Small cardboard packages which are collected over a period of time. Light-coloured, brick size or smaller preferred.

**Practical session:** Children draw brick surface pattern on package (or on paper and glue this before colouring). Paint package carefully mixing colours. When dry, they contribute their brick to a group 'Wall', decorated with 'graffiti' (authorized).

**Development:** Children draw and colour a whole wall. Small individual pictures? Mural? With clay they make small bricks which they texture on the surface to express the idea of 'worn brickwork'? Simple printing using a brick-shaped potato, repeat-printing to construct a building.

*Example 13  doodles into pictures*

**Concepts:** Development/change in drawing.

**Learning potential:** Fosters ability to invent, imagine and change. Encourages reappraisal of results. Fosters ability to turn 'mistakes' into something else or disguise them.

**Skills:** Drawing, imagining, inventing.

**Stimulus:** Drawing materials.

**Option:** Children exchange doodles with a partner/friend. Stimulus developed to include children responding by doodling to random sounds or stories.

**Materials:** Paper, pencils, pens, crayons, felt-tips, chalks, paper.

**Practical session:** The children doodle on paper first without looking, then by looking and adding to their doodles. Exchange with partner, or keep own doodles and develop them to fit a recognizable shape or become an imaginary creature.

**Development:** Make collections of doodles over period of time. Use for collage, source of reference for pattern. Copy part of doodle into another design. Assemble doodles into a 'Doodle Mural'. Doodle mobiles?

### Example 14 balanced shapes

**Concepts:** Balance, awareness of form.

**Learning potential:** Develops observation and awareness of balance in shapes, weight, volume. Sense of design in relation to weight. Modelling, weighing.

**Stimulus:** A weighing device, materials, resources for producing abstract shapes (such as a kaleidoscope, polished minerals, pieces of broken bone, fragmented tray-toffee).

**Options:** Children choose three-dimensional shapes, teacher and children discuss shapes. Use sources of reference for shape, e.g. numerals. Cut in black paper first in two dimensions. Roll modelling material flat? Use clay?

**Materials:** Weighing balance, scissors, black paper, Plasticine, dough, or clay.

**Practical session:** The children look at, talk about, geometric and non-geometric shapes, shapes of stones, mathematical shapes. They try to produce two three-dimensional shapes in Plasticine so that they balance when weighed. Shapes should have some similar characteristic. 'Make me two pebbles with a special shape' is an excellent starting point. Children weigh both shapes and adjust so they balance. Display, discuss.

**Development:** Weighing, mathematics, cutting black paper shapes which look as if they would balance. Mobiles. Drawing a picture of some shapes being weighed. Joining two shapes together after finding they balance. Making a drawing from the final joined model.

## Variety

Each of these ideas can be slightly rearranged to alter the presentation. Variety in presentation often makes the same idea look completely new to children, even if they have done it many times before. There are many occasions, in many areas of the curriculum, when we want to consolidate the same learning. By the time children tumble to the fact that they may previously have done something similar, their work is well under way, and in any case has different aims and a different outcome.

The presentation of ideas can vary principally by making changes to the 'Concepts' and 'Learning potential' listed here. A project which was designed to encourage awareness of colour might be changed to stimulate awareness of texture or form. Children could be presented with one half of a project this week, and the other half changed for the following week. Alternatively, ideas might be presented in three or four parts during a single art session, or spread across a whole week.

Most of the routes to creative teaching involve choices made from a number of options. In the set examples so far included, it is perfectly possible to reverse the content of two further categories, so that material contained in the 'Development' section, is transferred to that of the 'Practical session'. We might, for instance, want to change wax-crayon rubbings to a session in which we teach the basic principles and techniques of wax-resist. Plans to work on the concept of 'balance in shapes' might change to 'symmetry in pattern and shape'.

Successful ideas tend to become part of every teacher's repertoire. Yet this has its dangers, especially if we are unable to bring variety into presentation and development. There are already too many artistic clichés for more to be added. Children do enjoy making tissue-paper stained-glass windows, folded-paper butterflies and paper snowflakes. But how often are these just done for the sake of interest? How seldom do they form part of a sequenced development? The trouble is that these well-worn clichés are very entertaining. Their popularity is already proven, which makes them irresistible for a teacher who likes a well-mapped, guaranteed, end-product-only approach to art (Chapter 3). There is no risk, but little possibility of producing anything either unexpected or outstanding.

It ought to be possible to be more creative and generate ideas from an art activity which is already taking place. To achieve this is not as difficult as it seems. Each time there is artwork going on, a strategy which can work is to examine what is happening to see if the following questions produce new ideas for activities.

> 'Are there skills which need more practice?' (What task? What idea?) 'Do they need more work on pattern?'
> 'What would happen if we changed the materials?' (Would the ideas change?)
> 'Is it worth making changes to the activity? Reappraising the presentation?'

'Should they enlarge this?'

'How could we think of this as part of a mural?'

'Is there part of that which needs to be cut out to rescue it? How could it be used?'

A change of medium immediately changes the skills needed to cope with it. The effect is sometimes remarkable. Children who find an idea alien to the materials they are using will often come alive when they try to express it another way. This is not an argument for changing media just for the effect. The point here is that children occasionally become stuck in their expression if they have very little chance to use different media.

All these activities are the source of further learning if we allow them to be. There is, however, no point in assuming children have appropriate skills unless they have already learned them. Whilst art is not simply to teach skills, there are still many practice activities which are necessary for children to learn how to control materials. The keynote is learning, and without much effort on our part it should be possible to think of practice activities which develop control of media. Examples are activities which include skills like mixing paint, using a brush, smoothing a clay surface, or controlling adhesives. Children already have imagination, but we need to give them the psychological 'space' and freedom to use it even within a simple skill. That, and the ability to tie in art activities with children's previous learning, should make art teaching as demanding as any other aspect of education.

# 9  Using paint

No teacher or child in my school ever uses ready-mixed paint.

(First school headteacher)

We always use ready-mixed paint.

(First school headteacher)

These two opposing views sum up the diverse positions teachers sometimes take up when they want to use paints. There can be established camps and occasionally a no man's land where the cry is 'We don't use paint here because it's too messy.' Messy it may be, but the rewards for organizing painting effectively are not to be missed. Most teachers will put up with difficulties if they feel the end results are worthwhile, but it must also be pointed out that there are teachers who dislike using powder colours, block colours, or watercolours. So do a few children. To enforce any one particular method of using paint would not be profitable. Yet the advantages of one way over another need examining, not least to show how versatile the medium is.

Very young children may draw what they know, but it is said that they paint what they feel. Quite whether or not that is true is arguable. Their paintings often tend to look strong in feeling or emotion, perhaps because of the fluid nature of the medium, perhaps because that is how they respond to it. Certainly paint offers them expressive characteristics and qualities which no other medium can quite match.

Painting is so fundamental that no art education is complete without some experience of it. Children generally enjoy painting, partly because paint is an unpredictable medium, one full of surprises. For them it has the excitement created by moving areas of wet colour around and across the paper. They can fill shapes, push pigment about and watch the immediate effects created by their brush. Paint is a deceptively easy medium to use, yet it takes years to control and master. It can defy control to the last. However experienced we are in using paint there is always some way of using it which we have not yet come across, and this is one of its great attractions. Of course, how we use it with children seriously affects the outcome of what they do, a factor which can make apparently well-worn subjects like using paint worth closer scrutiny.

## Mixing paints

A child's first experience of paint may be 'finger-painting' where the excitement is more in the doing. Naturally, the results are of limited artistic value. The paints are mixed round and round but not much skill in handling paint is demonstrated. In the nursery, and sometimes in a reception class, children may need to use paints which have already been mixed up for them so that the consistency is thick enough not to run down the paper. When they try out paints with brushes, we can expect them just to dip in a readily available pot and make their exploratory marks. We can expect that, but it is surprising just what children can manage by themselves even at the age of 5 years.

> When I first came to this school I found an incredible resistance to the idea that children could mix their own paints. You really have to demonstrate how to mix up powder paints on a palette so teachers can see. Then they can try it with the children. I put a couple of generous drops of water on a dry enamel plate and wipe the brush on the side of the water pot. Then I dip the wet brush into powder paint, mixing more powder into the drops of water until I can tip up the plate and nothing runs down. The dry powder sticks to the brush. Children soon get the hang of it . . . they test their mix by tipping up the plate, but not for long . . . really it doesn't take much practice before they know how thick it should be.
>
> (First school headteacher)

Some of the organizational problems have already been mentioned (Chapter 7) but there is no doubt that the availability of water and sinks obviously affects what can be done. The teacher (Chapter 7) who was working under difficulties had eighteen different mixtures of ready-mixed colours for the children to use. But even so she felt that was not enough. Whenever she could, she had her children mixing powder colours together on palettes or enamelled plates. The children were not only mixing powder into a liquid paint, but they were also mixing colours of their own from the ingredients they had.

Water-based opaque paint is made from extender (powder), pigment and glue. In cheaper powder colours there is a great deal of extender and far less pigment, so the brightness of colours is not as good as it could be. Powder-colour has its own glue already added as a binder. The coarser the powder, the more likely the paint will be opaque, rather than being like true watercolour. One reason why watercolours are expensive and sold in small quantities is that they are very finely ground and the pigment is strong. They are expressly intended to be used very wet and thinly applied (Plate 35). Watercolour paper is consequently thick so that it does not buckle easily when made wet.

One of the advantages of using dry powder-colour is that a wet brush picks up the powder without leaving water to contaminate the remaining powder. The brush can therefore be dipped in one colour after another without needing to be washed. Some teachers call this the 'sticky brush' technique because powder sticks to a brush. Where children develop skill in mixing from powder, they also discover something about how paint is made too. Pigments for the manufacture of paint come from all over the world, but end up as finely ground powders held together in a paste. How they respond on paper is part of the art of their manufacture and children benefit from knowing that not everything in their artistic lives comes ready-mixed. Practice is needed, but the children develop a skill they would otherwise miss.

Where ready-mixed paints are the only ones available, children can still try out mixtures of colour in plastic containers, cooking trays, tin lids, or on laminate surfaces, a little paint at a time to see what happens. They will soon mix them to muddy colours, but that is an important teaching point. Children need to find out what colours do when they are mixed together, even if this is only at the bottom of a used margarine container or a yoghurt pot.

A question that arises is why there should be any rush to teach children to mix their own paints. Surely there is time enough when they are older? There is, but the difference in results between children being independent in their mixing of paint, or dependent on an adult, is staggering. They can have at their disposal a vast range of colour combinations once they are not restricted by using ready-mixed colour. Besides this, we can see that a project such as 'Multi-Coloured Spaghetti' (Chapter 8 and Plate 17) is one which is almost impossible to carry out with ready-mixed, thin and diluted paints. The paint needs a certain thick consistency if one colour is not to flood into others, and it should be mixed with other colours for desirable learning to take place. The specific skills children develop using paint are described in more detail in Chapter 16.

## Colour-mixing

Of all the characteristics of artwork displayed in any school, colour-mixing is perhaps the most striking. Where children have been limited to using raw primary red, yellow and blue (additionally with green, black and brown as extra colours), the artwork looks remarkably similar and far less personal. It is a disappointment to walk into some schools and see that children have never had the opportunity to mix any colours together themselves. The artwork is trapped in a clash of reds, blues, yellows, oranges and greens without a more subtle shade in sight.

Sometimes there is a particular quality of colour missing (usually a red where only one dark crimson red has been ordered) from the school requisition. This gives a further restricted and impoverished colour range. Even for making the most basic of colour-mixes we will need

- two different reds: a crimson (dark red) and a vermilion (scarlet or bright orange-red)
- two blues: an ultramarine (or royal, bright blue) and a Prussian blue (dark blue with a hint of green-black in it)

- two yellows: a chrome yellow (bright yellow) and a yellow ochre (earthy dark yellow).
- black, white.

This range is very austere but ideal for learning how to mix colours. Additionally, brown, purple, orange and green can be ordered. These give greater variety to the shades which can be mixed, but their introduction at an early stage of colour-mixing is questionable. The austere primaries are a restricted minimum for learning about such colours as green and discovering how they might be mixed.

Quite a productive time can be had mixing paints together and never transferring them to paper. It is remarkable how absorbed some children become as they watch colours change in their mixing-plate or palette. There is a stage at which they need to try this and may sometimes learn just as much about colour on the palette as they do using it on their paper. By contrast, they can discover a great deal about paint through looking at the paintings of other artists (Chapter 17).

If we want children to paint in a sustained and interested way, there is an obvious outcome to choosing small-scale paper and large brushes, or large-scale paper and small brushes. Children are going to cover a small piece of paper very quickly with a large stiffly bristled brush. Large and stiffly bristled brushes may last, but they have a specific function, which allows the artist to paint broad large areas of colour where the brushstroke is generally a feature. The worst possible use of a large brush is for children to try to fill in a small and neatly drawn pencil image. A good range of brushes is needed from size 0 to 7, nylon or hair to tough bristle. It is often far better for children to draw using a fine brush, rather than a pencil if they are next going to use paint and larger brushes. Some children will actually ask for a fine brush for detail, but others seem to plod on with quite inadequate materials.

Skill in handling a brush is not just a matter of handling one size of brush. Large stiffly bristled brushes, for example are held differently in the hand. They have long handles because they are meant to be held further away from the work than small brushes where a wrist-action is needed. Obviously, not all children want to work with large hog-haired brushes. Some are much happier working on a smaller scale with tiny brushstrokes. More than anything else, children need to experiment with scale, paints, brushes, mixtures and arrangements of materials to find out how they function.

The effect of paint on white paper and on neutral or grey sugar-paper is quite different. Where children are trying to cover the whole paper with paint, white paper is often very difficult to use. It tends to show small pinpricks of bright white when almost all the paper is covered. This is, of course, unless thin water-colour is being used. (A feature of using watercolour is that it allows for thin translucent washes to build up on the paper.) These pinpricks, where the paint has missed, are less noticeable with grey sugar-paper, but children must mix the paint thickly enough to cover the grey. The additional advantage of grey, brown and black papers is that children have the chance to include white paint.

(A natural tendency is to mix colours which are darker than the grey paper that children use. Quite a breakthrough in understanding occurs when they find mixtures which are lighter than their paper.)

Teaching colour theory is not appropriate with young children, especially 5-year-olds, who use any colour they please rather than the expected colouring of things as we know them (Chapter 4). We should not attempt to teach taste in colour; which is associated with personal preference rather than a sensitivity to colour. A good starting point is to have children work on newspaper, putting down dabs or patches of colour to try out their mixing skills; practising on newspaper is not intimidating for children and it is inexpensive. For added variety, children can use scraps of shaped pieces of paper, half-circles or triangles, for instance, in which they can organize colour and pattern. Painting with a very restricted range of colour (for example, mixing different shades of red) is another worthwhile introduction to discovering their own mixtures.

This can be followed by working on colour themes or subjects which particularly lend themselves to further development. The pattern which evolves from patches painted on newspaper, for instance, can become more ordered or complex. Children could paint 'Our Special Red Patterns', 'Our Green Patterns', or 'Our Blue Stripes and Circles'. Or there are subject themes like 'The Red Balloon', 'Fires', 'The Big Red Bus', 'Disco Lights', 'Caves', 'Snow', 'Autumn Colours', or 'Camouflage'. Colour is sometimes associated with emotion. An emotional response to colour is so personal that we cannot easily begin to analyse it, nor should we. Children can still try out colour-mixes associated with their feelings, but if they do, it is not for us to say what colour is supposed to fit which emotion. We can, however, ask children about their feeling-response to what they paint. Emotional subjects which appeal can often be quickly committed to newspaper or scrap paper, or even painted on a large scale. For example, children can put down patches of colour using a large hog-haired brush (no drawing) inspired by feelings which express

colours of anger
colours of sadness
colours of loud noises, colours of silence
colours of a frightening storm
colours of a sunny day
colours under the sea
colours of autumn leaves
colours of a day at the seaside

Opportunities for using paint can also occur very spontaneously. A feature of using paint is that the world itself can actually begin to look more painterly. A cherry tree in full blossom outside the classroom may for some child suggest brushstrokes of pink and white paint. Subjects like 'A Flurry of Snowflakes' or 'The Sunshine on Water' are useful sources of inspiration. In the imagination, subjects like 'Field with a Thousand Greens' or 'A Marmalade Sky' can similarly suggest varieties of colour to paint. Seizing the moment, painting subjects are often derived from local events and the surroundings of an artist. It comes as no surprise that children in rural villages paint farm animals, or that living on the coast encourages the painting of boats and beaches. An inner-city carnival produces something quite different again. A number of topic ideas for painting with a local flavour are,

> old buildings
> village landscapes
> patterns of a ploughed field
> boats on a beach
> garden design
> me in my duvet
> my bedroom
> pattern in Indian/African textiles
> kettle and pans

A valuable teaching device is to persuade children to choose and to change, each activity promoting inevitable learning experiences. Two obvious key questions can make children think in this way about what they are painting:

> 'What are you going to choose?', and
> 'How are you going to change it?'

Whilst children do not need to change things *at all costs*, without changes and choices their painting can become very fixed and predictable. They need to review and modify their own work. Choosing and changing gives back responsibility to them for their decisions and keeps ideas flexible. The session on colour-mixing may have been inspired by the teacher, but now it is the turn of the pupils to take the initiative and develop their own painting style.

A difficult point to press home to children is that they may profit from working on various parts of their artwork, rather than starting carefully in one top corner and losing patience as they work their way down. This applies to work where shapes have been drawn first and are being coloured, rather than more vigorous and direct painting. A piece of work which has been visited in more than one part, already looks more finished than one with a corner section carefully painted. Some children who seem to have great patience will happily work piecemeal from one side to anther, as did the English artist Stanley Spencer. Others appreciate seeing their work develop more as a whole, tackling the detailed parts wherever they are. Sometimes this avoids the problem of 'filling in the background' after having carefully painted other shapes. A way around this is to work on both background and other content at the same time, making decisions about what to paint next. Younger children often leave the background paper showing anyway as they tend to draw using paint, rather than plan elaborate backgrounds and foregrounds.

Self-responsibility in art naturally includes looking after painting materials. Often it is far too easy to create a mess with paint, and, unless checked, children will find that to go off and wash palettes, or paint each other, can be more fun than working on the painting. When children first colour-mix, they need practice in looking after paints so that the brush, the water pot, and they themselves stay clean enough to work. Without practice and insistence on care by their teacher, the colours they produce are entirely conditioned by the filthy state of water pots and brushes. Without further encouragement they are likely to clean up inefficiently and painting as an activity can become an experience which is not willingly repeated.

Teaching children to use paint requires effort and sound organizational skill precisely because it is not a straightforward medium to control. But it offers children such a wide range of effects in comparison, for instance, with drawing. Where drawing may be the string quartet of art, the richness of painting is nearer to being a symphony. Once children become skilful at using paints, their scope for producing expressive work can expand considerably. They have within their grasp the means to colour, eliminate, rearrange and add to the vast array of visual ideas which absorb them.

# 10 Sequencing printmaking

It is often not long after starting school that children return home with a familiar request to turn up the following day with a potato. Parents may guess what is about to happen. They have seen it all before when they were at school themselves. The idea was to use half the potato on which they made a pattern with a pair of scissors or a blunt knife. Then they printed with it for a time, and if the results were not too messy they displayed them at school or brought them home. Sometimes the potato was pressed on sponges charged with paint, sometimes it was loaded with a brush. Mostly, the activity was a novel afternoon's experience which did not develop much further.

Two distinct paths of development are possible and both of these imply a sequence. That is to say, the work which is done is not simply an afternoon's activity, but bears some relation to what happens before and after it. Either simple printmaking can develop from something else, such as a theme which is already under way, or we can begin at the very beginning and develop a sequence from the first printed marks children make. Along the first path, printing can also grow from rubbings children make, or from embossed wallpaper collages which they cover with a sheet of paper and rub over with crayon. Printmaking, in any case, is a natural development from looking at surfaces and already uses the qualities of a raised surface for its images. Sometimes a professional printmaker will rub over a wood or lino block to see what it looks like. The two techniques, printmaking and taking rubbings, have obvious similarities.

Alternatively, a second path of development can grow from trying out very simple printing techniques to find out where they lead. A well-known one is to take prints from finger painting (where the teacher takes a print from a laminate surface on which a child has enjoyed pushing paint about). Another technique children may have experienced is using a printing roller and water-based inks to roll over a leaf or a paper stencil. Whatever the elementary experience of printmaking, there comes a point at which children need to explore the technique more fully. For that there must be a different plan of campaign.

The very youngest end of the age range needs first to try out simple printing activities with very limited materials. Reception children enjoy ready-to-use materials so that they can press an object into paint and quickly transfer it to paper. For them the excitement is immediate and only the forerunner of what can eventually be a rich and expressive medium.

To anyone unused to looking at pre-school and infant art, the first attempts to print or paint may appear to be superficial and chaotic. However, this takes no account of the fact that there is a sequence of development to any artistic learning which (as has already been pointed out in Chapter 8) begins with exploration and play. The rhythmic stamping of a bottle top, a lid, or a potato on newspaper, is just as important to the learning sequence as is refined and careful placing of one printed shape next to another. At this young age, not much consideration of where the bottle top might be placed can be expected, nor is there generally a deliberate choice of colour.

Bottle tops, scraps of polystyrene, cotton reels, junk and vegetables are all ideal surfaces for elementary printmaking. For the beginner, printmaking can be organized with plastic margarine containers lined with sponge or rag. These serve as ideal reservoirs for paint and are not messy. If there are enough interesting mixes of colour available, children can produce excellent results by using them as a stamping-pad. Enough sponge-filled containers and a variety of objects for printing make for a successful combination, though very young children may need to have their potato cut to a shape they can more easily hold. The first experience of printmaking is novel and short-lived and, so long as all the materials are to hand, it can be enjoyable and educationally worthwhile.

Younger children may like these unsophisticated encounters with print-making but we must consider how a sequence of learning develops from here. What steps can we take to push development well beyond that of novelty and entertainment?

If children are going to progress further than a 'press-and-print' approach we must take account of acquired skills like colour-mixing (Chapter 9). Obviously there is a considerable difference in the range of colours and techniques which is possible when children can already handle colour-mixing. A whole new experience opens up. From colour-mixing activities, children can develop more ambitious organization of their materials. Their workspace can be arranged so that they can charge a printing surface with a drip-free mixture of their own making and not let paint splash all over the place. Printmaking, using margarine containers as a reservoir, can be abandoned in favour of a far wider range of colours and tones.

A crucial aspect of sequencing is to devise games which teach skill in printing before any specific subject-matter is introduced. One such exercise is to see how many times a potato can be printed on scrap paper or newspaper before the effect cannot be seen. Many children assume that a potato must be fully charged with colour each time they put it down on paper. Most of them will put far too much paint on their potato when they first start. Yet the mottled printed pattern of a potato surface can be attractive and add character to the design. To help understand this, children who have not quite got the message can try using a piece of newspaper as a preliminary blotter for the potato so that they only ever print the second pressing on their final designs. Or they can usefully be in competition with each other to see who can print with the least amount of paint on their potato.

Another valuable skill-teaching idea is to try to have them printing by pressing as lightly as they possibly can to see the effect. Children seem to have no difficulty whatever pressing down hard and to print lightly seems quite alien to their natural inclinations. It is surprising how much more care they will actually take once they try out these competitive learning activities.

The plan of campaign could also include cutting a variety of usable shapes from potatoes, wood blocks and ready-to-hand objects for printing. Initially, children do not then have to cope with the problem of cutting anything for themselves. The reason for removing this problem is to deal with other issues and for children to learn printing rather than cutting skills. It is perfectly possible to practise printing by dividing up a potato into chips rather than using the familiar halved shape. The activity can extend throughout a whole week and cost very little. Later, wallpaper scrapers can be used for cutting a flat printing surface on a vegetable. There are also blunt knives, potato peelers, shaped wooden spatulas, or inverted pen nibs (in holders), which are all useful cutting tools for making patterns. Twigs with an end cut and shaped like a glue spreader make simple and safe cutting knives. Blocks of potato which have a triangular-shaped printing surface, pieces shaped like cake slices, rectangular, square and curved shapes, all add to a miscellany of chippings.

An example of an activity designed to develop printing skills is seen in Figure 22. Here children begin by printing shapes next to a block of newspaper text

Figure 22 Text Blocks. Age 8. 300 × 400 mm.

or advertising matter. Shapes and colours can be limited so they concentrate on placing their marks carefully. An important teaching point is for children to learn to follow their own intentions. That is to say, they need sometimes to be able to draw a guideline and carefully print their potato next to it, making sure they closely match their potato edge to the line they drew. Some practice in placing printed shapes of potato edge to edge, point to point, or on a curved line (Figure 23), is also excellent as an additional way of developing this skill.

Drawing ruled lines at different angles, drawing around objects and creating meandering lines, all are variations of this practice activity. With each simple project children will usually learn a fraction more control. Some surprising patterns can be discovered and there is often a very rewarding development of skill evident for use in future work. Practice ideas for these activities might be of this kind:

- Draw me three lines like snakes across your paper. Choose mixtures of one colour and two shapes, and place them as carefully as you can against the line.
- See what pattern you can make with a ruler and pencil. Then add your printed shapes, carefully following your line with the edge of your shape.
- Choose two colours and work on squared paper (large squares if possible), carefully deciding where to put your potato printing.
- Draw round a dinner-plate and put patterns inside with your potato starting from the outside line and working inwards to the middle.
- Make a pattern of curved and straight lines. Develop your design using these as a guide.
- Put all your potato shapes point to point so that they touch when they print.
- Print your potato shapes edge to edge leaving very little or no gap between shapes.

In contrast to this controlled 'drawn line' approach (see also Plates 22, 23, 24) children can work quite freely using no guidelines whatever. An interesting problem to set them, for example, is to begin with a printed shape of their choice, work from the centre of their paper and try to make that central area look more interesting than the outside areas. The children learn a great deal about different ways to emphasize their work through choice of shape, tone, colour and arrangement of design. Emphasis is an important concept, one which has universal recognition in composition and interpretation in all the arts. This particular printmaking activity is one in which children can go on adding small shapes to the centre, so that they overlap each other. It involves decisions about when to stop and how much paper to leave showing, and judgements about its final impact.

A more sophisticated development is to change the shade of colour slightly each time the potato is printed. The printed shapes gradually change in colour from, say, red to orange, or blue to pink. To control such a colour change, especially where subtle colour-mixes are involved, demands skills which are

*Figure 23* Curved Line. Age 8. 505 × 387 mm.

not unusual but are determined by practice. Children may also be able to tackle working from light to dark colours or working with pattern on dark-toned papers (as in Plate 22).

As a variation on pattern, some children may be able to cut a letter of the alphabet on their potato. Even if they could not do this (and most can manage a straight-sided letter), alphabet letters still provide a useful way of producing patterns. The shape of each letter can be a substitute for drawn guidelines and incidentally reinforce children's awareness of letter formation. Patterns can additionally be cut into the potato surface, or round the outside edges, changes which give a different effect from using the potato as an entirely solid shape.

Sooner or later printed shapes will suggest interesting subject-matter. Snake-shaped lines will become snakes or caterpillars. Many of these subjects grow naturally from the creation of patterns. Children will sometimes see spirals as shells or snails. The triangular shapes of chopped-up potato may suggest to one child the spines of a prehistoric monster. To another they may be the cogs of a gigantic and futuristic machine.

## Putting ideas to the test

The purpose in presenting the following ideas in this particular format is to encourage some flexibility of approach. Most educational ideas are changed by the best of teachers. Yet it is worth knowing that there are two distinct ways of doing this, each of which has a very different outcome. One way seems to be to extract only a fraction of surface-level material from the ideas as they are presented. This strategy is one which can make the most excellent of schemes, maths, art, or language, fail miserably. The end result is a diluted version of the original. A better approach is to adapt and add to what is already there whilst retaining the principles of the idea. Some ideas which do not initially appeal may then serve to spark off others.

In the first example, which follows, some indication of learning potential is shown. From there onwards the whole emphasis of projects must be decided by the teacher in the light of the principles, concepts and learning potential outlined in other chapters (see in particular Chapter 16).

### Three kings

Learning potential includes colour-mixing, printing, sticking, language development, judgement of shape and designing.

This can begin with colour-mixing skills. Working in small groups, the children follow this by making patterns with potato prints on strips of paper, about 500 mm × 70 mm. This includes using black paper strips with white shapes printed by the children. These are then discussed as if they are lapels, or trimmings for an ornate and jewelled costume. After discussion, working on scrap paper, the children design for a large-scale costumed king which they draw out and print with various objects. They might print jewelled braid effects on black paper, cut them and collage with extra pieces of printed pattern, paper doilies and gold foil. There are options available to the teacher to vary materials, or limit them, allow choice, change scale and make a mural.

### Castles and houses

Teacher or children cut a potato into a useful block or brick shape. Children then discuss with their teacher castles, houses, windows, doors, moats and building techniques. The teacher also provides resources, books and visual aids. The potato block is used as a printing brick/stone for designing castles and houses. This technique has similarities with children's previous experience of using wooden building blocks, Lego and construction equipment. The project can be developed into three-dimensional work with model-making a useful outcome. Children print on cardboard boxes and assemble them. The scale of these can be large enough for the boxes to become a model which can be temporarily inhabited or used for drama.

### Spaceships

This printmaking theme is tackled using black paper and printing in white. (Reference can be made to the 'Black and White' project in Chapter 8.) The children draw out, in rough, spaceships, planets, spacemen. The teaching points arise from the difficulties of mixing whites, greys and light colours. Developments for teaching could include specific projects on space travel, murals, displays for the hall or corridor areas. Joint efforts can be assembled, collaged.

*Gardens*

A possibility here is to study petal shapes and leaf shapes. Printing may be done either on dark or light papers (or both) with obviously different results. Instead of producing a solitary flower or plant, children can develop ideas by printing over shapes until the garden contains a profusion of their own designs. Ideas: 'A Multi-Coloured Flower-Bed', 'The Giant Leaf Plant', 'Repeated Leaf Shapes'.

*Machines*

This project can grow from printing with bottle tops and lids. The children begin to invent machines which are meant to perform functions. Fantasy: 'The Fastest Machine', 'The Wheely Machine', 'The Football Machine'. Reality: 'Bus', 'Car', 'Railways', 'Farm Machinery'.

*Murals*

Murals can develop from any of the projects mentioned, but sometimes it is worth having a 'pattern mural' on which all the children print in turns. The organization of this, rationing of space, themes and decisions, makes for a productive learning experience. Such subjects as 'A Stripe Mural', 'Curves and Lines', 'Sponge Print Mural', can be developed as works in their own right.

*Circle segments*

Instead of children filling circles with pattern, this time they draw segments. Alternatively, they may incorporate ideas from mathematics. The aim is to use pattern which follows the design of a segment. This simple process allows for great variety in use of colour and shape inside each segment. For example, small triangular chips of potato can be used as the sole interior printed shape, or there might be a variety of different shapes. Colours can be limited to two or three, or children choose from a wider range.

*The sun*

There are various ways to develop this. Stories of sun gods, pictures of the sun, and fantasy songs, poems, rhymes and anecdotes provide a stimulus. A considerable variety of shapes and colour-mixes can be tried (an aim might be to build up a rich surface by overlapping shapes). The scale of the 'Sun' pictures is important. Imagine, for instance, two or three children printing a large sun shape on a mural. Developments include 'Sun and Clouds', 'Sun and Shadows', 'Sun and Rain', 'Hot Pictures' (fantasy).

## Birds

As with many other creatures, the theme of birds allows children to print shapes instead of painting with a brush. Many children find they have much more confidence using printed shapes for feathers than they do brush drawing. A development might be to print from real feathers using water-based inks and a roller. An advantage of themes such as 'Birds' or 'Fish' is that they may require very little drawing ability in the first instance. As a consequence they can often lead children to observe more closely and develop more sophisticated drawing skills.

## Fireworks

This subject is very successful even with very young children, especially if they can use thickly mixed whites, yellows, oranges and colours associated with fireworks. On black sugar-paper, the children can try out their printing with much more freedom than, for example, the 'Spaceship' project demanded. Here, they have the chance to let fantasy run riot as they create brightly toned mixtures for a firework display.

## Three-dimensional prints

Some of the patterns children produce make exceptionally good three-dimensional designs. Prints can be cut up and reassembled into sculpture. A finished print can be displayed as a cylinder, or the cylinder used as a Christmas decoration. Printing can be effective on masks and paper costumes. Children can design these working from skirt shapes, dress shapes, boxes, cones and shapes used for mobiles. The prints need not necessarily be large or elaborate.

There is an endless number of art activities which can have a carefully considered sequence. The more rigid the sequence, however, the more difficult it is to allow for children's differing work rates and this needs to be taken into account when organizing sessions. Sequencing should be sufficiently flexible to allow for individual differences. There is little point forcing children to jump through tightly organized artistic hoops under the assumption that they will eventually learn something useful. There are broader categories for a sequenced learning programme.

So far, the sequence described has been mapped out so that children develop ideas through

- play, rhythmic stamping of bottle tops, lids
- experience of colour-mixing
- simple practice games on newspaper (pressing objects as lightly as possible, printing until no effect is seen)
- controlled pattern, choices of colour, shape, drawn lines
- development of subject-matter
- large-scale projects, murals, three-dimensional work.

*Figures 24, 25*  Parrot, Boat. Age 8. 330 × 450 mm, 390 × 310 mm.

This is a useful but not sacrosanct sequence. Large-scale work is not, after all, the final objective for all printmaking projects. It is different rather than better. Of much greater importance is the development of a sequence of learning which arises in response to what children do. Such a sequence is likely to evolve as we ask,

> 'Do they need more practice in cutting?'
> 'Do they need to have a break from this and do some colour-mixing?'
> 'How can they cope with printing in artwork connected with the theme of . . .?'
> 'Could the work they're already doing be developed to include . . .?'
> 'What might that tree bark look like printed instead of painted?'

It would be a great mistake repeatedly to practise skills until only the technical side of things was perfect. Children need to try out ambitious ideas for subject-matter in the sequence, as well as to improve their technical skills. Rather in the way handwriting skills can still develop when children are inventing their own stories, colour-mixing or printing skills can be developed through other imaginative pieces of work. Sequencing any activities demands professional judgement especially when deciding what to leave out as well as what to put in. No sequence which is formulated in advance is ever going to replace a teacher's evolving sequence in response to the children's progress. If we want to develop printmaking to some depth and use it as a way of developing a wide variety of artistic skills, sequencing cannot be ignored as a crucial element of the process.

# 11 Collage as a medium

Collage began life as a serious medium with artists such as Braque and Picasso in 1910. Newspaper shapes found their way into the Cubists' paintings once work had begun to develop a fragmented jigsaw quality (Chapter 17). Braque had already begun to add sand and sawdust to paint, so it was a small step to add paper. The idea was not exactly new as it had been used to decorate screens for centuries. Today, the term is used for almost anything stuck to anything reasonably flat, including picture frames, decorated mirrors, gift wrap and packaging. Modern glues have allowed artists to combine items in sculptural 'collage' as well as being used for paper and card. Young children may begin by sticking down pieces of paper, but there are many more ambitious ways to create using collage. Enough layers of card stuck down, for example, create a small relief surface which can then be decorated.

Like all artistic learning, a project such as decorating a picture frame or the frame for a mirror is informed by principles of learning. A great deal depends on whether we want to increase children's knowledge about artists, develop their ability to choose interesting things to stick down, improve their ability to control cutting and sticking or find out the limitations of glue. Children might, for example, stick string of different thicknesses and colour the raised surface once it has dried. If the artist being studied was Klimt, then gold foil might be one of the obvious resources to provide. The artist and the learning objective will condition the original idea. Improving the handling of paint might generate an introduction where the teacher demonstrated how to mix a good consistency of paint. How absorbent is the paper being used? Is there, for example, an investigation of the work of the French collage artist Georges Braque going on and some need to look at the resources being used?

The medium of collage can be described as a recipe for visual confusion. This is because without careful control of abundant colour and pattern, the results of cutting, tearing and sticking things down tend to look jumbled and disorganized. The best collages, by contrast, show considerable skill in sorting materials and making them work together. If children thoughtlessly assemble anything that takes their fancy, the effect is to blur their designs, rather than organize them with clarity. Handled well, collage is a richly individual medium for designing. The main advantage of the technique is that materials can be tried out and moved around before being stuck down. The artist can put off the decision to finalize things until satisfied with the arrangement.

Collage has similarities with sorting activities. Children are often asked to sort numbers, colours, beads and blocks. If we take it as a teaching principle that activities should be sequenced (Chapter 10), there is every good reason why sorting collage materials could be used to this end. The opportunities for developing visual discrimination are limitless. Children can sort similar patterns or textures. They can sort colours, lines, different printed typefaces, fabrics, threads, foils, leather, metal, feathers, fur, grasses, or seeds. All this before they start to produce anything creative.

At the younger end of the age range, children particularly enjoy tearing shapes from paper, rather than cutting them. They also enjoy finding things which have different tactile qualities, like rough, smooth, rounded, or flat surfaces. The opportunity here for language development from these tactile experiences is an obvious one. Besides this, very little imagination is needed to devise practical maths tasks using various collage materials. Sets of five seeds and five lids, four blue wools and six black, three silver papers and seven sweet wrappers, could aid the teaching of number. Additionally, maths games where one colour represents a particular number can help to combine and support these different areas of the curriculum.

So long as children do not become totally bored by extra sorting activities, they can build up a useful resource for collages. A demanding but extremely worthwhile activity is to begin by sorting scraps of torn newspaper, a few centimetres square, into three different piles. One pile could be scraps of headlines with large letter shapes. Another could have parts of photographs and the remaining collection could be of small-sized text. It is quite surprising how interesting an effect the use of this simple resource has in a collage where there are bright colours. Even on its own, to use three tones of newspaper collage can be very attractive and a welcome change from screwed-up pieces of coloured tissue paper.

Scissor-cutting skills (see Chapter 16) are just as important as tearing paper, and awareness of shape can be encouraged by cutting repeated units. Cut and torn shapes rarely go well together so it is better to choose one or the other method. Children can cut shapes which represent fish scales, or feathers, and carefully use them to build up their own designs of fishes or birds. It is well worth encouraging children to choose how they themselves will limit materials so that the collages have some character. Could they, for example, work using newspaper only? Or could they limit themselves to two or three colours? Might they work with the same repeated shape?

When one design feature of a collage is very strong, it will often support a wide variety of colours and textures. Supposing children were to cut small brick-shaped rectangles from a varied range of colours and patterns. These they might assemble to make a richly patterned wall or building. Ordinarily, a multi-coloured design could look confused and over-fussy. But choosing such a simple shape as a rectangular brick binds the design together. It imposes its own unity and limitations of shape.

The repeated shape idea could easily be developed in other ways, taking titles such as 'Marbles', 'Beach Balls', 'Trees', 'Clouds', 'Fencing', 'Paving Slabs', 'Petals', or 'Patchwork'. In fact, from repeated shapes a whole theme could emerge. Imagine generating ideas around a theme of 'Sweets and Sweet Jars'. The theme could cover a spectrum of visual ideas from a 'Design for a Sweet Shop' (based on reality) to 'The Biggest Lollipop in the World' (fantasy). An additional development is to use different materials besides paper and to work in media other than collage, like paint and crayon.

Children accustomed to choosing what medium to use can bring a great deal of their own originality to each theme. As far as the teacher is concerned, the effort needed to develop ideas diminishes as pupils offer more. It also lessens with continual practice in thinking around possible themes. In fact, five minutes spent scribbling ideas on the back of an envelope can sometimes create the beginnings of enough useful work for days (see also Chapter 5).

The concept of 'contrast' in collage is an important one but not easily taught or understood. Most muddled collages we see are confused because one material merges into another. Sometimes this is because the shape is rather ambiguous, more often it happens because dark material has not been contrasted with light. Colour has not contrasted with colour, pattern has not found a place next to a plain area. Of course, more sophisticated adult collages work well without contrast, yet for children who have little control of the medium, contrast is a concept which they put to good use. They can develop awareness of it in any number of ways. They benefit from comparing the effect of sticking dark paper shapes over light ones, or light over dark. They can also try to discover which colours and shapes might stand out against each other, which ones tend to lack contrast. And they can compare strong patterns with subtle, large with small, brightly coloured with dull.

Many collage materials, like leather and fabric, are difficult for children to use. Leather does not cut sufficiently easily to create a clear and readable shape, so contrast of colour and tone is vital as an alternative way of making the work more readable to the eye. With the best of intentions, a number of teachers produce murals or friezes which are collaged without any regard for this concept of contrast. The same colours or tones are often used for both background and foreground, where with some thought they could be much more decisive as design features.

A simple guide to avoid confused images is to keep specific colours and patterns for different objects in the collage. A particular blue might be used solely for part of the sky and other blues reserved for objects elsewhere in the collage. Similarly, patterns can be representative of only one element, like vegetation or building materials. In fact part of the all-important decision-making process is to sort out which material suits the particular part of the content. Is black and white newspaper the best choice for that elephant? Should we save the red for this wooden fence?

Many of the drawings and photographs we see in books depict objects in their most easily readable view. Usually this is a side view or a silhouette which has an outline or edge which conveys the maximum information. In such a complicated medium as collage, silhouette shapes are helpful ingredients. That is not to say that the side-view silhouette is the best, simply that it is readable. Children will need to spend time finding out just what a silhouette is, or play with positive and negative shapes from the same piece of black paper to see what the effect of maximum contrast is. Most collages can be rescued with black paper shapes. A fact often overlooked is that plain black or white papers, even plain coloured papers, have a clarifying effect on collages that have become muddled.

Obviously whenever a shape is cut from black paper it leaves its negative in the remainder. Both positive black paper and negative space can be incorporated into a design. Picasso, Braque and, notably, Schwitters were artists who found that pieces they had left over from cutting out were fascinating resources for collage. Naturally, there is a unifying link between the cut shape and its waste surround, so it is not surprising that artists found using both was visually appealing. The message here is 'Don't discard the litter from collage because it is useful.'

Children may well discover that the assorted junk they collect themselves has strong visual attractions. Part of the learning experience is for them to collect their own collage materials and bring them into the classroom. Storage difficulties apart, the collections they make often provide a good talking point as well as being a cheap art material. Needless to say, teachers of this young age range, 4–9 years, become great hoarders of all sorts of material for collage. Practically anything which will stick down is worth collecting.

For most purposes, school glue, PVA, or even paste (so long as it has no fungicide) will do for sticking collage. Stick glue is good for paper, but not for much else. Occasionally, some stronger tube adhesives may be necessary under the teacher's supervision. A useful organizational device is to have children gluing on magazines so they can turn the page when the surface becomes too messy. Glue does seem to travel in the hands of inexperienced children and some skill in instructing children how to use it is called for. If about a centimetre

*Figure 26* Collage 'Eyes'. Age 5. Each 290 × 210 mm.

depth is put in the bottom of a pot, the glue is less likely to travel up the spreader. At its messiest moments, collage is a great test of skill in handling materials. Children and their teachers discover what will stick and what refuses to do so. Where there are problems these usually involve too much glue, or the wrong kind for the job.

Rounded surfaces, such as cardboard rolls, and curved junk refuse to stick easily, as do plastic containers and heavily waxed surfaces. The choice open is to use ingenious combinations of tabs, staples, strong glues and adhesive tape, or take a wise step and avoid curve against curve. A hot-glue gun is a possibility as it will stick almost anything but this would not be safe for children to use themselves. There is really no such thing as failure in collage because it is all about techniques of assembling what we can. A child who discovers something is impossible to stick with the glue being used may learn as much about technical problems as can be learned about art. The experience may not be very enjoyable but still educationally worthwhile.

Every so often, children will ask if they can add paint to their collage. This is usually an afterthought but it can also be tried quite deliberately as a starting point. From this beginning comes the combination of drawing and collage, or paint and collage, both of which are as valid as collage is in its own right. Coloured chalks, ink and felt-tipped pens can all add to the work. Particularly useful are chalk and ink which can add to and emphasize a collaged shape. Paint, if it is thick enough, can obliterate confused parts of a collage and unify it. In some adult artists' collages, where three-dimensional blocks of wood are stuck to a flat surface, it is not unusual to find the whole work has been painted in matt white paint. The shapes used were probably painted white because they needed some unifying element.

Many paintings which incorporate collage never began that way. The artist has arrived at the collage through a process of change and may even have rescued the work by incorporating collage. Sometimes in the classroom, a pattern-making session which went wrong can lend itself to a rescue operation. Instead of the results being thrown away, they can be cut up later and glued down again on another paper surface, the materials used and reused.

Closely related to collage, and often confused with it is 'photo-montage'. We tend to think of collage being a collection of colours, textures and shapes applied to a surface. When artists use parts of photographs and stick them together, this is strictly a montage. It is worth distinguishing this because the medium of stuck photographic material is altogether different from using coloured tissue and scraps of coloured paper torn from magazines. Photographs have to be found and some sense made of them. There is, of course, a certain fun element in making a photo montage of someone's face using eyes, nose or mouth from a photograph of someone else. Some practice is needed to take photo montage beyond the comic and use carefully selected parts to create an artistically worthwhile image. An organizational drawback is that of having enough (suitable) magazines and newspapers for a class.

## Other assemblages

We usually think of collage as being flat and two-dimensional in comparison with sculpture. But it becomes three-dimensional as what might be called 'assemblage'. The term is self-explanatory. Scrap materials are assembled into three-dimensional forms. These may well represent a fantasy creature or become interesting objects in their own right. Once the concept has been introduced that forms can exist independently of subject-matter, children enjoy making them to see what they can produce. The assemblage no longer has to 'be' something recognizable. Children are far less worried by the abstract than adults seem to be.

A number of remarkable assemblages can be produced by working on themes like 'Balance', 'Symmetry', or 'Tall Shapes'. Again, the use of units, like boxes or cotton reels, paper cups, egg containers and packing material helps. Simple three-dimensional shapes can be made from paper strips and assembled into larger forms. Paper strips are cheap to produce, can be bent, curved and stuck. Children can devise shapes which they repeat (a good learning activity in its own right) and the variations possible are endless once these units are made. As a development of this idea, children might stick some of their repeated shapes around a paper cylinder or around a box.

Displays of paper strip sculptures (Figure 27) can prove interesting discussion points. There is a great deal to look at in terms of shape, shadow effects, textures and colour. Ideas may be triggered by

*Figure 27* Paper Strip Sculpture. Age 8.

looking at shadows
making a 'shadow show' using coloured strips of paper and a light source
   (choice?)
using black and white
painting the sculptures
making paper strip mobiles
drawing the paper strip assemblages
finding different ways to display them
combining sculptures into a very large assemblage.

When cutting skills are well advanced children can use shapes cut from card or papier-mâché egg trays as a resource. Allowing the scissors to travel until an interesting unit is found produces a very original shape. Some of the units can then be made into creatures, or alternatively they can simply be glued together as three-dimensional forms. Sufficient learning often takes place through the cutting and painting activities which children do. Painted assemblages made from egg trays are often so striking that their original source material can become cleverly disguised.

The last thing we want to do is dampen children's interest by enforced sticking of small pieces of paper, layer upon layer. An approach which has much to recommend it is to use collage selectively in a work of art, or keep it small in scale. A class's collage of flower blossoms, for example, can be made up from very small units. Designing jewellery using small cut shapes is also a way to keep scale under control and limit the time taken to produce something. Depending on detail, an A4 sheet of paper can sometimes be far too big for children to complete in an art session. A5 size is worth trying, especially with very young children unused to cutting and sticking.

A technique which has developed since schools began using PVA glue, rather than water paste, is that of embedding coloured tissue pieces. This technique is as follows:

**Resources:** A piece of thick polythene about 300 mm × 300 mm, PVA glue, coloured tissue paper.

**Method:** Coat a small section of the polythene base with undiluted glue. Lay a small piece of tissue on top of the glue and add another layer of thick glue. Build up about three layers of tissue pieces, by which time the surface appearance should look white. Dry for a day and the embedded tissue layer may be peeled off the polythene. Fix to a card frame otherwise the tissue layer tends to curl up. Display against a window so that the light passes through the tissue.

**Comment:** This is a creative alternative to making 'stained-glass windows' using black paper and tissue. It can be particularly effective as a way of studying an artist such as Kandinsky. Children can tear or cut tissue and choose a restricted range of colour. The tissue tends to slide a little when being stuck down, but the final effect is worth the effort. It is difficult to believe that the layer has been peeled off the polythene and survived.

**Development:** If reproductions are available, make a connection with the stained glass of Marc Chagall, much of which is in the churches of France.

This technique is not quite the flat collage it seems because it has to be framed to display it. The frame itself might be decorated too, extending the use of collage and creating a setting for the translucent tissue. The windows against which these embedded tissue artworks are displayed begin to take on the feel of installations rather than something with a view. Four frames can also be stuck together to form a lantern for a very small wattage bulb, or might be hung from the classroom ceiling.

Other hanging collages can be in the form of two-sided shapes made into mobiles. Creating collaged mobiles is a lengthy task unless it is a group project threaded together by the teacher and attached to wire, sticks or twigs. This is collage used as decoration, but the shape of the card on which collage is stuck turns the activity into something more than a decorative technique. Subjects for this collaged mobile might be 'Rainbows', 'Colour', 'Flight', 'Angels' or 'Vegetables'. Most themes can include mobiles and collaged surfaces are an additional learning dimension which can draw in information about artists and designers.

Applying collage to surfaces also includes decorating ready-made cylinders, boxes and packages. Collage may be the medium, but decoration as a theme can take this off in new directions. Collage is such a versatile medium that it can be used to cover unusual objects such as an old shoe or a discarded straw hat. Plastic and polythene surfaces do not lend themselves to the use of glues found in school, but they are the exception. Most surfaces, including wood, can be used as a former for a three-dimensional collage. Whatever surfaces and forms are chosen, the principle of contrast remains. If collage is a recipe for visual confusion, then nowhere is contrast more important than in a three-dimensional shape.

Two minor organizational teaching points are necessary considerations when running a session of collage. Litter is generated and glue needs to be handled with care. Some provision for soaking glue spreaders may be needed unless the intention is to peel off glue when it has dried. Keeping glue off scissors, clothing and desks is always a problem. Rules about the organization of workspace and the collection of litter will apply. Collage is often a noisy activity, for reasons unknown, and care needs to be taken to ensure that practical materials do not become lost in newspaper and find their way to the rubbish bin. Teaching, however gloriously elevated an activity it might be, eventually comes down to mundane judgements about when to organize a search for scissors and begin to limit the litter. This does not diminish art, but certainly puts the effort needed to teach it in perspective.

# 12 Design and problem-solving

During the 1980s much discussion centred on design and problem-solving as worthwhile and necessary activities for children. The Design Council project of the 1980s, government departments and various teachers' journals raised the issue of design, particularly in relation to craft and technology. Two clear assumptions are that designing is a good thing and problem-solving a necessary function of everyday life. No one quite agrees on a description of either of these activities. Yet they satisfy the need in some minds for education to have useful vocational outcomes. In the new century this is no different as countries strive for economic survival. Art reigns supreme, but not without a hint that it is designers who will bring home the bread.

In the early years of schooling, design may sound an inappropriate and highly sophisticated area of activity. We tend to think of young children as more involved with exploring their first marks on paper and finding out about art materials. Some of them can hardly hold a pencil or manage a pair of scissors, let alone design something. How can we expect them to understand anything about design? How can we expect teachers to introduce design to their children when they themselves may be unsure of what it is?

There are several promising aspects of design and problem-solving to examine, but they need first to be put in perspective. Design is a new facet of art education in the early years. It would be tempting to allow it to displace an otherwise healthy art education programme in schools, and this could well happen (as it already has in one or two secondary schools). Design and problem-solving are an enrichment of any art education programme, not a substitute for all the other important art activities children do. Arguments will go on about the part design and problem-solving play in the curriculum, but it would be a pity if they were ignored and an even greater pity if they became the only justifiable art for children to experience.

If we assume that problems can be solved and that children should be involved in solving them, a likely effect is for us to applaud not only creativity but initiative, self-responsibility and fitness for purpose. It would be difficult to argue against children becoming design-conscious or taking responsibility for solving their own problems. Self-responsibility has, after all, been encouraged over the last century in many of our schools. We want children to consider

*Figure 28*   Design for a Key to Open a Treasure Chest. Age 9. 400 × 172 mm.

problems, generate new ideas and develop a wide range of alternative solutions for themselves. Without our deliberately involving them in design and problem-solving processes at school they are less likely to encounter strategies for doing this and less likely to give their creativity vocational relevance.

Children have the capacity to live in fantasy without taking account of economic realities, a state which may lead them to discover original, creative, if occasionally impractical design solutions. Subsequently it may be necessary to modify these in order to make them more realistic and workable. But we can sometimes learn a lesson in problem-solving ourselves through the experience of seeing the risk-taking originality of the children we teach.

Happy accidents, like the discovery of stainless steel, or glass tubing (see Osborn, 1948/72), are apparently few and far between. If the crop of fortunate accidents cannot be increased there must be alternative efforts made deliberately to promote creative thinking. De Bono (1976) suggested that creative thinking can be taught. If that is true, then art and design processes can make a significant contribution. Where else in the curriculum are visual and sometimes irrational fantasies so readily acceptable? Art often gives children the chance to develop impractical ideas as if they already existed. In their representations on paper children regularly enter a world where materials can be given unusual properties. The heaviest of them can temporarily defy gravity, the lightest be given unreasonable toughness. It could well turn out that the irrational, unreasonable and impractical can be an important part of the problem-solving process. If it does, then we may be dealing with a life skill, rather than merely indulging the fantasies of childhood.

## Introducing design and problem-solving to children

It is arguable how old children must be before they can cope with design and problem-solving as activities. Many 5-year-olds may be quite unable to follow a sequence or to predict what they think might happen. Generally their experience of the world and its materials is as yet very limited. The 7- and 8-year-olds may have the capacity to predict what will happen and are much more likely to follow a sequence of anticipated events. That does not mean that young children cannot be introduced to elements of designing, though the approach must be at a much less sophisticated level.

How might this be done? One way is to develop children's drawing as a way of classifying and explaining their ideas about design. When children are old enough to cope with a very simple sequence, one drawing can lead to another to establish the necessary concept of development in a design process. For example, many children's drawings tell a story, almost like a cartoon strip. Drawing 'what might happen next' is an activity closely associated with designing and one which obviously involves prediction as well as sequence. Through drawing out ideas on paper, a child also creates a resource for discussion of how things might work.

There are obviously problems to overcome with the very youngest of children. The essential point to grasp here is that although we may not achieve very much it is important to make a start. Subjects that can be attempted (either as one drawing, as a sequence of drawings, or in verbal and written form) could tackle problems like 'How do you think a bicycle pump works?', 'What happens if we change small wheels for big ones?', or 'How would you design a space craft?'

Besides drawing, basic to designing is an understanding of the nature, properties and qualities of materials. Good designers understand the limitations and potential of the material they choose and through experience gain insight into those qualities and possibilities which each material offers. It follows that worthwhile activities can be set for children so that they can begin to understand more about how different substances behave.

In the first instance this may be as elementary as comparing Plasticine with dough. Later on, children may be finding out the difference between one fabric and another, or comparing the properties of two kinds of adhesive. At the age of 4 or 5 tactile experience is very important and children need to push blocks around, squeeze washing-up liquid bottles, stroke fur and velvet simply to discover the feel of materials. Junk modelling is ideal for finding out about different materials. But the activity needs to be taken seriously if children are to understand that materials are different to handle. Traditionally they may only have used what materials were provided. If we want to develop their discrimination and introduce them to design from the moment they start school, they must begin to talk about these differences in terms of quality and function.

There are many objects of whose function children have no idea. This is especially true of objects from organizations such as the various school museum services. We can ask young children a wide variety of questions like

'Why isn't this made of sand?'
'What might happen if this was made of newspaper?'
'What do you think it would be like if lamp-posts were made of rubber?'

'Why do you think this is made of metal?'
'What do you think your favourite toy is made of?'
'What do you think this object is used for?'
'How would you use this?'
'Can you think of a way to draw this?'
'What else could we use this for?'

Older children might make these comparisons themselves by constructing the same model animal, for instance, from alternatives like sand, Plasticine, clay, Lego, or paper to see how different they are and why. Whilst to a very young child most art materials present practical problems, older children can be introduced to a far wider range to relate them to designing. They can explore materials not only for expressing their artistic ideas but also with a view to designing and making things which could have a purpose. Essentially this is a process of discovery, but seen now with the eye of a designer as well as that of a fine artist.

Materials like adhesives can be compared without specifically posing design problems. In the realms of simple science we may want to test the strength of various glues by hanging weights from the glued objects. Such activities are worthwhile but not necessarily art or design. They can be entirely the province of science and technology. For children to copy the shape of a pebble in clay, however, or to make silhouette shapes in black paper brings them nearer to design considerations. Their concern, in this example, is for form and outline, not solely function. It is also important for them to find out which shapes and materials might conveniently glue together and which will not. There is little point in exploring materials just for the sake of it. They also need to find out what their properties are, how they function, how they are used and how they might be used.

Children can start to develop some awareness of design through looking critically at designed objects in their surroundings. They may not be expected to do this particularly well at first, especially in their early years, but will have made a beginning along the route towards a growing design consciousness. Much later on in their lives we can expect them to have developed some sensitivity to good and bad design. In a good design there ought to be the feeling that no other way of doing things was appropriate. We ought to feel that to change the shape would be to destroy the aesthetic form and make it a poorer design. If the design is bad, we should know why and question what might be done about it.

In the classroom, the cross-curricular implications of introducing design are far-reaching. We can imagine children being set a task like 'Think of three ways of using materials for designing a pattern'. What begins as an elementary design problem may lead to solutions which have an aesthetic and visual content, but will of course offer much more in terms of discussion and learning. The children might make patterns in the sand tray or in clay, which might in turn lead to looking at sand patterns made by the tide on the beach, or patterns found in minerals. Both these natural materials could lead to work which develops in simple science or environmental studies.

Technology also features in many design processes. Children, for example, who are using layers of papier mâché (Chapter 16) are involved in the same process as is used for building up a fibreglass mould. When they model in clay or assemble using collage, they mirror design processes used in advertising. Modelling has been done this way in schools for years so there is nothing very new about it. The new element for teachers is deliberately to make links with these established processes of technology and design and bring them to children's attention. Design consciousness must inevitably take account of the technology which it encompasses.

In the more traditional way we have taught children art, problem-solving is generally of two kinds. Children face practical problems, like how to glue and fasten things together, how to mix paints, or how to control a medium like clay. And there are imaginative ideas-related problems. Like how to draw a machine designed to perform a variety of household tasks, or how to design a painting of 'Seven Swans a-Swimming'. Specific design problems emerge each time any project has a set of imposed limitations or functions (like seven swans rather than six or eight, or a device for household tasks rather than for brain surgery). In fine art there is a certain freedom and autonomy. In design there is often the imposition of limitations and functions. Fine artists need be accountable only to themselves, but designers are usually bound by a design brief. Where the limitations of that design brief are very clearly stated, the solutions often present a considerable challenge.

Of course, art and design overlap and are not mutually exclusive. This very feature blurs the edges between art and design and makes defining design extremely difficult. Whilst it may be true that function plays a much stronger role in design than it does in art, we can still see examples of the process working within traditional art activities. Children already engage in designing. It could even be said that design is the structure of any art form. Without design it lacks order, coherence and successful organization of the elements of line, colour, shape, tone and texture. These elements defy any rules we care to invent for designing because each artistic structure is different and therefore unique.

An example of the way these limitations are imposed on fine art is seen at Christmas time. There are already a number of expectations (e.g. Father Christmas will be red and angels need wings). Originality and problem-solving are severely put to the test, especially in an area where artwork has gathered a tradition of festive stereotypes. Yet precisely because there are limitations to the colours, forms and functions of Christmas artefacts, children respond as designers, answerable to a design brief. This may sound impressive and of exaggerated status, but children are designing and have been doing so in schools for many years.

We associate problem-solving with design perhaps more than we do with art. Yet problem-solving is not confined to design alone. Many problems in the traditional 'fine-art' area of drawing and painting are well known and arise with some frequency. In fine art there are visual problems for children to solve like

- how to arrange the subject on the paper
- representing imagined three-dimensional space
- making one shape or colour stand out against another
- choosing the most appropriate medium
- deciding on size and scale
- finding shape and content which best expresses the ideas
- organizing and handling painting materials
- trying to make the colour green from primaries yellow and blue.

The older they get, the more sophisticated seem the problems children set themselves. As children move from symbols to visual realism (Chapter 4) they face considerable difficulty in dealing with the illusion of space. Very young children are often far less worried about where to place things on their paper, whereas 6-, 7- and 8-year-olds become much more concerned with problems of how to represent space. Drawing problems are not new, yet they still need to be solved. A designer is not after all like a machine which switches off and on, depending on whether it is dealing with art or design. There is some support for the view that design has its roots in 'fine art' rather than technology. Most designers are from a fine-art tradition because there are few completely insular design programmes in UK art schools.

## Stages in problem-solving

When we turn to design ideas, it can be argued that problem-solving takes on similar characteristics to problems of designing in the 'fine-art' tradition. Function, fitness for purpose, or economic practicality are of course factors, but for the designer aesthetic considerations are also of equal and occasionally greater importance. A motor vehicle, for example, must not only function. We expect that if it is to sell to the public it will also be a pleasing shape. In a design process there is a design logic to take into account. Sometimes the logical process is that there are stages where facts are gathered, needs identified, ideas and solutions generated and finally put to the test. By contrast, in the world of industrial design, facts may be thin on the ground, needs difficult to identify and many mistakes made. Although we may think it is useful to teach children a reassuring and consistently logical process of design, it is precisely this logic which can limit outcomes. As David Pye, way back in 1978 pointed out, 'It is eminently true of design that if you are not prepared to make mistakes you will never make anything at all.'

Such approaches as there are must take account of a wide variety of factors and try out unlikely processes and solutions. If we are to introduce children to problem-solving as an art activity in its own right we need to be wary of a commonly experienced pitfall. Whenever we are faced with a problem to solve, a temptation is to expect that there is one problem and therefore ultimately one workable solution. In fact there are usually several problems and several possible solutions. Part of the skill of problem-solving lies in developing the ability to identify these several problems, generate many solutions to them and choose from the best.

Five important stages in design and problem-solving are evident and offer a flexible model. Most other models produced by design educators tend to be variations of this one, but its roots are in common sense rather than conceptual theory. The first stage is to examine and collect information about the problem. This is the point at which it is quite likely we will discover that the problem is (as already discussed) several problems. We can call this early stage 'information-gathering'. Suppose we asked a group of children to design a 'spacesuit' for a school play. They might consider a variety of questions like

'What would we need to think about if we had a particular person in mind?'
'What characteristics does it need if it is to fit most people?'
'Should it have any special working parts?'
'What materials would work best?'
'Should we just design it or do we need to make it as well to find out if it works, fits and looks good?'

Stage two would be to allow imagination to run riot and generate both practical and impractical ideas. This we can refer to as 'idea generation'. A spacesuit made of metal would obviously be heavy and impractical, but to consider making it of metal might be the very thought which later proves useful. To disregard the impractical at this stage would be unfortunate. For example, the suit might, finally, include metal foil and bottle tops in its construction. By discussing metal as a material we might eventually find ourselves talking about the design of suits of armour. There are many designs for armour which are both functional and artistic, and comparisons of both aspects of design can prove useful teaching points (even if we began by designing a spacesuit). What, for instance, does a suit of armour need as a design feature compared with the requirements of a spacesuit?

In an earlier chapter (Chapter 5) mention was made of the 'Scamper' technique of idea generation. In essence there is no difference between trying to think of ideas for teaching and trying to generate ideas as solutions to problems. Once we have thought of only a few ideas, the processes of rearranging, altering, substituting, eliminating and so on, are useful tools of design development. Unless, however, they are consciously applied (as in the Scamper technique), important alternatives can go ignored. Every possible means should be used to generate new lines of thinking and no strategy for doing this may be ruled out.

If we really want to generate ideas it is worth deliberately setting out to stimulate thinking by imposing odd limitations and trying oblique avenues of enquiry. The process is one which seems to send messages to what we could call the brain's 'creative department'. It may be that nothing needs to be adapted, added to, or rearranged. On the other hand, by consciously sitting down to make ourselves think of alternatives, adaptations, substitutions and rearrangements, we stand a far better chance of stumbling on something new.

Stage three is to construct the design, which may be a very crude prototype, something we can look at before proceeding further. During the making we will inevitably touch on other stages in the process, but for convenience only we can describe this stage as 'making'. From making we can move to 'evaluating'. Stage four is to test and evaluate the design solutions in order to change and finally choose the most promising of them. Naturally, the younger the children are, the less they can be expected to devise ideas which are brilliantly practical. They are therefore not going to respond well to an over-critical appraisal of their creative but impractical solutions. When we are in the judgemental realms of good, bad, better and best, the competitive element can easily become destructive of children's confidence. Yet they can be involved in simple checking and testing, which is a valuable experience for later more sophisticated problem-solving and evaluating.

In doing this, there is an obvious comparison for them to make their initial identification of the problem. How has it been solved? What problems emerged as work progressed? What changes were made to the original design and what difference did they make? Individual children can compare and discuss their own solutions, one with another, to see what they themselves think are the best features. Very little is to be gained at this age from urging children to pick out and criticize the worst elements of a design solution. If the aim is to find out what works, then children need to understand at the outset that condemning the solutions for their impracticality does not usually move them far forward (a view which flies in the face of much human experience but is true of very many instances of problem-solving). Asking how the best of their solutions might be improved can be far more constructive.

In the evaluating part of the process we should ask not only what looks best but why one idea is better than another. Children are not naturally inclined to analyse why one feature of a design is better. Neither in many instances are adults, and to be able to pinpoint what advantages one solution has over another is a sophisticated skill which needs practice and experience to develop it. We can at least make a start, however, by asking simple questions which are likely to promote evaluation. In group discussions we can ask,

> 'Why do you think this would work?'
> 'Why do you think this part is the best?'
> 'What do you think of its appearance?'
> 'How could you improve it?'
> 'What does this do?'
> 'How might it be made to work better?'
> 'If you had to change this what would you do?'
> 'If you had to add something what would it be?'

To 'Modify' the design is a very obvious step before finally adopting the best solution. Again there are shades of the Scamper technique mentioned earlier, though if we are to achieve total flexibility in handling design, perhaps we should not think of all these stages in this order alone. They usually react and interact with each other. We therefore have to think of five stages which in differing circumstances will demand different patterns of usage. The whole sequence, 1–5, might occur over and over again, or a stage might need to be left out, another one added. For convenience the stages are

1   information-gathering
2   idea generation
3   making
4   evaluating
5   modifying.

Sensitivity to aesthetic qualities which exist in good design is not learned by rote. Children will learn far more about design by designing things themselves and looking at everything with the critical eye of a designer. Inevitably, to develop any sensitivity to design is to encourage children to look at what surrounds them, not only the made 'designed' objects, but natural forms as well. A major area of study and discussion is the form and aesthetic characteristics of things which are in nature and have influence on the designer. These are the resources for shape, proportion and function. Nature offers the designer a great variety of examples from which to learn.

*Figure 29* Passiflora.

Nowhere is this more evident than in the superb designs to be found in sea shells, rocks, minerals, animals and plants, all of which demonstrate principles of design. We need only look at how leaf stems grow out of the main body of a plant to see how structurally sound they are. Thicker stems bear heavier weight and the whole plant grows according to its function and surrounding conditions. The Passiflora (Passion Flower, Figure 29) is a good example of design in a plant whose tendrils have a specific function, working rather like small springs as it clings to its surroundings. Beyond function, its flower head is considered a master-piece of artistic design. From nature we derive many of our most aesthetically pleasing curves, harmonies and contrasts. They are not difficult to find, nor can we find a much better starting place for awakening children's sensitivity to them.

## Practical examples

All the design projects which follow can have practical outcomes. However, the discussion and comparisons children make as they evaluate and change designs are just as important as the final product. In some instances the teacher may feel that discussion is far more important than drawing and designing. It may be that the only design-related activity is discussing an aspect of these examples. It would be unreasonable to suppose these projects could stay entirely in the domain of art and design. They may suggest all areas of the curriculum despite the fact that here they emphasize the aesthetic, artistic and visual side of design.

These ideas can be developed to encompass discussion of both contemporary and historical material. Here, and in the brief examples which follow, there is no indication of the learning concepts and problem-solving involved. This is quite deliberate. No activity is worthwhile without being a relevant part of the curriculum, but it is the task of the teacher to make purposeful links with children's growing experience, rather than begin a design activity which does not fit in with ongoing work. For the format to be educationally worthwhile, these ideas would certainly need to take account of many of the categories of learning already discussed in previous chapters (see especially the format of 'four areas' in Chart 5, Chapter 6).

### Shops and houses

Children's existing classroom surroundings are an obvious starting point for devising design activities. A home corner, for instance, can become a source of design. Whenever children organize space and furniture, they are designing, even though the level of this activity does not appear to be very sophisticated. They can usefully consider the design of their play space according to its function, layout and appearance. Questions might be,

'If you could change this room what would you do?'
'How does the builder design houses so that the rain doesn't run down the walls?'

'How do windows open?'
'How do you think the rooms in a house are used?'
'What is it like in the Wizard's Lair?' (story, drama).

They can also organize a classroom shop, a well-tried activity which is rich in potential for designing not just the one shop but extending to include

shop fronts, consideration of lettering, decoration and displays
food, sweets, sweet wrappers, chocolate boxes, sweet containers
packaging, posters, advertisements
shop interiors, counters, check-outs, tills
sale goods: clothing, hardware, bicycles, vegetables, groceries, electrical
    goods, televisions and radios, computers
gardening supplies, decorators
butchers, bakers, antiques.

Design ideas should also lead to other related ideas. For example, shop tills have changed dramatically from the hand-operated to the electronic, computer-based pay points of today. Comparison of their designs can lead to a study of shape in relation to materials, decoration and clothing fashions. Similarly, designing patterns for clothing may develop in the direction of looking at designs for hats, boots, shoes, dresses and skirts. Obviously, hats can be designed for specific jobs, like helmets for firemen, welders or astronauts. Alternatively, they can become more imaginative like 'My Automatic Hat', or 'Party Hats', which may prompt yet another design theme.

### Design for a party (older children)

The children are asked to design on paper and write about a place outside or inside where they would hold a party. The emphasis could be on the information-gathering stage of design. They must next choose their colours and dream up shapes and surroundings which they would like to find there. They should consider themselves to be like stage designers who have been given unlimited funds to design an environment. They have to think of what specially designed costumes they might wear and who or what else would come to the party. This could include imaginary creatures, changing scenery, lights and sound, and creating events or technical devices for entertainment. The whole theme could produce several different areas of design and discussion. An important aspect of this project would be to discuss what design problems there might be and how they could be overcome.

### Adventures

Problem-solving activities can grow from reading stories with children. The stories which have an adventure theme are particularly useful. They can provide inspiration for drawing and painting, or children may construct using modelling materials.

'Draw (tell me, write about) how you would escape from the cave.'
'What would you need to cross the river?' 'How do you think you would use these?' 'How would you climb over the rocks?'
'How can you cross this crevasse?'
'How would you get past the fiery dragon?'
'How would you find the treasure?' (Links with simple map work. Draw a map of how you come to school, a treasure map, or a map of school buildings.)

From the questions above, children might make models of their imagined solutions in paper, clay, or Plasticine. Or the solutions could provide them with subject-matter for drawings and paintings. The projects could be extended into simple science or mathematical activities, but to keep the art and design perspective, considerations of the shapes, colours, arrangement and function would still be essential.

## Jewellery

Geometric and mathematical designs can inspire some children to design jewellery. The process of enamelling is beyond many young children, but they can still produce large drawings of jewelled adornments. There is also a vast resource of illustrations available for the study of things like bangles, rings, brooches and pendants down the ages. Children love designing things which involve decoration and pattern, especially if they can be worn. If the scale of the designs is enlarged to make drawing and colouring much easier they become effective as displays for study and discussion. Only some of them need to be made to scale. A professional designer very often works on a scale much larger than the final product. Additionally, it may be possible to design using collage materials, strong glue and a glue gun (finally producing something to wear in drama, the 'Shop' or the 'Home Corner').

## Design some sweets

This can be treated as a study of pattern, or as a design for an imaginative confection. Children might design a special patterned sweet, such as 'Liquorice Allsorts', or create an imaginary sweet shop full of their own designs. They could collect and compare the design of packaging and sweet wrappers.

## Variations on the sweets

Birthday cakes, feasts, fantasies such as sugar houses, sugar mountains and foods of all kinds provide stimuli for design. The best chefs are involved in design as they create their special dishes. Children could imagine they are 'best chefs' and design as if they considered that the visual presentation of their food could be as interesting as its taste.

## Textile design

Simple prints, such as those discussed in Chapter 10, can be a good starting point for looking at printed textiles. Children can begin to design their own through looking at costume, furnishing fabrics like curtains, tapestries and wall hangings. Once children have developed the skill of following their own pencil line with a printing block, they can manage more complex patterns. Fabric designs can evolve from simple ruler-drawn patterns. Some may repeat, others be much more random.

## Designs for flooring

This has links with mathematics through tessellation and symmetry. The children begin by making a collage from small squares of paper. Different colours can be used, paint manufacturers' shade cards, anything which will produce a regular tile pattern. A mathematical link can be made with Logiblocs, rectangles, triangles, squares and hexagons. It may be possible to obtain flooring samples where children can see how designs fit together. They might draw on paper and fill in with pencil, felt-tip, or pen, arranging tiles using a number sequence. This could be done by numbering the squares, for example, 1, 3, 4, 7, 11, 7, 4, 3, 1 (counting on from the last square which was numbered), and choosing a numbered colour to fill in the design, continuing all the way down a whole page of squares. Variations and extensions of this idea are numerous and can readily be discussed alongside work in number. Children could alternatively make designs based on the maths work they are doing.

A further development would be to design floor mosaics so that although smaller paper shapes might be used, the idea would be to produce a regular floor mosaic with a decorative border. Reference to Roman mosaics, shopping arcades and murals would be a valuable starting point, though often children respond far better to historical mosaics after they have tried to design one themselves. There are also, for reference, a number of tiled mosaics decorating stations in the London Underground.

## Murals

Not all murals are neatly rectangular and many street murals are painted on gable ends and in odd shapes. Children can design murals to fit a cut-out shape of a gable, possibly an end-of-terrace house. Young children would need to see examples of the shape and might benefit from seeing photographs of murals other artists have done. They could also try to design a mural for a specific building, like a railway station, a school, a hospital, or a library. Reference for murals is much more common than it used to be, especially in London and other major cities of Britain where there are a number of gable-end murals.

### Aeroplanes and dream cars

When we think of design, man-made objects feature as important examples. Many children will eagerly see themselves as the designers of racing cars, custom-built cars, aircraft and spaceships. There are plenty of examples of children, especially boys, designing these vehicles time after time in their art sessions. In design education there can be a much more serious enquiry into function as well as fantasy. What would their ideal dream car do that other cars do not? How might an aircraft function if it could do other things besides fly? What else could we make it do that would be useful?

### Machines

A variation on the idea of designing vehicles is to think about designing fantastic machines. Instead of this being limited to designing a machine to solve problems we already know about, the project can be reversed. The brief is 'Design a machine which has wheels, levers and buttons. Now think of about six things your machine might be for. What do you think it does now you have designed it?' Variations could be devised to include robots, mechanical arms and imaginary machine-like creatures. Specific ideas might be 'The Best-Ever Food Machine', 'The Greatest Cleaner in the World'; or 'The Get-You-Up-In-The-Morning Machine'.

### Dirt eater

Here the children are involved in social, economic and technical issues as well as design. Their task is to design a machine (or think of a fantasy creature) which eats the rubbish left by humans. Designs can be three-dimensional, or drawings, or may for much of the time be something written down and discussed.

### Mind stretchers

These are design problems intended to stretch the imagination. Some of them are impossible situations requiring an acceptance of fantasy as well as development of creative thinking. (Judgement is needed to assess the appropriate age range for these tasks.)

- Design a fish which you think could live in transparent glue. Show how it would swim.
- Imagine we never needed to sleep. Draw a design for a house where there are no bedrooms and think of new uses for the rooms.

- Design a bottle that has outlets at the top, bottom and sides. How would you use it?
- Imagine that in the school corridor there are ten levers and five buttons. Draw a design showing what you think the levers and buttons might do.

Finally, it must be said that one effect of being involved in design education is that the teacher can participate in thinking about how to solve problems. An essential ingredient in a teacher's preparation is to think of questions like

'What might we need to think about if we designed a mural?'
'What do we need to think about if we design a racing car?'
'What do we need to consider to design a fabric?'

Although questions like these can motivate us to think in new ways ourselves, the temptation to supply answers for the children needs to be resisted. Design education, where practised in the early years of schooling, has changed the way in which we have previously thought about teaching art. Yet it need not conflict with any vision of artistic growth we privately hold. The responsibility for developing children artistically at school is ultimately ours. How much design education we include depends partly on our own interests and preferences, partly on the way we see it developing in the next decade. It is a facet of art which enhances and enriches our existing heritage. We always need to consider carefully what anything new will displace, and should be aware of the importance of design in relation to fine art, not as a subject divorced from any part of the art curriculum.

# 13 Talking with children

## Imaginative talk

In the tale of Hansel and Gretel, two children find a house in the woods. The house is made of sweets, candies and chocolate. An imaginative delight for any child. The power of imagination lets us distort ideas, so that we can make things any colour we like in our mind's eye, or any size, or any combination of forms we fancy. For the children hearing the story of Hansel and Gretel, the house becomes edible as tempting materials are combined to function as a dwelling.

A surprisingly large amount of this imaginative thinking depends on our ability to accept and use quite unrelated ideas. An example might be for children to describe 'A Million Pound Ice-Cream', or 'Life on Top of a Cream Cake', both of which defy our usual concept of scale and value. They require an unusual sense of the infinitely improbable, yet imaginatively possible. It is as if anything we like can be drawn on the paper of the mind. Imaginative talk can stretch children's thinking allowing them to create wild and weird pieces of artwork. Not only that, but it will probably help other areas of their learning, like their creative writing and problem-solving. By using their imagination they often generate a flow of creative ideas which can spill over into other parts of the curriculum. The impractical ones can always be rejected later on, leaving the best ideas for discussion and modification.

Stories are full of rich sources of imaginative imagery and children are used to listening to fantastic ideas locked into an impossible but believable logic. Imaginative questions, the more bizarre the better, can lead children to feel that imagination has some currency in the classroom. Discussion of mind-stretching visual ideas teaches children that their own fantasy is not only acceptable but can be used to great advantage in their artwork. In the realms of imagination, children play with combinations of images, making new relationships between them, enlarging, changing and adapting them to suit their fantasy. Examples of topics for imaginative talk, which can be tried to see how far children will stretch the unusual, could be to discuss:

- Do you know what a zebra looks like? Well, what do you think a Zebra Bird could be like?

*Figures 30, 31* Zebra Birds. Age 7. 450 × 320 mm.

- The highest mountain is Mount Everest. Imagine climbing a much higher model of someone's nose.
- The road in your street is probably a dull colour. Can you imagine it looking like a patchwork of coloured squares?
- What do you imagine a patchwork-coloured cat would look like?
- If you could live inside any object you like, what would you choose to live in? Why? What would it look like?
- What do you think would happen if all pavements were really made of banana skins?

The famous painting, by René Magritte, of an enormous apple filling a corridor may be familiar. We can speculate on the question being asked, 'What do you think it would be like if an apple was so large it filled the whole corridor?' This, and many other imaginative paintings, make use of the impossible witty combination of ambiguous scale or size. The canvas of Magritte is partly the canvas of the mind, and there is a fragile line to be drawn between imagination, memory and the senses. Children will happily change from one to the other as they work (see Figure 6, Chapter 4).

The following idea was tried with some 7-year-olds and makes use of looking as well as imagining, switching from one state to the other.

### The imaginary tree

**Concepts:** Shape, pattern, line, adaptation.

**Learning potential:** Use of observation, imagination, drawing ability, discrimination of structure.

**Skills:** Drawing, fine motor skills, selection of colours.

**Stimulus:** Begin by looking and talking with children about part of a tree. (Find a tree fragment, possibly a small piece of driftwood picked up from the beach. It might be weather-beaten, knotted and twisted into an interesting shape.) The children are asked to describe what they can see. Then they have to think what they might add to their drawing of the fragment to make up an imaginary tree. The tree can have anything added they wish, can be coloured and patterned as they like, and may be any size. Discuss, elicit and develop ideas.

**Options:** Children could draw their tree on rough trial paper first or begin on a larger sheet. They might find their own (local) source of reference for part of a tree. Choice of viewpoint, choice of materials, size, content and components of tree (e.g. creatures, a 'tree den', nest, leaves, blossom). Site of tree (garden? wood? city?).

**Materials:** Choose from paint, crayon, coloured felt-tips, collage materials, pencils, black pen.

**Practical session:** The children draw from the fragment itself, looking carefully for what they can see. When they have enough on paper to satisfy their need to have some basic shape, they add details (extra branches? leaves? blossom? spirals? tree-bark?). They colour in what they have done, embellish a drawing, or begin to paint.

**Development:** The subject could change to 'Who inhabits the tree?' and children also bring in objects to which they themselves could add ideas. These could be natural forms or man-made. Alternatively, the theme could develop into topics related to their bringing in, for example, a broken mechanical alarm clock or part of a machine. These become 'An Imaginary Machine', 'A Robot', 'The Workings of My Head', or 'A New Vehicle'.

There are other areas of imagination like dreams and nightmares to touch on. Some children may find these too disturbing to talk about but many will welcome the chance to bring the images of dreams into their artwork. Even if dreams and nightmares never become part of artistic expression, they form a valuable source of shared experience, not least because they involve children's feelings. There are many children for whom the images of dreams in art are a way of expressing their most feared anxieties. Often art becomes a vehicle for talking about such influential experiences as those involving themselves and their friends, violence, love or loss.

Of course, not all discussion need centre on the extreme, zany or dreamlike state of imagination. Memory, that unreliable window of the mind, proves to be a constant resource for discussion of imagery. The artists Henry Moore and Ben Nicholson used to play a memory game called 'Shuteye Golf', where they drew a map of a golf course on a sheet of paper. They practised their memory of the golf course by trying to find their way round it using a pencil, but without looking. They had to negotiate hazards like cows and bunkers, gaining or losing points accordingly. The claim was that the game improved spatial memory.

Memory games played with children can take many forms, of which the best known is probably the one played at parties where several objects are put on a tray and the children have to say, when the tray is hidden from view, what was there. Such memory games tend to be classed as an entertainment, but they can be played more seriously as a way of teaching children to develop their visual memories.

Discussion of memories can be made specific. Memory of shape can be encouraged by asking children to describe from memory what particular shape they think things are, then, where possible, comparing the description with the original source of reference. The process is a straightforward one. With practice children can learn to compare shape sizes, lengths and characteristics that they know they can talk about. Playing memory games is rarely ever wasted time and can be fitted in during those odd five-minute periods when children are waiting to do something else. Apart from this, there may be the chance, for example, to visit a wood, or go on a school trip, which can provide the opportunity to discuss and memorize leaf shapes or visual details of the journey. Such discussion is a necessary contrast to the more usual gathering of information which goes on.

## Using questions

One of the more obvious ways an interested teacher interests her children is through the comments made throughout the school day. These range from questions to discussion, including commands, instructions and a great deal of factual information. Art, as has been pointed out, does not readily lend itself to facts and has (Chapter 2) been described as a 'wordless' experience. But talking with children about their perceptions is unavoidable if we seriously want to develop their abilities. A distinction must also be made between talking *with* children and talking *to* them. Whether we act as benign dictator, democrat, or combinations of both, discussion with children provides us with valuable and necessary feedback. We do, after all, need to understand children's responses in order to make informed decisions about our own teaching.

Frequently, teachers ask children questions which arise from the work which is already going on. In mathematics, for instance, there is a mathematical language and mathematical concepts. Just as elaborate questioning can be appropriate for mathematics teaching, so with art there are a number of important areas of teacher and pupil exchange. Quite apart from talking about paint, paper and images, there are (Chapter 2) the well-established formal elements, such as colour, line, shape, pattern, tone and texture. We tend to think of these mostly relating to artwork, yet they exist in almost everything we see around us and can be applied to looking at the environment just as well as drawing or painting.

For the purpose of making this clear, we can analyse some questions and search for those which are clearly visual in their characteristics. What follows here may be familiar, yet it bears closer examination because in many classrooms, the use of 'visual questions' is often misunderstood or entirely absent.

Imagine we are examining a slice through a tomato. The question, 'How many seeds can you see?', is not necessarily a visual category of question. 'What

*Figures 32, 33* Violin Drawings. Age 6. 220 × 323 mm, 295 × 395 mm.

shape and colour do you think they are?' comes closer. 'What colours do you think you could mix to make the colour of those seeds?' pushes the question towards the use of art materials. These last two questions point to a fundamental function of art teaching. A teacher can consciously and deliberately bring visual and art-orientated details of the environment to children's notice.

Ideally everything should come from the children. But they do need prodding in a direction which allows this to happen. When this is successful, teachers extend children's vision whilst taking full account of what they offer. For example, in a class of 6-year-olds, the children are gathered round their teacher looking at a violin together (see Figures 32 and 33 and Plate 10).

| | |
|---|---|
| *Teacher:* | Let's have a close look at it . . . a careful look at it. Tell me some of the things you can see. |
| *Paula:* | An 'S' and an 'F'. |
| *Teacher:* | These are called 'F' holes and the sound comes out here [points]. What else can you see? |
| *Aaron:* | Knobs at the top . . . string things. |
| *Teacher:* | These are pegs [pointing] and round them go the strings. What are the strings like? |
| *Jodi:* | They're straight. |
| *Michael:* | [interrupts] I know what's curved at the top. |
| *Teacher:* | [ignoring him] Are all the strings the same? |
| *Kelly:* | No, some of them are thick and some thin. [Teacher talks about sound and plucks strings.] |
| *Teacher:* | Now if we look at the shape does it remind you of anything? |
| *Toni:* | Yeh, a guitar. |
| *Michelle:* | Like a pear shape. |
| *Teacher:* | See, the curve comes out here . . . then goes . . . can you see? Michael . . . you're looking at the back . . . what can you see? |
| *Michael:* | It's got stripes on it. |
| *Michelle:* | And that bit there [points to top pegs] goes round and round. |
| *Teacher:* | We can call that a spiral shape. Let's draw a spiral in the air. Start in the middle and go round . . . [Children do this.] |
| *Paula:* | It's like a snail shell. |

[Later on the children are drawing.]

| | |
|---|---|
| *Michelle:* | Violins aren't all sorts of colours. |
| *Lisa:* | Well mine is. |
| *Aaron:* | They're all sorts of different browns. |
| *Teacher:* | What do you think you've missed out from your drawing? |
| *Toni:* | The neck and the curvy bit . . . I need a brown . . . I need a brown you got a brown? |
| *Michelle:* | Where's the orange? . . . I need a brown . . . I'm using this one because that's shiny there. |

Here we have a good example of how children make comparisons and analyse shapes and colours. Their teacher steers them from general observations to specific comparisons of detail and generates interest by talking about the shapes that they can see. She also extends their experience by making them think about several qualities they would need to consider if they began drawing the instrument. The emphasis on visual detail is necessary to encourage concentrated looking and build up a strong mental image, which then acts as a basis for drawing and colouring. Of course, this is not a matter of telling children what details to include in their drawings. Rather than this, it is to engage children's attention in so many details that they are compelled to exercise choice about what they want to draw.

When this teacher asked 'What do you think you've missed out from your drawing?' there was no intention of providing answers. The decision was theirs, by which route far more original work can be forthcoming. Later on that day, more was said about the sound of the violin and the teacher played a recording of some violin music. The children practised letter shapes and wrote words and sentences connected with their experience of the instrument. Their comments and questions were wide-ranging in comparison with the visual ones introduced before the children began drawing. An interesting feature, however, was that they drew first, then wrote, rather than the other way round.

The process of looking and questioning has an added bonus for the teacher. Together, teacher and child can talk in terms which build a vocabulary for looking at things. Both of them sharpen observation by sharing what they themselves see. Before long, and really with little prompting, children become very good at describing the appearance of what they see. The teacher might have stimulated interest in the first place, but she soon discovers that children are very ready to respond. They can analyse what they are looking at even to the extent of including comments on specific qualities they find, like shapes being spiky, smooth, winding, curved, or twisting.

Sometimes the children learn to find a 'visual vocabulary' of shapes in what they see, not in words as such, but as letter shapes.

> We talk about line, what a line can do and where it's going . . . up, down, sideways, or perhaps in spirals . . . I teach my children a vocabulary of letter shapes . . . letter families when they can manage capital letters . . . 'E' 'H', 'L', 'T', 'V' or 'S' shapes . . . they can be found in patterns and shapes . . . They're all around and finding them gives my children a confidence in drawing.
>
> (First school teacher)

Usually the children can find a letter 'L' or a 'V' in something. And though this way of looking should not become a rigid method it does help them to focus attention on shape. The angles of doors, desks, windows, boxes and chairs are examples of source material for finding letters. A further development is also to ask, 'Is that letter "V" the same as this one? How is it different?' By this means the children gradually build up a strongly differentiated framework which helps them to look even more carefully than they previously did. Once they try to find different 'L's, (and, more importantly, recognize the differences) they are making very sophisticated comparisons indeed. A start has been made which is no different in kind from that made by many artists down the centuries. It is said that the painter Cézanne often looked for circles, squares and cubes in his own paintings. Comparison with known shapes is nothing new, but it may be very new to those children who have never had the chance to try it out.

Through discussion, children often give back what we give out to them. If, for example, we spend a whole week periodically looking out at the different shapes and colours to be seen in the sky, before very long the children begin talking about the changes that they have seen. The following days and weeks are often times when they recount memories of clouds seen the previous evening or perhaps during a weekend rainstorm. This vision regularly finds new expression in their paintings, where the colours they see and the shapes they create become as absorbing as the skies they are trying to paint.

Naturally, apart from all the discussion that is possible, there are times when to talk with children is actually detrimental to their progress. Once they have been stimulated to work with art materials, children need to be left alone to get on, especially at the earliest stages of production. They may well feel apprehensive, but so do many artists when they make their first marks on canvas. If children do not think they are expected to make a start by themselves, they often engineer ploys for extra help. The extra help is almost entirely unnecessary at this stage and to offer them further help simply puts off the moment when they have to start. If they regularly needed more and yet more help, they would never do anything by themselves. As a general habit it is good practice to walk away and leave them to start by themselves. They quickly take in the message that they are on their own.

Later on, when the work is well under way, if we were never to comment and feed in encouragement, we would find ourselves teaching in a rather ineffective way. Some teachers would say that to talk to children about their artwork in progress is to over-influence it, whilst others find questions can be well handled and constructive. Teachers are rightly more cautious about commenting for fear of harshly criticizing, destroying a child's fragile confidence, or stereotyping the work. But fear of being insensitive can lead to giving praise as the only apparent safe response. Yet it is a response which bewilders a pupil who is not having much success. How often does a teacher lose credibility this way as well as the opportunity to teach something useful? Without support and encouragement we know that children lose heart, but need the encouragement be so vague? Are there other areas of comment which are important?

## Commenting on children's work

The age of the computer-controlled robot is with us and, if pursued thoughtlessly, the ideas which follow might be more like a computer's response than that of a human being. Certainly if we followed each idea in sequence the effect would be mechanical. Yet the categories suggested here need not be used inflexibly. They only describe the most likely areas we have for contact with any group of children about the artwork they are doing, providing a marked contrast to the unending vague praise children's work generally elicits. We can talk about

- what we asked the children to do
- further ideas around the theme on which they are working
- feelings evoked by the artwork
- their use of fantasy and imagination
- shapes, colours, patterns, lines, tone, texture
- scale, size, arrangement of the design
- use of materials
- a particular technique
- the effort put in
- ways ideas could be used in another medium another time.

Praising the use of well-mixed colour, careful attention to shape, or control of materials are obvious enough areas to warrant praise for most children. Few teachers have not experienced circumstances where they want to praise pupils who are having difficulties simply to spur them on. An experienced teacher finds ways of commenting that are not immediately judgemental. For example, the comment 'That's better than yesterday's work' is a safe area for praise, whilst 'That's good' can sometimes sound rather generalized and unconvincing by comparison. Fortunately, few pupils quite know, or remember well enough, how good yesterday's work was.

It is natural to want to praise children. Praise is a two-edged sword because it can limit as well as encourage children. Many children want to know what is valued and what to do in their art. In recent years 'descriptive praise' has become a more productive way to encourage children. Examples of this technique, where the teacher describes the good features of the art being done, can be found in Chapter 17. An example of this teaching skill is,

> You've taken trouble to find interesting coloured paper from magazines. This is getting better the more you get rid of the background paper colour and make some of these shapes dark ones.

Praising children is rarely easy because we do not always know how they react. We assume praise is a good thing, but we are more likely to know how we ourselves might feel being praised than how children feel. Descriptive praise is safe to use and has the advantage of referring children to specific positive points about their work (see Barnes, 1999, for an extensive chapter about the use of descriptive praise).

There is little doubt that rewards such as approval or praise are valuable motivators. But children usually want to please and will respond to our own personal values and judgements. There is no way entirely to avoid influencing children, and if we had no influence on children would we honestly believe we were teaching? Comments can have a positive motivating effect if they are well aimed and specific. An effective example of ways to encourage would not just be to say something global such as, 'I like that', but to add a particular *descriptive* dimension such as, 'I like the way you have

> drawn that shape . . .
> added those details . . .
> arranged this on the paper . . .
> mixed those colours . . .
> chosen those colours . . .
> tried to remember what that looked like . . .
> found that pattern . . .
> worked on your own . . .
> worked together . . .
> glued this, cut that . . .
> threaded these together.'

Searching for rewarding things to say to children has a secondary spin-off of teaching us to look for special qualities in their work. It also helps children to understand some of the values and qualities which are to be found in what they do. Sadly, a great deal of comment from teachers tends of necessity to be on a very mundane level of organization and control of materials. This is true of many activities. The valuable creative component which is specific rather than general can include rewards which have some credibility in our eyes and those of the children.

Questions can swiftly follow on from rewards. Superficially they may have the flavour of an evaluation but effectively they encourage children to think about what they are doing. Questions can be challenges which spur children on to find out more, such as

> 'How did you mix that colour?'
> 'What do you think about . . .?'
> 'Where did you see this?'
> 'Can you see how . . .?'
> 'Can you think of another way of . . .?'
> 'What else could you add to . . .?'
> 'What would you do next time . . .?'
> 'How do you feel about . . .?'

In any busy class, possibly with over thirty children, time for talking with them is precious. Which is all the more reason for making discussion purposeful. There may be no immediate goals. A question like 'What other way can you think of doing this?' may not actually produce any answer but can be asked with the purpose of making children think about what alternatives there might be. That in itself makes the use of unanswerable questions educationally worthwhile, even if personally we would rather there were always answers.

## An artistic vocabulary

Children learn to use words like shape, colour and line, if their teacher refers to them with some frequency. But there are a variety of specialist words which children may also enjoy using. From some teachers they may pick up words like exquisite form, embellish, or clever design. Children love to use these special words even if they do not really understand them at first, so that words like medium, media, vermilion, umber, ultramarine, mobile, sculpture, spectrum, collage, mural, or ceramics can become part of their growing artistic vocabulary. Whether this vocabulary should develop by chance or by choice is a matter for individual teachers. But the most likely route for learning by choice is through looking at work done by other artists, even if this is artwork done by children.

Here, especially by seeing the work of famous artists, they can begin to develop critical awareness of what artists do (see Plates 15, 37 and 38). It is almost impossible to talk with children about a reproduction of a work of art without them learning some special words to describe it. The words they use may be their own inventions, like 'curvy', or 'scratchy', but might also include technical words the teacher has taught them. Words like 'glaze', 'brushwork', 'scale', 'impact', 'balance', or 'expressive', are examples.

Four very useful questions for discussing a work of art are these (identified by Gaitskell and Hurwitz, 1970). More searching examples are to be found in Chapter 17.

- What do you see? (Description)
- How are things put together? (Analysis)
- What is the artist trying to say? (Interpretation)
- What do you think of it? (Judgement)

Question three may provoke the most interesting responses and can be a problem for some teachers. How irresistible it could be to tell children what the artist was trying to say, rather than asking them first. The point of looking at artwork is to become practised at looking at it and develop some critical skills. The sophistication of expressive content in a work of art may take years to understand. Yet the categories suggested here are useful as a starting point for looking at work, though initially we should not expect them to produce much in the way of a response.

There is not much point knowing what the colours of the rainbow are unless they also have some meaning. Similarly, there is little to be gained from children's learning new words for everything in sight, just for the sake of doing so. Complementary colours, colour wheels, or the nuances of perspective can be spoken about, it is true. But impressive though knowledge of them might seem, they could obscure the real reasons for talking with children about their art. The main purpose of discussion is to involve children in building up their skills in verbalizing, visualizing and remembering. Even if the words used are very unsophisticated ones, the aim is to vitalize children's imagery and expression so that they are sufficiently confident in talking about their ideas, as well as working them out in a practical art medium.

# 14 Assessment and evaluation

The 1990s were years where English education became obsessed with assessment. In a new decade, assessment and benchmarking has not disappeared in core subjects. Testing, testing and more testing has characterized the early 2000s as teachers and pupils respond to the demands made on them. Few areas lend themselves so readily to the unquestioned criticism of being subjective as do the assessment and evaluation of art. Can it be assessed? Some teachers would say that nothing worthwhile can be assessed or evaluated in art and anyone who tries is fooling themselves if they think it can. The argument grows from the stance that, however carefully we judge anything artistic, because that judgement is personal and therefore subjective, it is not valid in comparison with other judgements. Of course, if our starting point has been that art itself has no value, is a frill, a recreation, or a time-filler, there is little to be argued. The basis of informed judgement is that we should know something of the values which permeate the area of our concern.

Assessment of major works of art by painters such as Van Gogh or Rembrandt would prove just as difficult a task as the assessment of children's work. Would Picasso fail his art examination in the UK Key Stage 3 of the new century? The criteria for assessing can lead to a nonsense. Could we say that Van Gogh's handling of colour was masterly where Rembrandt's was not? Could we say that Rembrandt achieved a higher standard of drawing? Would we say, as we handled a tear-stained piece of paper, that because a famous poet cried bitterly whilst writing the lines, the poem must be deeply emotional? Each artist's work is valued for qualities over and above the mundane. To assess in a naive or mechanistic way is to ignore what brings fame to the artist.

We are not dealing with the famous, but suppose we were teaching children art in the United States of America. It is more than likely we would pay as much attention to the development of their personalities through art as we would to the artwork they produced. We might even see the development of a child's personality as the main reason for teaching. In some other countries and cultures art education clearly has a different emphasis. There are also questions of how reliable or credible assessments and evaluations are, what their function is and how we should arrive at judgements. To complicate matters further it is not always clear what can be evaluated and what may not.

Who is to assess and evaluate? What seems excellent to one teacher may not be seen the same way by other teachers, Ofsted, HMI, parents, or children. A piece of work, or progress in maturing personality, may be exceptional compared with previous examples from an individual child. But how are we to know?

For the purposes of this chapter, evaluation is perceived as a process through which we determine the value of what we are doing or have done. This is usually understood to be the educational value, though by that broad term we could also mean learning about oneself in relation to the arts, or ultimately to life itself. Evaluation tends to take place over a period of time or is encountered period-ically at an appropriate point in a course of learning. It is often characterized by reflection on the extent to which our aims and objectives have been achieved. Evaluation particularly focuses upon our own teaching though of course we can also evaluate children's progress in terms of achievement.

Assessment, in this instance, is taken to mean making judgements using known criteria to determine whether particular qualities or changes are evident and skills or abilities have been acquired. There are many forms of assessment and many terms which can be used to describe them, ranging from ongoing informal assessment, formative assessment and formal summative procedures involving detailed testing and grading. Yet if the process is not to become unwieldy (since the aim is to produce a useful account of a child's artistic development), the definition and method of assessment must be accessible and readily understood. Assessment in the model proposed here seeks to identify qualities and skills.

All assessment procedures have limitations, even those associated with measurement. In fact for some teachers assessment is solely associated with measurement, though as David Best (1983) has commented,

> It is crucial to recognize that only some kinds of progress can be measured. Moreover, the most important aspects of educational progress, such as the ability to understand people, and moral and emotional development, cannot be measured, although they certainly can be assessed.

Assessment is concerned, for our purposes, with trying to discover what the child has achieved or become. Evaluation enables the teacher to reflect upon a session, programme of work, or period of teaching. Through evaluation an attempt is made to identify the effects and effectiveness of teaching, and assessment is a necessary part of this. We may, for example, assess a child's progress in relation to his or her previous work or in some instances that of his or her particular class or group.

To assess or evaluate anything in the arts we need first to be aware of the context in which the art is produced or the process takes place. The time, location, values and attitudes all have a bearing on how we form judgements. There would be little point in judging a 4-year-old's painting against that of a teenager, sculpture against painting, or colour against black and white.

Nor should we become victim of arguments which suggest art cannot be assessed because it is too subjective. We need to revise common assumptions about what it is to be objective, not only in the arts, but in the sciences. Judgements in science are, despite the empirical research which they encompass, given their sense by underlying theoretical interpretation. That is, interpretation is just as important in the sciences as it is in the arts. Not all objective assessments are scientific, and scientific examination cannot tell us all that can be objectively known about human behaviour. It certainly cannot tell us what is most important in human life.

> It is not that the arts are like the sciences in yielding definitive conclusions, but, on the contrary, that the sciences are like the arts in their ultimate answerability to new and different interpretation of objective features.
>
> (Best, 1985)

We should not be misled by the fact that testing and measuring are frequently not only associated with assessment but erroneously equated with it. Testing and measuring sometimes have irresistible attractions in that written proof can be pointed to and data produced as clear evidence of progress. Yet the measurable, quantifiable aspects of education are not very helpful when it comes to assessing whether or not certain qualities are evident, qualities such as expression, feeling, imagination, or invention. That they cannot be quantified, or scientifically verified, certainly does not mean that they cannot be assessed, for instance, by a sensitive teacher's judgement.

The range of professional interpretations of progress in artistic development can be wide but it is by no means unlimited. There is also some consensus amongst experienced teachers about what constitutes poor or exceptional progress. Even so, an understanding of children's capabilities and their expected development is clearly something we would need for assessing any progress children make, whether in mathematics, language, or art. Where judgement does not include testing and measuring we may simply need more tolerance of differing interpretations. Even if we are faced with a set of figures or test results, the process of assessing anything still calls for experience and professional interpretation. Test results are not always conclusive proof of existing ability.

For this reason it is essential to develop educational and artistic values which can be articulated and defended. If we are to recognize specific qualities in children's work or personal progress we must first have experience of what those qualities are. There would be little point, for example, determining whether or not a child was capable of mixing colours from a strong red to a paler shade of pink, unless we knew what these shades looked like. We would similarly need to have experience of what might be expected from children at a certain age to judge how far individuals had developed artistically for their age.

## An assessment model

We can compare five categories and a variety of criteria for forming judgements. Were it not for the plethora of statutory assessment in other subjects a scale of one to five could be used to assign a grade. Improvements to these criteria can be added or substituted, given that we must be aware of the context in which children work. The following bulleted examples could be imagined as comments on a school report if they were expanded or developed to fit individuals.

1  *Process of working*: this covers the important aspects of artistic development during the action of creating artwork. Certain abilities like developing an idea, changing the design, substituting, adding and improving are not otherwise evident except during the process of working. In fact, the categories of observation which follow can be applied to other subjects too. Response to ideas and visual stimuli are sometimes far more evident during the process *than* they are in the final product. Ideally in art we are working towards being able to state the pupil:

- is inventive, full of ideas
- shows initiative, independence
- shows curiosity and interest when working
- puts in effort
- perseveres with artwork
- is keen, absorbed when working
- works well with others
- responds to visual stimuli, ideas
- is able to overcome difficulties
- can follow instructions when necessary.

2  *Handling of materials*: it is important to know whether or not children have developed good organizational skills and can use a variety of materials appropriately. This is quite without regard to the artistic outcomes. We need, for instance, to know if children can organize and use paints as a prerequisite to producing a worthwhile painting, or scissors if they are cutting out a shape. Otherwise there is a considerable gap between intention and skill needed to handle materials. We are working towards being able to state that the pupil:

- is able to mix paint to good consistency
- can use a variety of drawing media
- is able to use scissors well
- understands nature of media, e.g. Plasticine, clay
- can organize workspace for media.

3  *Use of media*: apart from the control of materials we need to know whether or not children are developing an understanding of the media they use. Can they,

for example, mix colours together to produce shades? Do they simply draw with paint or can they use it in other ways (e.g. to produce textures, patterns, blocks of colour)? Can they design models in clay which make the best use of the medium? The child

- discriminates when choosing colours
- shows skill in mixing colours
- is able to use a paintbrush appropriately to the medium
- is able to use modelling/3-D media
- can select appropriate media where choice is offered.

4   *Critical skills*: this category deals with discriminatory skills and is concerned with looking and analysing. Children do not only produce artwork, they develop the ability to discriminate between one colour and another, different lines and different shapes. They can be involved from an early age with looking at designs and artwork by other artists as well as at their own work. They will also need to look at their natural environment in a critical way, comparing such varied designs and patterns as those on leaves or sea shells. Critical skills can also include self-assessment which older children (7–9 years) might use. The child:

- responds enthusiastically to looking at artwork
- is able to discuss ideas and experiences
- can point out similarities and differences in things seen
- is keenly observant of environment
- notices displays, things brought in
- is able to use artistic vocabulary, e.g. colour, line, shape, dark, light
- is able to make judgements about own performance or achievement.

5   *Stages of personal development*: this covers assessment in relation to the expected stages for the age range. These stages are simply an indication of what children might be expected to do when left to their own devices. In order to make judgements we need to refer to stages of developing imagery (as outlined in Chapter 4) but bear in mind that the aim is not to rush children through these stages. The aim is to see how far they have developed as a result of engaging in artwork. Besides this, there are social and personal attitudes to art such as the degree to which children value their own and other children's work. To what extent, for example, are they able to accept praise and criticism of their own work? We would need to know that:

- the work is at an appropriate stage of development for the age of the child
- the child is able to draw things from more than one viewpoint
- he or she sees links with other areas of learning, e.g. mathematics
- he or she has confidence in producing artwork
- is able to tackle subjects involving the emotions

- adapts to changes of ideas
- values own work
- values the work of others
- helps others
- is able to accept criticism
- is able to cope with praise
- listens attentively
- is able to say why she or he likes or dislikes aspects of artwork.

## Evaluation

As teachers we are sometimes our own worst enemy when evaluating. Self-criticism is frequently interpreted as merely finding fault with our own teaching, a practice which could lead to frustration and a poor sense of personal worth. This is not true of all teachers but is far more commonly found than it need be. None of us really believes that we teach perfectly or that nothing can ever be improved. Although the very word evaluate suggests that we determine the value of something, in practice we can often misinterpret this as looking for what is not of value, rather than what is.

These two aspects of evaluation are admittedly like sides of the same coin but need not become unbalanced and tend to the negative. If evaluation is to be useful (and this usually means it leads to changes in the way we or the children work) it should be seen as a signpost for the future rather than a condemnation of the past. The future cannot be evaluated, but there is something to be said for evaluating past performance with an eye to making changes. Where evaluation is solely a judgement on the past, it can quickly become fixed and impotent, a fair account of the past but no indicator of future developments.

Teachers evaluate most of the time. It is hardly possible to think about what children might do next without evaluating what has gone before. They may need more practice in colour-mixing, for instance, or a drawing might reveal skills which could be used in another context. It could be that particular developing skills in using pattern should be put to a different use. By this (often subconscious) means of evaluation, artistic learning can be given direction rather than remaining random or without impetus.

There are evaluation questions which refer to several aspects of art teaching. It would be very difficult not to discuss artwork without simultaneously evaluating something in connection with the work. Mention has also been made (Chapter 12) of the evaluation process as a stage in the proposed model for designing. Other than this, there are questions we can ask ourselves, for instance,

> How well are the children motivated?
> Was the stimulus appropriate?
> Does the organization (e.g. water pots, paints) work well?
> How original is the thinking (e.g. compared with copying other children's/
> teacher's ideas)?

Was good use made of things brought in from home?

How well is the drawing developing?

Can the children use reference material like pictures and photographs without copying?

How inventive is the work?

How well is the chosen medium used?

How extensively is this theme/project developed?

How well can the children mix colours which are light in tone as well as dark?

How varied is the range of materials the children can use?

How well do they tackle subjects concerned with emotion?

Have they any particular flair for using pattern?

How imaginative are the pieces of work?

Are the children able to take care in colouring a shape they have drawn or cut out?

No two teachers assess exactly the same way and each interprets assessments slightly differently from the other. Assessment and evaluation can never be entirely reliable processes. Yet there is no reason why they should not be valuable. Their success will depend on our making the best possible judgements we can at the time. We are dealing with assessments of quality, for which there are no absolute yardsticks. There are sound judgements which, it cannot be emphasized too strongly, call for considerable sensitivity to the qualities of art and design.

In the end, the most likely assessment data we have is the work itself. Teachers often build a portfolio of work for each child, and artwork is sometimes part of this. Some comment needs to accompany work completed and a glance at the above categories reveals that many of the comments would not be out of place in a pupil report. That is mainly because processes in art, life and other subjects generate assessments of this useful kind. We may be looking at art, but there are many more subjects to which these categories apply.

# 15 Art and the digital image

When young children use paints and crayons, the direct involvement they have is of handling physical materials. The physical, rather than electronic nature of paint is one of its main attractions. The pressure of a crayon on paper, a container of colours to choose from and wearing an apron is all part of the excitement. How, then, is it that children are also interested in using a computer to generate images? Could it be that computer programs have something special to offer just as engaging as paint and paper? Computers can certainly be found in nurseries and reception classes besides being used by older children. Many children also see computers being used in the home and in shops so these are familiar objects no more mysterious to them than washing machines.

In a nursery, a computer is likely to be used alongside other equipment as part of a 'learning through play' programme. This is just as important as the possible appeal of what appears on the screen. Children need to affirm who they are by playing with equipment they see adults using. There are plenty of examples of this need being fulfilled in role-play activities, dressing up and finding out what jobs adults do. Some nursery-age children are very adept at pointing and clicking using a computer mouse. Others are happy to pretend to use the computer, just as they play at driving cars or using the telephone. This stage of development is complemented by their use of paint and crayons. The exploration and 'play' is still part of their discovery of what marks can be made in paint and what excitement there is in filling paper with colour.

The connection with digital images is very close. Where teachers use art software in a nursery or reception classroom, children can be seen filling the screen with colour using a mouse instead of a brush. In 'paint' programs, the excitement is still that of changing a blank area and having some control over what happens. This process is immediate and vibrant on a computer once children know how to click on a colour palette to change the screen image. While there may be no paint to mix and water to organize for children, the teacher may still have to do more complex things in setting up the program. Nothing very interesting is going to happen unless the teacher can set the size of the 'brush' and click to change colours for those young children unable to do so.

The parallels between the traditional materials of the artist and the digital effects of a computer are not particularly strong. This is because computers can

*Figure 34* 'Dazzle' Picture, Thick and Thin Lines. Age 5. 200 × 150 mm.

do things that art materials cannot. The reverse it also true. Thickly textured brushstrokes are impossible to build up on a computer screen even though the effects of this can be recreated. The screen size is usually the same compared with huge differences in scale achieved by trimming or sticking together paper to use whatever size is needed. There is no appreciable difference in physical hand pressure like that felt when pressing a pencil to paper. Immediate changes to colours, tiled effects, symmetry, rainbow colour effects and 'cut and paste' are intrinsic to the way computers work, depending on the software chosen. These effects cannot easily be replicated in paint and certainly not so quickly. We need to drop all notions of the computer being a substitute for traditional art materials or being deficient as a medium. Computers are valuable in art because they produce images not produced any other way. Additionally, they can display reproductions of works of art from compact disc, DVD and access galleries through web sites, a feature where search facilities provide a rich source of stimulus.

This rarely stops teachers making comparisons between traditional paints and those on screen. Software tries to emulate effects such as watercolour and uses similar words on screen-buttons such as brush, draw, fill, spray and line. (The art program 'Dazzle Plus', marketed by Grenada Learning in Manchester, UK, is an example. There are other educational art programs, but this one has the advantage that colours can easily be made lighter and darker as well as mixed into tints of many subtle colours.) There are skills being learned that help children develop computer literacy for the future. The age of the child is not much of a guide to how or when this happens, but some children quickly understand that in order to make anything appear on screen they need to hold down the left button on a conventional PC mouse. They learn to 'drag' lines across a screen. They learn to point and click to fill areas with colour and pattern. A conventional PC mouse has two buttons. Software designers usually use the right button for displaying a menu to change brush size, shapes and even colour palettes. Whatever the preferred software, the development of skill lies in finding out how to make small adjustments to colour and shape, or discovering built-in effects such as symmetry. Minimal skill is needed to develop some control over what is happening, providing teachers are prepared to step back and allow for experiment.

The least likely digital art activity would probably be that of video installation, requiring editing. It deserves mention here because it is increasingly to be found as an art form in its own right. Use of the digital video, screen capture or edited image require so much input from an adult that it is difficult to justify in the lower age group. Once the balance of input shifts from the child to the adult, it is difficult to believe early-years art education is happening. Imagine an activity where children point a video-camera and create a record of what they see, or record what is acted out. Control of this as an art form rests far too strongly outside the children, unless the aim is to bring to their notice that video is a different way of seeing. The digital image can reveal aspects of the world not noticed, or it can create a world of its own by being displayed in a gallery. Both these approaches touch on sophisticated contemporary video art, just about possible with 9-year-olds, but needing a great deal of input from an adult.

## An early-years computer-art lesson

What do children need to be able to do to use computer art 'paint' software? There are obvious advantages in having a colour printer if children are going to take away anything as a reminder of what they did. A further advantage of having a printed version of the screen image is that children can add pencil-crayon to the image, cut it up and reassemble it. A sequence of activities might therefore be something like:

- Produce a screen image and three printouts in colour.
- Display one of these just as it is.
- Add coloured pencil to one of the remaining printouts.
- Cut, collage the remaining image for display, decorating a greetings card, enhancing a menu or making a picture frame for a drawing.
- Display a screen image as part of a web page on the Internet.

The minimum of computing skill needed by children is to be able to drag a mouse line across the screen. This is not very ambitious and the real break-through comes when a child can do two further actions – pick out a new colour and change the size of the 'brush'. There are of course ready-made effects to be had just clicking on buttons called things such as 'shape', 'stamp' or 'water effect', but much more control is possible once changes can be made to lines and colours without needing help. Children will explore buttons by themselves, but few software programs operate without some teaching being necessary. In practice teachers smuggle a variety of learning objectives into using a computer. An example is where pupils create a decorative border for a book. The computer skills are all geared towards this, but children might also learn to 'tile' patterns on a computer, cut and paste these to a word-processor and discuss the design of book-jackets in general. There are chances to learn about saving a file, loading an existing one and editing it. Few worthwhile activities involve only one skill or objective, though it is worth remembering which of the skills are artistic and which are generic computing skills. Art and design are concerned with shape, colour, line, placing, balance, designing and making things. Computing is a way of developing these, sometimes with the dullest of objectives such as skill in using a mouse.

There are three main ways in which digital images are used in art. First, there are images created as artworks like those already described. Pupils use 'paint' packages and manipulate images. Second, there are images taken from sources such as the Internet or CDs. These can include galleries of computer-generated images, even mathematical fractals and web-page patterns. Third, there are images created on a digital camera in such a way as to have aesthetic, abstract or artistic qualities. The images themselves are most often saved as computer files in one of two popular formats. They are either 'bitmap' images saved as *filname.bmp* or 'jpegs' saved as *filename.jpg* where the file name is anything the user decides is a good name to use. Digital cameras and Internet images are normally jpeg files. Art packages are normally bitmap images. Both these formats can be converted into other formats and many art packages accept both kinds, converting them into something that can be seen on screen. Increasingly, word-processors accept a wide range of different files and pictures created in art programs can be imported into a word-processed page. However, the jpeg format has the advantage of being easily displayed on the Internet. Teachers wanting to display Internet web pages of children's work done in an art package will need to ensure the format is jpeg as bitmap images do not display. There is plenty of free software on the Internet to convert images from one format to another.

## Using an art program

An advanced skill for older primary children is to be able to 'cut' and 'paste' parts of an image. This also relates to 'tiling' where a pupil needs to isolate a preferred part of the image to tile it. This involves 'dragging' across the image holding down the mouse key, then choosing an option to copy, cut or tile the image. Tiling, like many instantaneous changes, will interest children for a time, but it is a limited technique because it produces similar shapes. The built-in features of art programs need to be used in other ways. So far, collage has been suggested, but the costs of printing may limit this as an outcome. The art topic of tiles can be taken much further if children cut and tessellate shapes, look at mosaic and interior design and design their own tiles using the computer as an initial stimulus.

If tiling effects using a computer are to be made interesting, then the options need to be known. Some characteristically different effects can be achieved by varying the drawing tools before filling in with colour.

- Create a drawing using ellipses/circles, then colour and tile.
- Create a drawing using ellipses/circles within rectangles, then colour and tile.
- Create a drawing using thick and thin lines, then tile.
- Create a drawing using 'freehand' drawn lines, then tile.
- Create an image where white will be the final dominant colour.
- Create an image where black will be the final dominant colour.
- Create an image where pale pastel shades of colour dominate.
- Tile a very large shape.
- Tile a very small shape.
- Tile a section of photograph imported into the art program.
- Tile a section of an image where the 'watercolour' tool or an effect tool has been used.

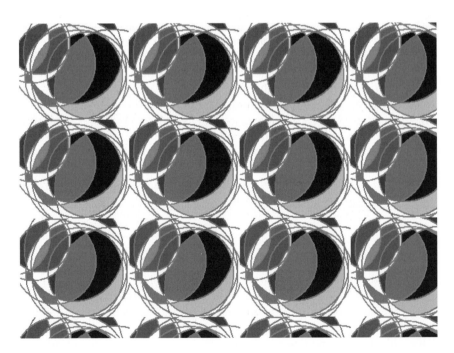

*Figure 35*  An Image Using Curves and a Tiled Effect. Age 9. 200 × 150 mm.

- Tile part of a design using 'symmetry' options first.
- Use other options such as triangles (no curves).

Some of the most striking effects are to be achieved contrasting images with curves rather than a mixture of straight lines and curves. Some art packages will also cut and paste ellipses and circles. Tiling effects often look like fabric designs and the link with this area need not be lost.

Extending this idea further, the starting point for using an art package can be the study of interior design or fabrics. In Figure 36 and Plate 34, the starting point has been reproductions of designs for Miss Cranston's Tea-Room in Glasgow. Designed by Charles Rennie Mackintosh, they have provided not only a means of pattern-making, but much more. An important point here was for pupils to know the difference between the thin pencil tool and the smallest brush size. This may seem just a refinement, but it is fundamental to adding variety in the emphasis of the line. What begins as rather a crude image becomes more interesting because the areas filled are bounded by both thick and thin lines.

Art is one of those subjects where history, commerce and afternoon tea recipes can meet. In *Miss Cranston's Tea-Room*, Mackintosh designed notices, cutlery, menu cards, chairs, cupboards and tables. He designed light fittings, leaded windows, and even beads for the waitresses to wear. Most extravagantly he

*Figure 36* Design for Miss Cranston's Tea-Room. Age 9. 200 × 150 mm.

designed doors of wood, metal and glass. The combination of these items can form the basis of a class project taking the principle of coherence in shape and colour. (There are additional opportunities to role-play the tea-room and bring design problems into numeracy and literacy.) Sophisticated though Mackintosh's designs are, pupils might design several artistic items with or without the help of a computer. Some suggestions for starting are:

- Talk to children about how Mackintosh designed every item in some of his houses and tea-rooms.
- Carefully study reproductions of Mackintosh designs for doors, windows and fabrics, looking particularly at curves and the use of flowers such as tulips and roses.
- Design a frame for a Mackintosh mirror using card strips and silver foil. Emphasize the need to look carefully at curves, flower and leaf shapes, but not copy directly.
- Design a necklace using the colours and shapes Mackintosh might have used.
- Draw a design for an entrance door seen from the outside of a building.
- Design curtains using a computer art program which repeats, tiles or uses symmetry. Pay particular attention to Mackintosh's favoured colours such as purples, pinks and greens.
- Design a fabric using Mackintosh shapes but using completely different colours. Explore the computer's ability to change colour effects rapidly.

The advantage of using a computer program is that effects such as symmetry and colour filling are rapid. The disadvantage is that controlling a mouse at best gives a crude and ragged line. This is all part of the process and it is far better to accept the limitations and strengths of each medium than complain it does not do what we want.

The 9-year-olds who worked on this Mackintosh project were absorbed for an entire afternoon making changes to their designs. They avoided other features of the art program such as tiling and watercolour effects. The teacher period-ically saved work to make sure it was not lost. More than once the pupils asked to return to a previous image as they were unhappy with the way they had developed it. An advantage of saving frequently is that there is a record of progress and every chance to return to previous saved versions. The teaching was minimal and consisted of referring children back to the features of the Mackintosh design, such as long vertical curved lines, tulips, leaves and jewel-like shapes. Pupils had no difficulty drawing with the mouse, nor did they find it difficult to use both the thin pencil tool as well as the thin brush tool.

## Linking the Internet to an art project

In some schools the Internet is going to prove a useful resource for art. Browsing the Internet has limited appeal if young children cannot easily read the text on a web page, so any project linked to the Internet needs careful planning. One way this has been done was for a group of children to work from reproductions of work by Joan Miró, then look for information on the Internet. The project also included work with pencil-crayons and paint as the number of computers and time needed to use them was limited.

The art module was to study the painter Joan Miró and use Information and Communications Technology (ICT). The children looked at a reproduction of a Miró from the 1930s and 1950s and had to decide what was in the background, mid-ground and foreground of his work. They had to draw an image in the style of Miró developing control over the mouse and learning to mix colours in a precise way. Other 'tools' used were the 'fill', 'cut' and 'paste' buttons. Several pupils worked from postcard-sized reproductions.

The structure of this was over a four-hour period of sessions.

- Show reproductions of the work of Joan Miró and discuss some features of these.
- Look through small card viewfinders to examine parts of the reproductions.
- Children working take turns using the computers or use crayons to make a study of the Miró. One pupil creates a Miró image and the other then changes it (encourages discussion and learning about the art program).
- Reproduce only part of a Miró painting and change it. Some children may want to use a magnifying glass to examine part of a postcard reproduction.
- Search the Internet using teacher-prepared question cards.
- Display and discuss changes made.

Some of the processes involved in this prompted much excitement as the following conversation shows.

*Pupil A:* Wow . . . this is great!
*Teacher:* What is great?
*Pupil A:* Changing your brush size with the mouse.
*Teacher:* Well, you change your brush size when you are painting with paint and paper.
*Pupil A:* Yeah . . . but this is better and quicker because you don't have to keep changing them and cleaning them.

Some children liked the fact that mistakes could be changed with an 'undo' button. Others were very pleased with themselves for being able to teach others the technical skills needed to change images. Computers can generate a competitive climate which may or may not be healthy. This can favour boys keen to show off what they can do and some channelling of their enthusiasm is necessary to ensure that opportunities to progress on the computer are as equal as possible.

When the children searched the Internet for information about Miró they found that there was a great deal of information about painters. The actual sites used may by now have moved, so it is safer simply to say that the pupils used 'search engines' (Yahoo, Google, Lycos) and typed in Miró. As one pupil wrote, seemingly aware of the perpetual criticisms of parents and teachers,

> It's good to have the Internet at school because then you learn things (lots). In a technilogital [sic] way. Which is very good, at least it's one way to get kids to learn something.

Most pupils wanted more time to explore and some already had computers at home connected to the Internet. Some images were downloaded into an art paint program and the pupils made changes to them still in the style of Miró. This is rather like coming into Miró's studio and adding paint in his absence, trying not to be caught out for doing so. The value of this is that children can try to absorb the painter's style while developing some control over what they do on a computer. Like the project studying Charles Rennie Mackintosh, the discussion this promotes about style, colour and shapes is all part of a growing artistic development. There are also many opportunities to review work in progress and discuss why changes are made.

There are teaching points to observe in this project. Some means of going back to a previously changed image is needed. Not all computer programs have an 'undo' feature and the teacher cannot be there just at the point where it is worth saving an image. Teaching children to save versions of their work as it progresses is not so difficult as adults think. Provided the teacher has set up the directory in which to save files there are only four mouse actions needed – File, Save As, type a file name and Save. Failing that, most children can send their image to a printer as a record of the progress so far. This is not repeatable if in the

*Figure 37*  Images Based on Paintings by Joan Miró. Age 9.

next moment the image changes, so persisting in file-saving pays dividends, especially as images can be burned to CD and displayed as a slide show.

Browsing the Internet for the work of artists can be very dull if children have no purpose in mind. The teacher who designed the Miró project decided that questions would be put on cards and pupils would each have a booklet in which to write their answers. The questions were initially simple, such as 'When was this painted?', 'What colours has he used', 'What effects can you see?', 'How large is this painting?' and 'What is in the bottom right-hand corner of this?' Other questions were about Miró's life, such as 'When did Miró move to Paris?' A more comprehensive range of questions is suggested in Chapter 17, but even here it can be seen that studying the digital image crosses curricular boundaries.

## Digital camera and scanned images into art

The digital camera, which has fast replaced conventional film, produces images stored in memory or downloaded to a computer. Even if teachers working in the early-years age range do not use cameras and scanners, parents and other teachers certainly do. There are opportunities for involving parents in a project needing digital images. Education is a service full of enthusiasts and people who know of someone capable of tackling technical challenges. Their involvement is welcome, so long as control of the artistic outcome transfers to the children. Two of the more interesting ways to take and use photographs are:

- Children photograph an existing work of art, preferably their own, then manipulate and change the image.
- Children take photographs that already have an abstract quality (such as close-ups of textured surfaces, stacked chairs, pipe-work around the school), parts of machines, cloud formations.

Young children will need their teacher to download digital images from camera to computer if this is too difficult for them. Never underestimate their skill. A 2-year-old is reported to be capable of deleting all files on a computer hard drive. Once in a form that can be loaded into an art package, changes can be made to digital photographs and, if a copy is kept, the teacher can reload the original image. Remember that digital photographs are normally saved in jpeg format (.jpg) and art software might need these converted to bitmaps (.bmp). An alternative to converting images is to load the .jpg file to see the photograph, then Edit, Copy it to the computer memory, load the art package and Edit, Paste the image back again. Children have fewer problems taking photographs than they do loading them to a computer. There is no real mystery to be solved for teachers here as most modern digital cameras need very little skill to download images. Some (Sony cameras, for example) have a memory system which behaves like an additional set of folders on the hard drive. There is nothing to do but copy and paste the photographs like any other document or image file on a PC.

The 9-year-olds who produced the 'tiled' images (Figure 35) took photographs around the school. They learned how to load a photograph which had been converted by the teacher to a bitmap. Some photographs were naturally more interesting than others, such as a photograph of stacked chairs in the school dining area. They learned to select a small area of photograph and 'tile' it. The artistic variations and aesthetic content of this activity depended on:

- the photograph being of interest in the first place;
- the chance to change or add to the photograph before tiling;
- knowing how to keep loading the original photograph and save the tiled variations.

The only difficult aspect of tiling was being able to load a file and save it with another name. Throughout the afternoon using the art program pupils very quickly adapted to the loading and saving routine.

A scanner (device that will produce a digital image from a photograph or magazine) is a means to an end. It acts in place of a digital camera if the image already exists on photographic paper or printed in a magazine. Photographs can be cut, pasted, tiled, inverted and recoloured to produce digital art. This tends to be a development of 'tiling' and fabric designs already mentioned. Colours can be changed, the image loaded into an art program and effects applied.

*Figure 38* 'Tiling' a Section of Digital Photograph. Age 9. 200 × 150 mm.

*Figure 39* Changing a Digital Photograph by Adding a 'Stamp'. Age 9. 200 × 150 mm.

What can be said with some certainty about digital art projects is that children's interest is sustained by trying to refine a particular image, rather than play with effects. The clicking of effect buttons in a program soon seems to bore children. Tiling, for example, is such an automatic effect that other ideas need bringing into that project, such as taking photographs, scanning and changing images before selecting the tiles. At its least sophisticated, images are cloned to give a pattern of rectangles or squares. A development of this is for the selected rectangle to be copied to memory and 'stamped' within another image. The greater the opportunity to change an image and refine it, the greater the interest there seems to be. Within the process of changing and refining images there is an inherent bonus. Each stage of change and refinement can be saved, revealing in the final analysis a sequence of artistic thought and judgement. There is 'the story of an image' behind the final result, a feature which offsets the limitations of printout size and image format. More useful than this, digital images can stimulate closer examination of the visual world. Manipulating and changing the sky in a photograph, photographing buildings and parts of the school interior presents them differently. Observation is being tapped and the creative possibilities of digital media explored.

The essential guiding principle remains. Skills develop through engaging with interesting projects, not by themselves. Playing with an art program is like playing with art materials, a beginning, but one which may lead nowhere. Structured projects, the need to change images and discover how to do that, drive skills forward. Some art programs certainly offer more than others. At times the Internet resembles the contents of a rubbish bin rather than the treasure of the Aztecs, but the digital image is here to stay. Large-screen display, laser lights and 'tiled' stacks of display-screens in public venues help overcome limitations of scale. In the classroom the digital image may be limited by the quality and size of printout, though collages as group displays can increase the impact. To some extent, producing a digital image and manipulating it is a study process rather than an end-product. Most importantly, in manipulating digital images, the contribution this makes to art education is not being ignored.

# 16 Using media and techniques to build skills

## Crayon, pencil and paint

Children's early school experience is often one of colouring in shapes they have drawn. This is an obvious way to apply colour to a drawing and basic to making artworks. The deeply ingrained habit of drawing in line and filling in with colour can remain the only way for some children to work when there are other skills they need. The filled-in shape also implies that artwork is finished if it has been filled with colour. The habit of thinking this way is less obvious using paint and large brushes, but can still limit the development of a wider range of skills. Reviewing and changing work becomes more difficult to implement. Schools' art lessons are often full of good starts which lead nowhere when they could develop skills which are transferred to other work.

Building and extending skills is worthwhile because doing so can sustain children's interest beyond a passing novelty value. There is simply more to do when creating, colouring and changing a work of art when enough skills are developed. Building and extending skills is the antidote to children finishing their artwork in five minutes flat. In this chapter some, but not all media, are discussed in order to exemplify ways to extend and vary skills.

One way to overcome limited use of media is to teach children to try out overlaying their colours and superimposing them (Plate 35). The advantage of this is that the range of what children can do is widened. Children have more choices they can make about how to affect existing colours. In the case of pencil-crayons this can be started off by using card stencils made by the children. Cutting an irregular shape with safety scissors is probably the hardest part of this. There are alternatives, such as folding thin card and cutting it, or just using scrap card shapes left from another project. A feature of shading, using pencil-crayons within a card stencil, is that there need be no obvious line, especially if the stencil is moved slightly to a new position and more pencil applied over an existing shape. An edge is created where the pencil stops, but no outline. The skills and learning involved when investigating this include:

- Learning to vary the pressure of a pencil-crayon.
- Learning that stencils can be moved and colours overlapped.
- Learning to hold down the stencil tightly to shade within it.

- Learning to shade right to the edge of the stencil shape.
- Learning that colours can be mixed differently depending on pencil pressure and the marks made.
- Learning that shapes may be overlapped to produce patterns.
- Learning that yellow, in particular, is a colour that (superimposed) changes other colours.
- Learning that an outline is not always necessary to start off a work of art.

Art materials are not cheap and the economics of providing a good range of colours can be a surprising one. It could be thought that the more colours in a range of pencil-crayons, the more expensive this will prove to be. In practice, providing a very wide range of colours means more time spent choosing and changing from one colour to another. A wide range of colours lasts and there may be less time spent sharpening all the pencil-crayons. The story is not quite the same with paints because they mix together very easily, so not such a wide range is needed. Pencil-crayons now come in up to 100 shades. It is not difficult to see that the quality of a crayon drawing is greatly enhanced if there are at least four shades of blue from which to choose.

Skill in using a graphite pencil goes beyond making a single line which is the same pressure throughout. Some children never do more than press using exactly the same pressure, producing a line which resembles wire rather than pencil. A card stencil provides a useful start because it can remove the need to make outlines. Simple though it might seem, it does not always occur to children that they can vary the shading they do with an HB or B pencil, adjusting the pressure (HB is a medium-hard pencil, 6B the softest and 6H the hardest). The variations of pencil-mark are infinite, from thin lines to thick, heavy to light pressure, solid continuous or broken lines. Shading with a pencil can have direction, be light, heavy, solid or relatively sparse. A card stencil makes a pattern, so a development of this would be to have children create a pattern using different pressures of line, then try out as many different ways to shade as they could devise. (Some practical projects are described at the end of this chapter.)

Using paint has already been described in Chapter 9. A further dimension of this is learning to overlay with translucent paint. This presents a very different set of problems and skills from those gained using pencil-crayon. Paint needs to be almost dry if it is used in a stencil, and wet if a watercolour. Opaque water-based paint will not work as an overlay. The technique with opaque paint is to mix colours together first or gradually and deliberately change each mix of colour as it is applied.

Colour-mixing skill involves memorizing simple mixtures. Even at secondary school, it is strange how difficult some children find it to remember which colour needs to be mixed to produce green. (A good learning device is not to tell them, but give them a start by saying 'Begin with yellow'.) If colour overlays and mixes are created the skills and learning include:

- Learning that thinly mixed watercolour layers need to be done without a stencil.

- Learning that thinly mixed colour needs to be used on a light or white paper to be seen.
- Learning that thinly mixed colour can easily overload a brush and be difficult to use.
- Learning that thickly mixed colour needs to be blended with other mixtures if it is to do more than fill in a shape.
- Learning that thickly mixed colour is not at its best on white paper, but on slightly darker, neutral shades of absorbent paper.
- Learning that colour can be overlaid within a stencil so long as the mixture is almost dry and applied with a stubby stencil brush.
- Learning how to mix green and purple.
- Learning that wet colour on top of wet behaves differently from wet on top of dry.
- Learning that opaque white paint needs skill in mixing and using with other colours.

The last point on this list concerns the use of white paint. As has been mentioned in Chapter 6, white is achieved in watercolour-painting as blank white paper, but in opaque paints white is an essential colour. It is worth teaching children that every colour has its own strength. Adding white to yellow to make it pale is not too difficult because yellow is not a dark colour. The difficulty of mixing light opaque colours is partly due to the nature of the dyes in the darker paints and partly the inevitable state of the water pot used for mixing colour. A real test of skill is for children to be able to mix colours so well that the opaque colour will cover black or slate-coloured paper. Adding white to blue is not good practice because of the very strong dyes used to create a blue. It is not enough to remind children to add small amounts of blue to white for a pale blue because they do not really understand why. Adding blue to white is not an artistic rule, it is just easier to achieve the desired result by understanding why colours behave as they do. Development of skill in using white and other light colours changes painting technique considerably because children realize that different pigments have different strengths.

The basic skill of painting a colour sharply against a drawn line may also need demonstrating. Children who are right-handed can paint up to the pencil line to the left of their brush, and vice versa. Often this means turning the paper 180 degrees so that they can see where bristle and pencil will meet. The other brush technique needed to paint sharp edges is to charge the brush with paint then drag the bristles along the side of the line. The rest is practice, mainly at having the wit to remember to position the paper so that the guidelines can easily be seen.

Stencilling can also be done by spraying paint using a stiff brush or a blow spray. Spraying paint has implications for behaviour management, but can produce interesting effects. Children can use a brush or blower to spatter or spray a stencil, though this fails if the stencil is very wet. Stencilling is really a semi-dry process, which is why using ready-mixed paints can actually rule out stencilling. Choice of paints is to some extent a personal taste and some experiment is needed before unleashing painting activities on a class. Ready-mixed,

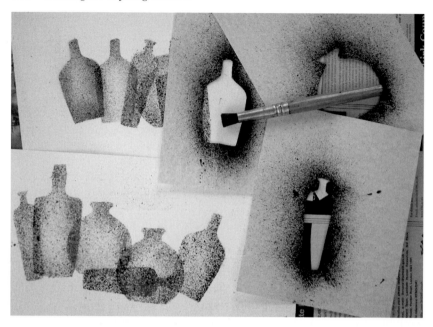

Figure 40  Stencil Spraying. Trainee-teacher project.

ready-provided paint solves some practical problems of organization but it creates others. It can limit the skills learned using it because it is generally apt to run down the paper or buckle it. Sloppy trickled paint is the death of many an art session and simple rules about not overcharging a brush, mixing colour thickly if it is in powder form, and organizing a work area are essential.

Once some of these basic discoveries about crayon and paint techniques are made a next step is to use them more freely, deciding when and how to blend or overlay colours. Instead of a 'shape and fill' approach to colouring, there are now several options from which to choose. The business of pattern-making, blending, overlaying and mixing colour is a source of delight and can absorb children in ways they did not expect. They have decisions to make and a repertoire of mark-making from which to create. Filling in a shape with colour will still be done because it is a commonly used technique, but pupils will have a wider range of skills. An important teaching aim is to give pupils the skills to work independently and in a *sustained* way.

Any skills which might have been learned are not automatically used by children in their next piece of work. They need reinforcing. Rather than intervening to comment on a painting's content, the teacher may find practical issues can dominate. Typically intervention by the teacher to reinforce practical skills may concern,

- Improving the thickness of mixed paint (powder).
- Reducing unnecessary waste as a result of mixing too much paint.

- Reducing instances of overloading paint on a brush.
- Stopping children destroying small soft-haired brushes by pressing hard on the ferrule.
- Monitoring the use of thin mixtures so they are applied in a way that allows for drying and overlaying more colour.
- Organizing changes of water for painting.
- Reorganizing workspace.
- Pointing out that a range of brushes is available.
- Explaining the choices available in respect of materials provided.
- Demonstrating on scrap paper, colour mixes and brush techniques – including holding a brush (without actually working on the child's paper).
- Praising and encouraging good technical organization and choices by remarking on the use of different shades of colour and how they are being used.

From the outset it is worth remembering that good art teaching has always required some effort to provide usable materials. Very wet, thin paint will buckle the paper it is on, so stout paper is needed or the thinnest of washes frugally applied. There are consequent drying and storage problems with wet paint, which is why using thicker mixes of paint, or frugal thin layers of paint have much to recommend them as techniques. (Watercolour artists soak and stretch paper, fixing it to a board if they intend to make it very wet. Teachers are not likely to do this for a whole class of children.) Collage materials (see Chapter 11) involve using glue and scissors. If card shapes are to be cut, the card needs to be thin, yet tough enough to stand up to vigorous shading of a stencil or stabbing with 'dry' paint and a short-bristled brush.

A development of colour overlays is to use diluted PVA school glue, the consistency of milk, to layer coloured tissue papers on white cartridge paper (Plate 35). Tissue paper is an underrated medium and with practice can produce stunning overlays. It is usually easier to coat a small section on the surface of white cartridge, rather than glue the coloured tissue itself. Once stuck down, another coating of glue will act as a glaze. Overlapping different colours, handling thinly mixed glue, cutting and sticking are obvious skills which may be learned from this activity. The cliché in schools is to produce stained-glass window designs. Breaking out of this cliché, children can produce anything they wish, but using overlapping coloured tissue, rather than paints or pencil-crayons. In making overlays of transparent paper, there is an obvious link here with science. Coloured acetate sheets behave differently from coloured tissue and much discussion can be promoted about what colours can be seen.

One use of paint mentioned in Chapter 10 was as a printing medium. The organizational skills developed here are considerable if children try to control the amount of paint and pressure used to print. Children learn that shapes can be repeated without recharging a printing tool such as a potato. Organizing workspace, colour-mixing, drawing and using an unfamiliar technique all come together in simple printing techniques using paint. The consistency of the paint used for printing has to be discovered by experiment. A safe bet is that initially children will overload their printing tools and brushes, under the impression that 'more' is 'better'. Skill in handling a printing tool, loading it with paint and controlling what is happening, ensures that the quality of teaching and learning are high. Overloaded printing tools create unimpressive solid shapes where paint has been squashed outwards under pressure.

## Building skills using clay

Using clay is a one-off experience in many classrooms because of costs, workspace, time and enthusiasm needed. This is a pity, especially as it is likely children already have previous experience of modelling, using Plasticine and play dough. Claywork includes sculpture, models, and pots created in a malleable plastic material, then fired in a kiln. When children use clay, they are exploring form in relation to space, expressing a three-dimensional world in three dimensions. This is quite a contrast from the mainly two-dimensional work they produce and has the added magic of a high temperature firing which vitrifies the clay.

An important feature of anything produced in three dimensions is that it is usually meant to be seen from different angles, not just one. By comparison, two-dimensional work is often a flat representation of three dimensions. In some cases the 3-D work can be explored in a tactile way by being touched or handled. Work such as sculpture has weight and will sometimes cast shadows to reveal its form. As work is viewed from different angles, slight changes of form and angle shift the balance of shapes and give a new experience of the 3-D work.

Plasticine and dough are quite different from clay and different skills are needed. Clay dries out as it is worked and pieces of clay do not simply stick together like Plasticine or dough. Once dry, clay will fall apart unless it has been 'welded' together. Welding clay is joining it, smoothing it in such a way as to make one piece of clay become part of the other. Sometimes there is enough clay to push one piece into another. Sometimes it is necessary to roll a thin piece of clay to the size of a small earthworm and 'weld' a joint together pushing the clay until it becomes absorbed into other pieces. The legs of clay animals, tails, ears and decorative additional clay needs 'welding' in this way if they are not to fall apart in a firing. The joints need to be slightly thicker and heavier than seems necessary if they are to survive kiln-firing. Children are unlikely to understand this, so it is important that once fired, especially if glazed too, pottery objects can have very sharp edges. This is particularly common around the base of a pot if it has been left to dry stuck to a board. A real skill for children to learn is that of smoothing possible sharp edges and points from some surfaces before firing takes place. Smoothing clay is good practice, even if a rough texture is added as decoration. The structure of clay models and pots needs to be sound or there will almost certainly be disappointment when the kiln door is opened.

Clay does not improve by being soaked with wet hands and sponges. Unless it is seriously dry and cracking, pupils need to keep water well away from their claywork. A combination of clay, water and children produces exactly what might be expected. Clay can also be a superb missile, dries on the surface of a floor and creates a trail of footprints around the school when trodden on. A strong behaviour rule is to keep all clay on the surface of a table or wherever it is officially being used. Pupils will probably need aprons and a damp sponge to hand if necessary. These days, clay arrives without its being full of air-holes, so there is little need to do any more than take some of it out of its polythene wrapper and begin. It does not need bashing down on a surface to remove the air, but in modelling, care needs to be taken not to create pockets of air. These expand during firing and fragment the model into pieces. Skill in handling clay includes constructing and modelling so that air-pockets are not created.

The surface of damp clay lends itself to impressing objects to make marks. Patterns and textures can be added by scratching when clay is semi-hard, but never when dry. Clay dust is actually dangerous if inhaled over a period of time. Professional potters use a face mask if scraping or scratching dry clay, but such practices can be avoided by using clay in its plastic state and firing it once it is dry. Of the many technicalities needed to take account of, points to consider are:

- Learning that a bag of clay (unlike Plasticine) needs refastening or it will dry out.
- Learning that poorly made joints, not properly welded, will fall apart.
- Clay that is too thick, more than 3 cm, will most likely crack or blow apart in the kiln. Clay objects need to be hollow if they are wider than about 3 cm.
- Models of animals may be dried upside down if the weight of them causes other parts, such as legs, to collapse.
- Clay needs to be thoroughly dried before it is fired in a kiln.
- Claywork needs to be done on porous surfaces, such as wood. Never on laminate surfaces where it sticks.
- Clay is not 'baked' but 'fired' to a temperature of between 950 and 1,050 degrees Celsius. Artistic language, such as 'fired', 'glazed', is part of children's art education and no favours are done calling it 'baking'.

Apart from these technicalities, making models involves skill in adapting shapes. Clay animals are often more interesting if twisted into movement and a great deal can be done through quite simple shifts of a model's head, legs and body. All this combines technical skill with observation. Models need something characteristic of the way the creature lives if they are not to appear lifeless. Even a slight twist of the creature's head will make a difference. Subjects for modelling include favourites such as 'Angry Cockerel', 'Twisting and Leaping Fish', 'Bird in Flight', 'Screaming Singer', 'Tumbling Clowns' and 'Prehistoric Creature'. Some models are best structured by fixing them to a clay tile or base. This makes them more stable and solves many of the problems such as making the model stand on its own feet. There are important design decisions to be made using clay, simply because models, pots and sculpture need to survive,

*Figure 41* The Village Choir. Trainee-teacher project

stand up without falling over, and in some cases cope with the wind and weather outside.

Other teaching points include using an artistic vocabulary of words such as 'balance', 'contrast' and 'surface texture' as well as impressing on children the importance of technical points such as taking care when welding parts together. Some alternative starting points when developing skill and technique in modelling are:

- Begin by looking at movement and discussing it. Refer to physical education sessions or demonstrate movement.
- Begin by looking at pictures of animals, birds or sportspeople. Look for shapes, thick and thin, turning, and twisting.
- Begin by demonstrating how to join clay.
- Begin by having children sketch a design for a sculpture based on the work of the British sculptor Henry Moore.
- Find out if children have family pets. Discuss the movement of, for example, a cat cleaning its fur or a fish in an aquarium.

A generic skill is that of observation, but this does not build unless children are highly motivated or have a natural inclination to remember what they see. Several photographs of a cat in movement, for example, could be a useful resource for children who do not have a developed visual memory. Unless children have a chance to observe for themselves they are left with imagination or photographic and drawn examples. Showing them a clay model of a cat is not a very good start because it diminishes and limits the choices they might make. The more prescriptive the source of inspiration, the more similar results will be.

It is tempting to show children a finished example of 3-D work and hope they will emulate it. This is not how art skills develop. The trainee-teacher example of the 'Village Choir' (Figure 41) sculptured heads came from a project devised by Peter Moore, an art consultant. The final example went through several stages. He began as if students were going to make a pinch or thumb pot. This then changed to become a human head. So far so good, but the pot changed again as students were told that they had to create a facial expression as if someone had dropped a brick on their foot. There was skill needed in reviewing and changing the work. Eyes on the model needed to bulge, there would be screaming mouths and tongues sticking out. The next change was to develop this into an opera-singer, singing a high note at the end of an aria. Finally, the truth was out. This was really a collective sculpture of a village choir, with lace doilies for ruffs. The story is a process of evolution, just as a drama is rehearsed and develops as a result of rehearsal.

Art is the outcome of skill, technique, observation, inspiration and development, not the shadow of someone's finished example. This does not mean there is no place for examples. It means that slavishly copying examples has little value unless review, change and development can take place. Artists have always copied other artists, but rarely have they let things rest there. They have gone on to adapt and change what first inspired them.

## Using paper, papier mâché, card and glue

Folding paper may not seem like much of a skill, but many adults, let alone children, find it difficult to fold paper accurately. Practising folding paper along a vertical drawn line involves folding in such a way that the top edges of paper align perfectly and paper is folded far enough over itself to crease exactly. The critical skill here is to shift the intended fold towards the line just before creasing it, while watching to see that the top edges align. Naturally, this is easier to demonstrate than describe, but developing this skill often involves breaking down an activity into simple stages. Some children find it difficult to press down on paper to hold it steady. Others have no idea how to crease paper unless they are told to slide a finger along the length of the crease to make it sharp. Folding a piece of paper in half sounds easy, but it involves hand and eye coordination, checking opposite corners and edges.

Developing skill in cutting paper and thin card can make or break artwork. When they first begin cutting, children will not necessarily hold scissors with blades vertically over the line they are trying to cut. A common mistake is to try to cut holding the scissor-blades almost flat to the paper. Assuming some progress is made holding scissors, there is a useful teaching device to improve the skill of cutting along a drawn line. Children tend to cut too enthusiastically, ignoring the line they may have drawn. Improving cutting skill can be achieved by asking them to cut along a blunt pencil-line slowly enough so that the scissor blades split the line itself in two. The aim is to be able to look closely at the cut edges of paper and still see traces of pencil-line on both of them. Of course, children will not be able to do this very well, but it does improve accuracy. The cutting is better than it would have been without having anything in particular to aim for. Like many skills, a balance between accuracy and speed is necessary. The more complex the skill, the wider the variation in pupils' abilities to cope, and the greater the difference in the time it takes pupils to complete work.

Papier mâché in its true form is pulped paper and glue squeezed until most of the moisture is extracted. Teachers sometimes confuse papier mâché with paper lamination. This second technique is far more common in schools than making a pulp and involves sticking layers of paper over each other to create a thickness which will take paint and be sturdy. The recipe for pulped papier mâché is simple enough. Papier mâché needs mixing the day before it is used and it is worth remembering that it shrinks on drying.

### Recipe

This makes a huge quantity. Put the quantity of about two bin liners of shredded paper into a plastic dustbin (shredded white paper is far better than newspaper). Put four bucketfuls of HOT water into the dustbin and leave overnight. Pound and grind the paper to pulp with a large piece of wood or use a food mixer to grind the paper. Add a little paste as the mixture is being pounded, about two average packets of school paste, or less, will do. Squeeze out the mixture by hand or through a sieve. Never add any detergent as this destroys the effect of the paste.

True papier mâché takes ages to dry. It therefore needs to be very thinly applied to a surface such as card or Plasticine. Two to four millimetres is quite enough for most purposes. It is almost impossible to remove dry clay from papier mâché, so Plasticine or card provide a better former. An alternative is to use papier mâché as a small-scale modelling medium in itself for making animals and other models no more than a few centimetres high.

Skills and learning involved in using papier mâché include:

- learning how paper can be pulped and glue added to make a mâché;
- learning about using an appropriate thickness of papier mâché;
- learning to model over a form;
- learning about drying time;
- learning about the toughness of the finished object.

Paper-laminating can be easier to use in school than true papier mâché simply because it dries more quickly. Laminating is a process of tearing newspaper into small pieces about 2 cm by 2 cm, then applying them with glue to a surface. The form to which they are applied can be Plasticine, card or a balloon. Any reasonably solid shape can be covered in paper layers. Using white newspaper and 'Yellow Pages' can help to differentiate which layer is which and a minimum of three layers is needed for stiffness. The layers need not be fully dry before another layer is applied, but need to be thoroughly dry before being coloured. Paper-laminating can be done using thinned PVA glue, but a water paste (school paste without fungicides) is preferable. Using a balloon tends to produce very similar results within the class and has the added annoyance of having no flat side to rest on a table. Storage of wet objects is worth considering, especially those balloons, which almost always need to be hung up to dry.

## Organization

A practical point is that papier mâché will easily block a sink. Users need to rinse hands in a bucket of water before washing hands under the tap. Contents of the bucket should be poured down a drain outside. Papier mâché if dropped on the floor can be lethal because it is so slippery. Take care in handling it.

Skills and learning involved in paper lamination include:

* creating a form which can be covered in layers of paper;
* tearing paper into sufficiently small pieces to bend around a form;

*Figure 42* Paper-Laminating, a Sun Mask on Plasticine. Trainee-teacher project.

- keeping glue thinly applied to speed up drying time;
- organizing the desk or table space so that glue and paper do not travel to the floor;
- using differently marked or coloured paper so as to know which layer is which;
- decorating the surface and making decisions about this decoration.

## Some additional practical projects

Gather some different textured surfaces together, such as Hessian, corrugated card, stones, fossils, weathered wood, sea shells. Discuss them and talk about any surface marks. Have the children try to make pencil drawings of how they think the surface looks and feels, noting light and dark markings, and patterns. Emphasize the importance of changing the pencil pressure from light to heavy, choosing areas to shade. Emphasize close observation of parts of stones and shells, using hand-lenses if necessary. Look for patterns under the lens. Younger children may prefer to create patterns using a graphite pencil and just one other colour.

Some skills developed include:

- skill in observing and translating textured surfaces to pencil;
- skill in creating a variety of shading effects;
- skill in varying pencil pressure;
- skill in creating patterns from a known source.

Develop this by using pencil-crayons to create designs for gift-wrap or wall coverings. Restrict choice of colour initially (two/three) to emphasize choice in mark-making and shading. Begin with a theme such as 'thin lines/thick lines' rather than triangles and geometric shapes. Compare the effects made, for example, with a yellow and a blue crayon. Yellow has a narrow tonal range so dark lines are not possible. Blue has a wide tonal range and behaves differently. Cut up the patterns created with pencil-crayon and use them as collage. Rearrange the crayon pattern on black paper and stick it down. Discuss the effects and compare the different outcomes. Use the patterns to decorate a gift box or the cover of a workbook.

Skill development is open-ended and benchmarks for evaluating skills achieved are not always useful. Using paint well, for example, depends on the purpose and circumstances in which it is used. Learning objectives can be very elementary, such as 'painting right up to the edges of the paper' or more sophisticated, such as 'matching a previously mixed colour'. Developing a skill is also a matter of practice. Teachers are there to remind, demonstrate, encourage and praise, all of which makes for a dynamic art session rather than a passive one. Some children find out how to use a medium without much prodding, but without input from a teacher before during and after an art session, important skills will go by the wayside simply because bad habits are reinforced by default.

# 17 Learning about artists and designers

Not every child is going to become a famous artist, but most will have a chance to visit galleries in other countries as well as in the UK. Studying the work of artists (called Critical Studies) can help children develop skills, understanding and knowledge they would otherwise miss. Reproductions of major works of art are easy to come by and children can gain a great deal by seeing them. At worst, they merely copy, but at best, they gain knowledge of artist's methods and turn them to advantage.

There is a narrow distinction between copying and 'working in the style' of an artist. UK classrooms and corridors are not short of copied Picasso portraits, Monet water gardens (the Japanese bridge) and Van Gogh sunflowers or 'Starry Starry Night'. There is nothing wrong with working from these artists' ideas, but plenty to suggest that copying can limit the artistic outcomes. Copying is actually forgery, though much can be learned by the intense looking which is needed to make a copy of something. Art students throughout the nineteenth and twentieth centuries have copied in order to learn. The more creative act is to transfer some of this knowledge to original artwork and add something new.

## Two ways of looking at a work of art

Looking at a work of art in reproduction tends to elicit two main responses from children. First there is the content of a painting in terms of what is there. In the case of painters such as Marc Chagall, there are floating people, a cat with a human face, a donkey and the images of dreams or poetry. Van Gogh gives us portraits, fields, sunflowers, a church, cafés, boats and cypress trees. It is not too difficult to dwell on each detail in the picture under the general question 'What can you see?' This approach begins to fall apart as soon as we look at abstract paintings, such as those by Mark Rothko or Frank Stella. Here the second way of looking at a painting becomes more dominant. Apart from content, we can look at the way a painting was done and the effects that have been created. What brush-marks are there? How do colours change, if they do. How has the artist used marks, lines, shading, colour and surface effects? How much contrast is there in the work? Are there light effects, sharp edges, blurred areas or colour contrasts? And (not always possible to know in reproductions) what scale has the artist chosen to present the work?

These questions are not a checklist of desirable qualities or methods. If they were, then all children would need to do is make sure a work of art contained them. Each work of art has its own characteristics, so comparisons are useful so long as they do not turn into value judgements. Van Gogh's use of blue is not better than Monet's, it is entirely different. The fact that one artist uses strong shadows and another does not has little bearing on the quality of that artist's work. Learning from the work of artists is about noticing what has been done rather than wishing for something else to have been included. Comparisons can illuminate the way each artist has worked and widen the range of choices children make when they work themselves. Studying a work of art is partly a growth of knowledge and understanding, partly a means to developing children's artwork in unexpected ways.

These two ways to look at a work of art are just as important when dealing with a child's painting. In particular, the way the media are used is an important talking point in respect of art and its history. It is also important in getting to grips with the organization and practical problems art materials present. Discussing brushstrokes can lead discussion into looking at examples from styles of painting where it is impossible to see brushstrokes and styles where the brushstrokes are clear. At almost exactly the same time that Victorian painters in England were using fine sable brushes, for example, in France far bolder brush-marks characterized Impressionism. The sober Victorian narrative painters resisted the strong colours of painters such as Claude Monet, even though they were painting at exactly the same time. Artists have occasionally disguised or emphasized the fact that a brush was used to create a painting. Some canvases have been painted using a knife, some dripping paint over them, some covered by paint-roller or sprayed and others scraped and smoothed after paint was applied.

Investigations about artists' use of a brush are quite different from feeding children a few isolated facts about their lives. It is commonly known that Van Gogh cut off part of his ear and later shot himself, but many people are unaware of Van Gogh's time in England living in Clapham, London. What we know of Van Gogh's methods comes from letters written to his brother Theo. He described that he would exaggerate the fairness of the hair in a portrait using orange tones, chromes and pale yellows. He elaborated on his theories of the effects of colour and wrote about the subject-matter he intended to paint.

The business of looking at anything with a critical eye has always involved how things were made as well as why. Marcia Pointon (1986) writes:

> Obviously, to look at stained glass only through binoculars is never to see it as it was intended to be seen. On the other hand, however, the full quality of colour and effectiveness of technique cannot be appreciated without a closer look. The art historian wants to know not only what it is but how it has been made. Similarly, the magnifying glass is not only used by art historians to authenticate a work or to examine a signature but can assist towards knowledge about how a picture was painted.

The most commonly found artefact is probably a painting or a drawing, but questions can be asked of other aesthetic items. The Musée D'Orsay gallery in Paris, for example, has a superb collection of Art Nouveau chairs, tables, wall panels and room settings. These are examples of interior designer's style within a specific period of art and architecture. A class of young children may not readily connect with the style, but looking at photographs can lead to looking at all manner of chair and room design. Children are 'enculturated' through the things we bring to their attention whether we are aware of that or not. Pointon (1986) asks of any work of art:

- What is it?
- How did it come to be here?
- Where is it?
- What did people think of it?
- When and where was it made?
- What was going on in it?
- How is it organized?
- For whom was it made?
- Is it effective?
- What condition is it in?
- What does it mean?
- What did it mean?
- How is it presented?
- What is it made of?
- How much did it cost?
- Is it the only one of its kind?

A pick and mix of these questions can help children understand how to look at works of art. Some works of art are more obviously about emotion – tenderness, jealousy, for example – and events. Claude Monet emphasized light and colour, while Edvard Munch peopled his paintings with the despair, death and jealousies of his own life. Paintings are rarely about exactly the same thing. The questions listed so far also suppose that there is an art object to discuss, rather than an art event which ends when the participants go. That may not be the case. The meaning of a work of art changes with time too. When William Turner painted *Rain Steam and Speed* his railway engine, racing across a Thames bridge, was the latest dramatic form of transport. It was the ultimate in transport technology. Steam engines are now nostalgic museum pieces or the pride of preservation societies so Turner's painting means something very different today. The patronage of art changes too. Artists no longer spend most of their time decorating churches and painting portraits because art is sold by gallery directors. When teachers decide to study work of an artist in their art lessons, it is no wonder that the more accessible and popular artists prevail.

## From popularity to originality – three familiar artists

School art is full of well-tried clichés though this is not by any means a sign of quality. Three artistic projects regularly crop up in the corridor displays. The examples given here are intended to develop the practice of looking at the work of artists while sweeping aside some copied art which arises through ignorance. Rather like doing 'The Vikings' some schools do Monet's 'Bridge over the Lake of Water-Lilies', Van Gogh's 'Starry Starry Night' or 'Sunflowers' and Picasso's Cubist period 'Portraits'. There is nothing wrong with studying any of these artists, unless the way they worked is completely overlooked. The results can involve a lot of work for a rather impoverished result. Something that rarely seems to occur is that the study of the way artists work involves comparison between artists living approximately around the same time as one another. Monet, Van Gogh and Picasso are accessible to children partly because of the way they used paint. Painters such as Rembrandt or Leonardo da Vinci are more difficult to interpret and learn from because their drawing style is so difficult to emulate. This does not rule them out, but the fact remains, some artists prove popular with young children. Monet, Van Gogh, Klee, Miró, Kandinsky Braque, Picasso, Delaunay, Chagall, Mondrian, and Matisse are some of the regulars. In most cases, their work strongly emphasizes painting technique rather than hiding it and presents children with fewer drawing problems. Children can more easily manage pattern and the effects of brushwork.

## Practical points

When studying the brushwork of Van Gogh or Monet, (Plates 37, 38) the appropriateness of materials matters. There is little to be gained by working in thin overlays of watercolour on white cartridge paper. As has been said elsewhere in this book, white cartridge is mainly used for drawing and thin watercolour. Monet and Van Gogh used oil paint in opaque colour. The nearest to this in school paints is to use powder-colour, poster paint or gouache. These are most effective on grey sugar-paper or similarly neutral shades. There is no point limiting the outcomes of study by using paints very different from the artist, if we want to learn about the way paint was used.

It is not necessary to know a great deal about a wide variety of artists and styles. A handful of names and details is enough to make a good start. The following structure has been used to describe three artists. The second example, Van Gogh, includes example questions for children, comparing with the work of Claude Monet.

- Find out something useful concerning work methods and the ideas behind the works of a particular artist.
- Contrast these with the work of another artist.
- Bring these ideas to children's attention once they have described what they themselves can see.

- Design art projects based on the working methods of the artist and follow the principles that artist was trying to show.
- Use the results as a way of developing knowledge of culture, knowledge of the artist and understanding of the variety of ways an artist might work.

## A Claude Monet project

**Background for the teacher:** Claude Monet had become interested in Japanese prints and Japanese gardens. In later life he created his water-garden at Giverny in France, not immediately realizing that it was to become his source of inspiration for the next twenty years. Much of his painting was developed directly outdoors using the relatively new paints with their strong chemical dyes. Before 1850, paintings were dull in colour because strong dyes were not known. The lightness, freshness of colour burst on the artistic scene with the French Impressionist movement. Like artists of the time, they suddenly discovered that they could use these new colours and abandon the gloomy tones previously needed to create the effect of bright reds and yellows. Emphasizing light and colour meant relegating detail as less important. This was probably because detail would distract from the stronger effects of light and colour.

Monet painted some twenty canvases of Rouen Cathedral in different light conditions, producing effects such as fog and gritty surface textures. His range of colours widened and towards the end of his life some of his garden paintings are almost abstract. He continued to observe how his lake reflected trees and the sun changed the effects of light on water. His Japanese bridge became the central focus for many of his paintings, but the main emphasis of light and colour remained. If Monet ever used a fine brush it is not evident. What we have in his work is a wealth of effect seen as if through a rain-spattered window so we are aware of the vibrant colour and light, but not detail such as the veins of a leaf. Some of the later works are very large in scale, four or more metres wide, so reproductions are a poor substitute which give only a guide to the originals. Monet was already well established in the 1880s. He began painting his 'series' of repeated subjects in 1888, later painting haystacks, poplars, the garden at Giverny and Rouen Cathedral. At this time he was well into his fifties. He died in 1927.

**Working with children:** How can this source be developed to produce more original artwork? Obviously we can give children some choice about the subject-matter so that they are not all reproducing Monet's bridge. Like Monet, they might begin by drawing something they can actually see, such as a view from a window, part of a garden or a church. Second, make it clear that an aim is to paint in such a way as to lose the sharp edges of anything they have drawn. Close examination of Monet's brushwork will reveal that the edges of buildings, trees and lily leaves exist, but blend with surrounding paint and are softened. Try to find more than one example of Monet's paintings of his Japanese bridge or water-lilies, particularly late examples in the twentieth century. Discuss differences and similarities such as the use of pale or strong colours. Try to find some of the examples of water-lilies where pink and yellow brushstrokes mingle with whites and greens. Look at the tangled knitting-wool effects of some of the later paintings Monet made of his bridge in 1923 (Plate 38). Talk about weather and sunlight, water reflecting trees on the water's surface. Look at how Monet used many mixtures of almost the same colour in one part of a painting. Notice how, in some canvases, water-lilies are in groups of leaves going mainly horizontally. Between the water-lilies the brushstrokes are often vertical, representing the reflection of his willow trees at the edge of the lake.

Have the children try mixing different shades of green using white as well as yellow, applying them to a dark or neutral paper. If they are using watercolour, the white will be the paper seen through thin colour, but opaque paint is more appropriate for interpreting Monet's work. If the bridge is included, children need a free hand in how they use the curved design of the bridge. The practical learning involved is mainly that of colour-mixing and observation of Monet's brush technique. A real challenge here is for children to mix opaque whites and creams while keeping their water pot sufficiently clean. Monet often added these light colours to a darker under-painting.

**Development and discussion:** Producing a collage based on Monet's subject-matter would be a reinterpretation. This would not be very strongly connected with his work unless an aim was to study changes of colour and light. A collage of torn paper would be more appropriate than one cut with scissors. (Collage needs to be small in scale as it takes time to tear and stick.) Sharply cut edges are not really in the spirit of Monet. Further discussion of Monet's work could be derived from other bridges he painted, such as the series of the River Thames in London. Other directions might be to shift the art topic to one concerned with reflections of all kinds, not just in water.

## A Vincent Van Gogh project

**Background for the teacher:** If ever an artist was consumed by the emotional qualities of colour it was Vincent Van Gogh (Plate 37). In his letters to his brother Theo, he described his ideas for using bright strong colours to create the effects he wanted. It is worth remembering that bright pigments were still relatively new in Van Gogh's time. What most people see immediately, however, are the strongly directional brushstrokes he used. The brush was used almost as a tool for drawing in colour on canvas, sometimes swirling thick bright lines next to duller dark ones. His favoured subjects were portraits, sunflowers and landscapes, each with its high contrast of colour and broken line. Whole areas of paint were made up of different mixtures side by side giving a rich texture to the surface. Even today, some canvases look so freshly painted they could have been done yesterday. This is mainly because Van Gogh painted thick paint over thin, not using too much oil. The work of other painters has cracked over time, but this is not so with most of Van Gogh's work. It is reported that he sold only one painting during his lifetime, so he depended largely on his family for money.

The commonly known stories are of his cutting off the lobe of his ear and sending it to a woman he loved, being committed to a mental asylum and finally killing himself. This is the distracting dramatic side of his life, and we can remember that most of it was spent actually painting. Sometimes he produced a painting rapidly, in a day, compared with artists such as Cézanne who worked for hours on the same canvas. Canvas after canvas was produced almost as if the brush was a knife, carving slashes of line into the landscape. Van Gogh would take familiar objects, such as a bedroom chair, and use them to play one colour and texture off against another. Whatever else can be said about Van Gogh's painting, it is full of strong marks and clearly defined furrows of paint.

**Working with children:** Discuss what they say they can see. Their response will initially tend to focus on content: trees, churches and portraits, for example. Ask them about how the brush was used, what colours are often repeated, and they are more likely to reveal more. Two strongly obvious features can be brought to children's attention. These are movement and contrast. In Van Gogh's paintings, we see cypress trees swirl with a life of their own. Movement is implied with short directional brushstrokes as marks track their way across

*Figure 43* Designs Based on the Brushstrokes of Van Gogh. Ages 4 to 6.

*Figure 44*  Van Gogh meets Monet in a 3-D box. Trainee-teacher project.

a starry sky or down a street. Contrast can be seen in light brushstrokes laid against dark, blues placed against yellows and the use of black lines sharpening edges as a drawn outline. Not for Van Gogh the blurred edges of Claude Monet's landscapes and lilies. Compare examples with the way other artists work and see what children's response is. Neither artist is right or wrong to use dark lines, blurred effects or contrast because there are no rules that apply. Close observation is needed to understand anything we can see an artist has done. Again, close attention to looking after pale cream and shades of white is needed.

**Comparison:** Questions for children might include:

- How has Van Gogh used lines compared with Monet?
- What might you guess about the size and type of brushes they used?

- What subjects seem to be Van Gogh's favourites?
- What bright, dull, light and dark paint can you see?
- How did Van Gogh paint trees?
- How did Van Gogh paint the sky?
- What can you see about the way he painted eyes?
- What do you think Van Gogh would never paint/do in his canvases?

Questions are a means of drawing attention to the artist's methods. The last question is speculation, but a chance to point out that using thin, smoothed paint which gradually changed shade, was not Van Gogh's method of working. This can be contrasted with artists whose methods included far more fine detail, but less dramatic use of brushstrokes. None of these considerations touch on the unfathomable aspect of an artist's work. It affects us in some way beyond this analysis when we see it.

## A Pablo Picasso project

**Background for the teacher:** Pablo Picasso worked in such a variety of ways that he defied convention, and the cliché commonly found in school is that of copying the style of Cubist portraits. They are humorous, interesting and popular because of the way noses, eyes, mouths and ears can be put in almost any position the children want. Drawing problems are minimized, but so may be the children's understanding of what Picasso was trying to do. It is not enough to rearrange the features of a face and suggest this is a study of Picasso's work. At the time these portraits were produced, there were many influences on Picasso, including African masks and sculpture. Some of his portraits have a mask-like quality, but the main feature at that time was that of depicting the human face in multi-view. Picasso and his friends philosophized that the way we know anyone is from a great variety of angles and perspectives. A single viewpoint was not enough. Portraits reflected this and superficially resembled a fragmented jigsaw of angles or pieces of pattern resembling broken glass. There is no apparent depth to paintings of this period and an eye is often seen from the front while portraying an ear or nose from the side. If this explanation is a surprise, then the point about mindless copying is reinforced.

Being the creative artist he was, Picasso did not stop there, but developed a more pattern-like quality to the broken shapes he used. Instead of a painting being like a snapshot in time, it became an object in its own right, one full of clues rather than a representation of a single viewpoint. Though he was born in Spain, most of his life was spent in France, the Cubist period lasting only a short time from 1900 to 1910.

**Working with children:** Discuss with children how we see things from many different viewpoints. Children could draw a story-board to show several different viewpoints. Look at the silhouette of a person's head seen sideways and from the front. Look at Egyptian paintings of the human figure where a face is seen sideways and an eye from the front. Look at examples of Picasso's work where he treats the canvas as a surface for pattern as well as for drawing shapes. A feature of Picasso's work of this period is that it looks as if it was 'assembled' from pieces rather than flowing from one grand design.

**Development:** Look at some of Picasso's collages and his combination of paint and collages. Create a work of art which uses both paint and collage. Look at African masks and sculpture with the intention of designing masks, emphasizing a multi-cultural dimension and other artistic traditions.

## Questions about the artwork

There may be some shared views in response to 'How does the painting make you feel?' and certainly some responses to the following.

- What did you find easiest to do in painting like Monet/Van Gogh/Picasso?
- What things did you do to paint in the same way as he did?
- What can you tell me now about Van Gogh's skies and sunflowers, Monet's garden and Picasso's portraits?
- What could you tell someone about how to mix paint?
- If you could paint another picture in this style, what would it be?

Evaluating artwork can be done by both teacher and child. Evaluation needs to be positive because children generally progress in their artistic work if we emphasize their successes rather than their failures. It is a matter of personal choice when and how to intervene. A group or plenary discussion has its uses, but so does intervention to bring children back on track looking at the work of the artist they are studying. Reviewing work in progress is very important for children to do, but does not need to be a criticism which demotivates. At the very young end of the age range it is unlikely that much artwork is handed back to be finished. Older children benefit from having the positive aspects of their work described before continuing, which is a teaching skill needing some practice. Some examples are,

> I noticed that the way you use your brush shows me you thought about how you wanted it to look on paper. That's helped you get the effect you wanted to achieve. You've certainly got those brushstrokes Van Gogh would have used.

> I like the way your picture is not just copied from Van Gogh which shows you really thought about it for yourself.

> You thought about the colours you were going to mix. This is getting better the more you get rid of the background paper colour.

You made good use of the space on the paper by the careful way you laid out your work. It needs some thicker paint here and there like Van Gogh would have done.

The extra time you put into this is really paying off.

A danger of evaluating (both positively and negatively) is to have unwittingly transmitted the idea there is a right way to do things. There are technical points to grasp about mixing paints together, cutting, folding and sticking, but the major dimension is making decisions from choices. An advantage of closely studying the work of one artist and contrasting this with the work of another is that it demonstrates that success comes in different ways. The more carefully an artist is studied, the more likely it is that differences from other artists will be revealed. The teacher can evaluate pupils' work under five categories already mentioned in this book. Comments can be made about

1  the process of working (e.g. shows initiative, independence)
2  handling of materials (e.g. able to mix paint to a good consistency)
3  use of media (e.g. discriminates when using colour)
4  critical skills (e.g. can point to similarities, differences in things seen)
5  stages of personal development (e.g. has confidence in producing artwork, drawing advanced for age).

## Gallery visits and visiting artists

Two further ways of 'enculturating' children to the ways in which artists work are through gallery visits and visiting artists. There is no substitute for seeing an original work of art in the scale it was intended to be seen. The vibrancy of Chagall's use of yellow, the luminescence of a genuine Monet painting all contrast with the weak shadowy reproductions limited by printing technique. Watercolours probably come closest in both scale and colour to their very best reproductions. Anyone who has visited the Tate Modern in London or the Uffizi gallery in Florence has seen paintings and sculpture for real. The Tate Modern, for example, displayed a painting in 2001 by Richard Hamilton which gained its impact from being on such a large scale. A postcard reproduction shows nothing of the scale and in some cases actually crops the design to fit. At the Tate Modern, the viewer cannot ignore the way the Hamilton painting excludes everything else in sight when we stand in front of it.

Children can also discover what things galleries display compared with their experience of school corridors. We may, as adults, take it for granted that art galleries contain art, but children are mostly brought up on an artistic diet of book illustrations and their own work. Competent though book illustrators are, their intentions are different when working for the small-scale printed page. The great galleries of the world are not full of book illustrations and no amount of exposure to colour reproductions is a substitute for seeing art in a gallery.

An obvious question this raises for a school visit to a gallery is 'How is the original different from any reproduction we might have seen in a book?' Without some preparation beforehand the visit could be wasted. Once inside a gallery, teachers' focus inevitably includes organizational, health, safety and behaviour issues as much as looking at works of art. These can obscure the more important tasks unless children are well-prepared beforehand. Some guidelines for visits are,

- Visit the gallery yourself before taking children.
- Try to find out something in detail about three of the artworks, not just when they were created, but how and with what characteristics.
- Devise specific questions for pupils to answer.
- Devise specific things for them to do/draw.
- Have in mind 'follow-up' work before you set off. If possible, see this as a project comprising more than one piece of work.
- Spend time looking at, discussing and describing the artists' work and methods with children before the visit takes place.
- Make use of the gallery educational service if there is one. Some galleries suggest activities as well as providing information.

Visiting artists and designers usually do their own work alongside children, explaining as they progress and helping to produce something along similar lines. The availability and employment of practising artists varies across the country, but projects can be started if there is funding. Not unreasonably, weavers and textile artists use threads and fibres with children, while potters use clay. A visit from a 'real' artist can be very successful, particularly as children model themselves to some extent on adults. The artist or designer is not the class teacher and there is generally a surprise element in the work being produced. A visiting artist will usually have a programme to offer or may be guided by an art advisor if the local authority has one. Follow-up can take the form of discussion, an exhibition of work and writing about the experience. Some artists are actually art educators who will offer specialisms ranging from mask-making to advanced papier mâché sculpture. There are no guarantees that children will learn anything alongside an artist, but a great deal can be gained from hearing an artist talk about the work in progress and demonstrating techniques.

The experience of a gallery visit or a visiting artist contrasts with the paucity of some school art activities. In particular, older children's art may be a diet of historical illustration in their humanities topic. Painting pictures of Egyptian gods, just because Ancient Egypt is the history topic, is not as aesthetically productive as studying artists. In some schools it has nothing to do with Egyptian art and everything to do with getting a history project displayed. This lost opportunity ignores working methods, observation of the outside world and creativity in its interpretation. Some children may never see how an artist works unless there is a school visit to a gallery, or a visit from a practising artist. The influences on young children cannot easily be predicted and there are plenty of adults who would never visit a gallery themselves. Instead of children's experience of art being random, gallery visits and the work of practising artists can change perceptions of art and how to create it. These experiences are formative and, who knows, may be the catalyst to enjoying art in later life.

# 18 Conclusions

The new millennium began with teachers and a UK government passionate about raising standards in education. This was nothing new for dedicated teachers, but a diet of target-setting in basic subjects frequently pushed the arts into the background. The curriculum and its implementation sometimes became dreary and dull as teachers struggled to deal with assessment data and strategies in literacy and numeracy. As Michael Fielding (2001), quoting John Macmurray, put it, 'we worship efficiency and success: and we don't know how to live finely'. If living finely is equated with learning to shop until we drop, and teach only what we can test, then education has lost its intellectual way. Living finely is a journey of connoisseurship rather than one of prodding pupils to perform. No child can absorb a fine culture of art without seeing a great deal of it and doing enough of it to realize some of the processes involved. Art is one of the antidotes to a life which becomes increasingly busy and exhausting, yet far less humanly productive or satisfying (Fielding, 2001).

A number of maddening contradictions pervade art education. The UK government art schemes in the early 2000s included 'expected outcomes'. This was despite the fact that the holy grail of art is actually to be found in *unexpected* outcomes'. Galleries across the globe are not filled with expected outcomes. Art as a subject simply will not behave itself in the way target-setters, curriculum deliverers and data-collectors would have it. Fortunately, there are enough teachers who value the emotional and spiritually uplifting potential of our education system. Art is not quite a subversive activity in schools, but without it we ignore a profoundly human need. Expressing feelings and ideas in a visual way is a question of making judgements about things like colour, scale, texture, shape and drawing. Nobody ever learned about using combinations of colour unless they could experience using them. Benchmarks in art are by the agreement of connoisseurs, and being a successful artist has little to do with known criteria for success.

A contradiction of this book is that specific art activities are described but a whole chapter about developing ideas (Chapter 5) avoids details about art activities. A maddening contradiction in art teaching is that some of the best art activities come from wide-ranging themes where the starting point does not have a single learning objective or medium suggested. What makes art risk-worthy is the courage to invent and dream dreams long before anything specific springs to mind. This hardly suits a rigorously defined curriculum of art activities which 'must be covered'. The trouble with some art programmes is that deciding in advance that children will print or weave creates a straitjacket from which it is difficult to escape. The remaining contradiction is that being a dreamer of dreams is not in itself going to sort out the organization of practical materials and activities to promote art. Developing the courage to be skilful, creative and an ambitious teacher is not a soft option. Mindless art activities are the alternative.

Some years ago, BBC television ran a series in which portrait painters and sculptors demonstrated their art. One artist was working on a bust of Lord Lichfield, the well-known photographer, and made hundreds of measurements of his face using callipers. These she transferred to a life-size bust made in clay. When she was quite sure that measurements like the length of the nose, chin, mouth and forehead were absolutely accurate, she stopped for a moment. 'You see?' she said. 'It doesn't look right, does it?' She then proceeded to put clay where flesh did not exist and to make lines and twists of expression within the face. Gradually the bust seemed to bear a closer relation to its sitter, rather as if artistic expression had nothing to do with all these preliminary measurements. The artist had to find her own way.

In much the same spirit, good art teaching depends on becoming a teacher who does more than make measurements and look for textbook ways of doing things. Once we have grasped some of the essential characteristics of teaching art, we can leave them behind and find our own ways. It is not nearly so important to read about the value of art as it is to discover for ourselves what artistic values we hold. There is similarly little point in using ideas from preceding chapters without trying to adapt them to suit the artistic learning we have in mind. Ideas and examples often provide the stimuli for developing our own personal artistic ideology (something we ought genuinely to believe in) rather than a repertoire of activities which have no relationship one with another.

A crucial aim of this book has been to present material in such a way that it provokes thought and demands judgement. No book can ever do justice to the variety of teaching styles which affect how we use ideas. Even so, we can examine almost any idea and extend it ourselves by thinking of slight variations. If we suspect that is impossible, more than likely the children we teach will show us how. The essence of good art teaching is to harness the creative ability which is already part of every child. We are catalyst, enquirer, developer and delegator to the creative young minds we try to teach. Those teachers who say that everything comes from the children themselves are quite right, although what they say is not always very helpful. Our children are ultimately the creators of any original work which is produced in the classroom and it is they who must learn to look closely, use their imagination, and express their surroundings through art – providing, that is, we allow them the opportunity to do so.

The clichés of art teaching may always be with us. It would be foolish to suggest otherwise. Art at Christmas time, decorated paper plates and art for

Mother's Day are activities which are best seen for what they are. They are of important social value and will not go away as readily as some art educators would wish them to. Yet they need only take up a fraction of the year's art programme and should not be taken too seriously as constituting artistic learning. As has been pointed out earlier (Chapter 3), they can be adapted to become creative and educationally sound.

A principle which underlies many of the ideas put forward is that of self-responsibility. Each chapter has been written with the intention of providing for, and even encouraging, the exercise of personal choice. When children or teachers are involved in the process of making choices, they are inevitably manipulating thoughts and ideas. This is as true for the child who chooses a range of colours as it is for the teacher who decides why a particular artistic theme will be worth exploring. In the most creative of classrooms we will often find children deeply absorbed in solving problems for themselves. Their teachers act as guides and illuminators of yet more areas of enquiry and curiosity. The occurrence of this is by no means as rare as might be thought. Most of us have our best and worst moments in teaching and some of the best learning seems to take place when the outcome is a little uncertain. Teacher and children work together to find out what they can about what they can see and feel. It takes little imagination to realize that one of the rewards of teaching art is to become just as interested in what children discover as they are.

An obvious and fundamental teaching skill has already been mentioned: that of drawing children's attention to the appearance of things around them. For some children, their teacher may be the first person to do this with any serious intention of initiating artistic learning. The effect of this apparently simple activity can be very profound and in many instances have a long-lasting influence. It is, however, a skill which needs to be handled with considerable care and insight. Within the apparently simple process of leading children to give attention to looking at things, there is a wealth of subtlety to be discovered.

This is not a plea to put the visual appearance of things above every other educational consideration. It is just as important to count, measure and describe in words as it is to discover through art. The claim made here is that the means of developing artistic awareness are often far less easily understood than more conventional forms of knowledge. In view of this, teaching children to be visually aware may need greater deliberate attention than we presently give it in our schools. Although children's artistic development requires the same attention to detail that other subject areas enjoy, in practice it frequently seems to have less than its fair share of the teacher's time.

Through art we have the opportunity to give a significant start to children's early education. The arts are not only for communicating ideas, *they are ways of having ideas*. As such they can often be the main source of inspiration for the remaining areas of the school curriculum. Through art, children can retain that sense of wonder and delight which all too easily becomes lost as later concerns of adult life take over. Where being an adult can mean there are a variety of unavoidable routine commitments, art, as Elliot Eisner said over thirty years ago, can vitalize life by drawing attention to the quality of experience as such. He comments,

> Art reminds us that the act of looking intensely, of opening one's sensibilities to the environment yields a qualitative reward in the process of living.

This relationship of art and life can be taken still further. If in later life we take up one job in preference to another, we may develop special skills but are bound to neglect others. Consequently we rule out a variety of experiences which there is no time for us to enjoy. The quality of our jobs and interests can determine the quality of our lives just as easily as can the relationships we have with each other. Art, especially the teaching of it to young children, can enrich life by bringing to our attention the quality of such enlivening experiences. There is clearly and inevitably a link between the quality of an experience in art and the quality of life as a result of having had that experience.

A way forward for educators of young children is to persuade colleagues and administrators of the importance of the early years of schooling. A personal view is that within early education, artistic learning has a crucial and indispensable contribution to make. Some educators need no persuading of this. Others wrongly make assumptions about the unsophisticated nature of small children. If we are to improve the quality of art teaching, or for that matter teaching in the early years of schooling, there is still much to be done through in-service work and teachers' groups. Direct experience, such as an in-service course provides, is an increasingly vital part of extending professionalism.

We have experienced increasing emphasis on accountability in teaching and can no longer afford to regard our role as anything else but professional. We owe it to young children to give them the best art education we possibly can in the short time they are with us. For that reason we need to understand, not only why art education is important for young children, but why early-years education should be given a more prestigious place than it has been.

Dr Lilian Katz, Professor of Early Childhood Education at the University of Illinois, has observed on her travels worldwide that the younger the children, the lower the status of teachers seems to be. Yet the most important contribution teachers can make to the education of the young is to make sure they develop the ability to go on wanting to learn. To achieve that requires the greatest of professionalism and expertise, qualities which should place teachers of the young in the highest possible regard.

# References

APU (1983), *Aesthetic Development* (Assessment of Performance Unit, Department of Education and Science).

Arnheim, R. (1966), 'Expression', in M. Rader (ed.), *A Modern Book of Aesthetics*, 3rd edn (New York: Holt Rinehart & Winston).

Barnes, R. (1999) *Positive Teaching, Positive Learning* (London: Routledge).

Bennett, N., Desforges, C., Cockburn, A. and Wilkinson, B. (1984), *The Quality of Pupil Learning Experiences* (London: Lawrence Erlbaum).

Best, D. (1983), *The Function and Assessment of Art in Education* (Association of Art Advisors).

Best, D. (1985), *Feeling and Reason in the Arts* (London: Allen & Unwin).

De Bono, E. (1976), *Teaching Thinking* (London: Penguin).

Dewey, J. (1934), *Art as Experience* (New York: Minton, Balch & Co.).

Eberle, R.F. (1971), *Scamper: Games for Imagination Development* (New York: Buffalo D.O.K.).

Eisner, E. (1972), *Educating Artistic Vision* (London: Collier, Macmillan), chs 4–10.

Feldman, E. (1982), 'Varieties of Art Curriculum', *Journals of Art and Design*, vol. 1, no. 1 (National Society for Art Education).

Field, D. (1970), *Change in Art Education* (London: Routledge & Kegan Paul).

Fielding, M. (2001), 'Words that Don't Come Easy', *Times Educational Supplement*, 6 July 2001.

Gaitskell, C. and Hurwitz, A. (1970), *Children and their Art* (New York: Harcourt Brace and World).

Gardner, H. (1980), *Artful Scribbles* (London: Norman).

Gulbenkian Foundation (1982), *The Arts in Schools* (London: Calhouste Gulbenkian Foundation).

Hughes, R. (1980), *The Shock of the New* (London: BEC Publications).

Jameson, K. (1968), *Pre-School and Infant Art* (London: Studio Vista).

Kellogg, R. (1969), *Analysing Children's Art* (California: Mayfield Publishing).

Kenny, C. (2001) 'Friendship Pairing Boosts Creativity', *Times Educational Supplement*, 6 July 2001.

Lowenfeld, V. and Brittan, L. (1970), *Creative and Mental Growth* (New York: Macmillan).

Osborn, A. (1948/72), *Your Creative Power: How to Use Imagination* (New York: Scribner).

Parnes, S. and Harding, H. (1962), *A Source Book for Creative Thinking* (New York: Scribner).

Perry, L.R. (1973), 'Education in the Arts', in D. Field and J. Newick (eds), *The Study of Education and Art* (London: Routledge & Kegan Paul).

Pointon, M. (1986), *History of Art: A Student's Handbook*, 2nd edn (London: Routledge).

Pye, D. (1978), *The Nature and Aesthetics of Design* (London: Barrie & Jenkins).

Read, H. (1943), *Education through Art* (New York: Pantheon).

Robertson, S. (1974), *Children's Growth through Creative Experience* (London: Schools Council, Van Nostrand Reinhold).

Ross, M. (ed.) (1983), *The Arts: A Way of Knowing* (Oxford: Pergamon).

Rowntree, D. (1977), *Assessing Students: How Shall We Know Them?* (London: Harper & Row).

Taylor, J. (1971), *Organising and Integrating the Infant Day* (London: Allen & Unwin).

Watts, A. (1957), *The Way of Zen* (London: Thames & Hudson).

Witkin, R. (1974), *The Intelligence of Feeling* (London: Heinemann).

# Index